The Book of
SOUTH STOKE
with MIDFORD

THE HISTORY OF A PARISH

EDITED BY
ROBERT PARFITT

HALSGROVE

First published in Great Britain in 2001

*This book is dedicated to the people of
South Stoke Parish, past, present and future.*

Frontispiece photograph: *The Grove and
Tithe Barn roof early in the 20th century.* (Samler Collection)

British Library Cataloguing-in-Publication Data
A CIP record for this title is available from the British Library

ISBN 1 84114 103 8

HALSGROVE
PUBLISHING, MEDIA AND DISTRIBUTION

Halsgrove House
Lower Moor Way
Tiverton, Devon EX16 6SS
Tel: 01884 243242
Fax: 01884 243325
email: sales@halsgrove.com
website: http://www.halsgrove.com

Printed and bound in Great Britain by Bookcraft Ltd., Midsomer Norton

*Whilst every care has been taken to ensure the accuracy of the
information contained in this book, the authors disclaim responsibility
for any mistakes which may have inadvertently been included.*

Foreword

South Stoke is the name of three parishes in England. This book concerns that which was in Somersetshire, but which is now in the county and district of Bath and North East Somerset. This is a small parish that adjoins the southern boundary of the city of Bath and has within it the village of South Stoke and most of the hamlet of Midford. Throughout history the parish name has had many spellings, but in recent centuries South Stoke and Southstoke have prevailed. In this book the form preferred by the Parish Council for the name of the parish – South Stoke – is used. The single-word spelling appears when quoted directly from documents or when it is used in a house name.

As the year 2000 approached, thoughts turned to how it could be commemorated appropriately in the parish. To mark its centenary in 1994, the Parish Council held a modest one-day exhibition in the Village Hall. '100 YEARS IN SOUTH STOKE' was surprisingly popular, and from this stemmed the idea of a more ambitious project to present the history of the parish through 2000 years, first in an exhibition and then in a book. The proposal was supported by the Parish Council and by the Annual Parish Meeting, and a steering committee of interested and dedicated volunteers started work in September 1997, meeting at roughly monthly intervals thereafter. The South Stoke 2000 exhibition was staged in the Village Hall at the end of May 2000. And this is the book.

It might be wondered whether a small parish like this, little more than a square mile in area and with a population of 419 at the last count, has any history worth telling. Well, it enjoys the distinction of a Saxon charter that defined its bounds over 1000 years ago, and these may have existed for 2000 years or more. Men and women have been here throughout that time: what have they been doing? The book seeks to explore that question, to show how the parish has developed, what was happening and what life was like. It makes no claim to be definitive; it is the product of a relatively short period of research and preparation, and of course it reflects the fact that documentary sources of information are sparse until at least the middle of the second millennium. The book aims to afford a kaleidoscopic view of the evolution of a community and to persuade the reader that even this small parish does indeed have a fascinating story to tell.

The Book of South Stoke commemorates the history of the parish and its people at the end of the second millennium of the Christian era. May it provide interest and pleasure to all for whom the parish is, or has been home, and indeed to a wider public. May it also be a reminder of the heritage of which present and future generations must be guardians: a heritage succinctly expressed in two 20th-century quotations about the village of South Stoke. The author Arthur Mee wrote (even if rather romantically): 'it lies in as fair a scene as Nature has given us from her chalice of beauty', and the great art and architectural historian Sir Nikolaus Pevsner observed South Stoke to present 'the happy sight of a village still entirely unsuburbanised, though only two miles from the main station of a city.'

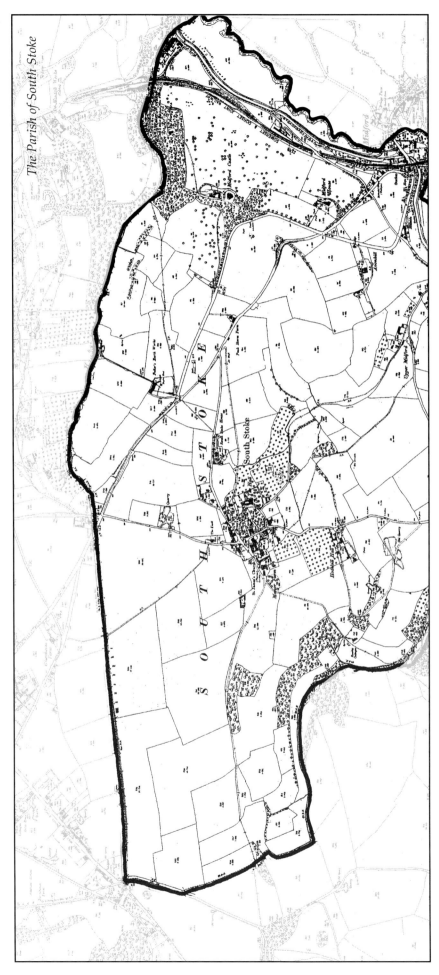

The Parish of South Stoke

The Ordnance Survey second edition 25-inch map published in 1904. This edition does not differ greatly from the first edition of 1888, but, for example, Hod's Hill Farm has become Hodshill Hall; The Vicarage has become The Hall, with a new vicarage (now The Old Vicarage); Lansdowne Villa has become The Knoll, etc. This map is perhaps most interesting for what it does not show, because it demonstrates vividly the extent of development that has taken place during the 20th century – north of the Wansdyke, along the Midford Road, Old Midford Road, Packhorse Lane and South Stoke Lane. The compact bounds of South Stoke village 100 years ago are very evident.

Acknowledgements

The South Stoke 2000 History Group gratefully acknowledges the encouragement and financial support given by the South Stoke Parish Council, and the Millennium Festival Awards for All for a lotteries grant. We also owe an inestimable debt to the late H.G. (John) Canvin whose earlier research formed the foundation of our study. The Master and Fellows of Corpus Christi College, Cambridge are gratefully acknowledged for permitting us access to the only extant copy of the Parish Charter.

Our gratitude is extended to the many people of the parish and beyond for their contributions, the loan of photographs and drawings, and for their reminiscences without which the production of this book would not have been possible. Special thanks are due to:

Rod Adams, Brian Auty, Tony Biggs, Stephen Bird, John Broome, Mike Chapman, Roger Clifford, Royston Clifford, Mark Corney, John Cross, Barry Cunliffe, Nigel Dagger, Lilian and Richard Daniels, Michael Davis, Molly and the late Ray Elliott, Ian Fraser, E.K. Green, Roger Halse, Ernie Hamlen, Brian Hawkins, Robert Hellard, Charles Hignett, Ceri Lambdin, Paul Langham, the late Kenneth Langley, Jane Lawes, Ian Locke, Jenny Mackewn, Neil Macmillen, Jean Manco, Paul Mann, Robert Masters, Andrew Mathieson, Lilian Meecham, Sandy Neill, Mark Palmer, Ann and Christopher Parsons, Julian Peters, Anna Philpott, Richard Pitt, Noel Pizey, Julia Ponsonby, Philip Raby, Andrew Reynolds, Tim Samler, South Stoke Show Committee, Rene Smith and family, Jim Summers, Charles and Brenda Swatton, Bob Sydes, Frank Thorne, Rollo Torrance, Gordon Tucker, Bob Whitaker, Robert Williams and John Wroughton.

The omission of anyone from this list is unintentional, but if that has occurred we apologise. Although we have made every effort to verify our facts, including names and dates, inevitably in a work of this sort there will be mistakes. We regret any such errors and ask readers to bring them to our attention.

The History Steering Committee. Left to right, standing: *Amy Barkshire, Betty Cavanagh, John Brooke, Sylvia Williams, Derek Satow;* seated: *Jenny John, Bob Parfitt, Judy Parfitt, Gill Carter.* (Photograph, Rollo Torrance)

A pair of frames showing most of the parish taken by the RAF on 14 January 1946. The low winter sun casts long shadows and lightens the south-facing slopes. On the far right, a steam train on the Somerset and Dorset line approaches the Combe Down tunnel. (© Crown Copyright 1946/MOD)

Contents

Midford in the foreground with South Stoke on the hill behind, c.1920. (E. Smith collection)

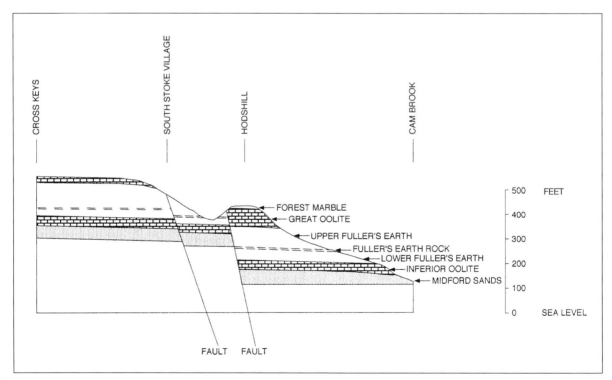

The strata beneath South Stoke: a simplified cross-section looking east (drawn along grid line 748).

CHAPTER 1

Prehistory

❖ *Geological Times: The Rocks and Landscape* ❖

In seeking to learn more about a community of people and the patch of land upon which they live, the question 'why here?' arises. What is it about the land that made early people set roots in this place? For South Stoke the answer is relatively clear; it lies in the springs and brooks, the south-facing slope of South Stoke village, fertile land, good grazing and an abundance of woodland for fuel. But the surface is determined largely by what is below the ground.

The Parish of South Stoke lies at the southern end of the Cotswold Hills, which form part of the great limestone ridge that runs across England from Yorkshire to Dorset. To this geological formation are attributable major features of the local environment – the landscape, to a great extent its flora and fauna, and most notably the presence of freestone so characteristic of the buildings of the parish and area and the shelly ragstones used in boundary walls.

The flat hilltops and steep-sided valleys of South Stoke parish are the result of the erosion of almost flat layers of rocks with varying hardness, massivity, permeability and hence erodability. The plateau is covered by a protective cap of hard great oolite limestone while the layer of soft clays beneath has been worn away to form the valley slopes. Rainwater soaks through the limestone but cannot pass into the clay, thus giving rise to frequent springs. The water washes away the clay and undercuts the limestone above, so that blocks of the stone often collapse. Indeed, in very wet weather, landslips at the level of the fuller's earth have moved down the valley slopes, reminding us of William Smith's comment that fuller's earth could be identified by declivities on the hillsides. Even without springs, the limestone has slumped, as, with the softening of the fuller's earth mudrock, the strata beneath become unable to support the weight.

ROCK LAYERS FROM THE TOP	
Forest Marble	Limestone that usually splits into thin slabs, often rich in broken fossil shells. Some sandstone/sands are present at Hinton Charterhouse.
Great Oolite	The limestone that was quarried and mined all around Bath, as quality Bath and Combe Down stone for stone facing of buildings and shelly limestone used for dry-stone walling.
Fuller's Earth	Mudstones and clays, including the beds worked as a source of commercial fuller's earth.
Inferior Oolite	Variable limestone containing many fossils, including a 'Coral Bed'. The Doulting stone provides a good freestone.
Midford Sands	Uncemented sand with some calcareous sandstone bands.

The inferior oolite and Midford sands are found at the bottom of South Stoke hillsides and were exposed during the construction of the Somersetshire Coal Canal (SCC) and Limpley Stoke to Camerton Railway. The harder and more permeable limestones often form a step on the hillside, while the softer sands, being more easily eroded, form steeper slopes. Again the inferior oolite has been undercut when underlying Midford sands were washed away with

the result that the competent limestone strata have cambered downslope.

The simple picture of flat layers of rock is complicated in the parish of South Stoke by two faults where the rocks have been displaced vertically by the east–west feature that runs through the area. The faults have the effect of repeating the hilltop geology south of the village of South Stoke, with a clay valley between.

The marine origins of the rocks are clearly indicated by the fossils that most of them contain. The original sands, muds and lime-rich sediments were deposited on the sea floor where corals and many other sea animals lived. The presence of corals and oolitic limestones suggests a shallow sea, as today they are found in such locations. The fuller's earth bed is mostly made of the clay mineral calcium montmorillonite, but it also contains tiny pieces of volcanic glass, suggesting its origin is a wind-blown volcanic ash, although the location of the volcano has not been determined. The rocks in the South Stoke area were deposited about 170 million years ago, in the Jurassic period of geological time, when much of what is now England was under a shallow sea and much nearer to the equator. Today the rocks are mostly buried beneath lime-rich soil but they can be seen in a few places. The great oolite limestone is exposed in South Stoke Lane as it rises from the centre of the village towards the plateau. The exposure is tilted to the south, perhaps due to the softening of the fuller's earth that is found a short distance downhill. Inferior oolite limestone is visible beside the Combe Hay flight of coal canal locks, while the upper coral bed is seen just west of the B3110 at Midford, near the bottom of Midford Hill. The Midford sands can be seen in the sides of roads in Midford. Both rocks are also exposed around Tucking Mill, where they are being conserved in memory of the work of William Smith.

William Smith: The Father of English Geology

'One of the most remarkable figures in the whole history of Geology is William Smith a man of humble origin... '. (*Encyclopaedia Britannica*)

It was while surveying and supervising the construction of the Somersetshire Coal Canal between 1793 and 1799 that William Smith discovered one of the cardinal principles of geology, namely that the succession and age of the stratified rock formations of the country could be established from their contained fossils. On 11 December 1799 at 29 Great Pulteney Street, Bath, he dictated his pioneering 'Order of Strata, and their embedded Organic Remains, in the neighbourhood of Bath; examined and proved prior to 1799.' He coloured a contemporary map of 'Five Miles Round Bath' to show the locations of the various strata, thus producing what is justly claimed to be the earliest geological map in the world. Between 1819 and 1822 he published the first *Geological Atlas of England and Wales* comprising 21 separate county geological maps; surprisingly, Somerset was not included. Of his work, the *Encyclopaedia Britannica* declares: 'his large coloured wall-map of 1815 was a monumental achievement for one self-taught man.'

William Smith was born on 23 March 1769 at Churchill in Oxfordshire, the eldest son of a blacksmith. His father died when he was young and he was brought up by a farmer uncle. At the age of 18 he became an assistant to a surveyor at Stow-on-the-Wold, and was sent to work in Somerset in 1791. From 1798 to 1819, he lived at Tucking Mill, which he greatly loved. In 1809/10, he opened a stone quarry at Kingham Field on the edge of Combe Down, which was part of the Midford Castle estate, intending to transport the stone to Tucking Mill for transfer to the canal. Ironically, Smith of all people failed to recognise the poor quality of the stone: the venture failed and he forfeited his house to the owner of Midford Castle in payment of debts. His later years were spent as a land agent at Scarborough. He died in Northampton on 28 August 1839.

Smith often took local and common names for rock strata: for example 'Midford sands' and 'fuller's earth'. But his adoption of the quarrymen and masons' name 'freestones' (because these limestones could be worked so freely) was later superseded by oolites (from the Greek for 'egg rock' as they are made from tiny limestone spheres that look like fish roe). As a result of Smith's work, the fuller's earth and great oolite are known worldwide as the Bathonian stage of the Jurassic system.

William Smith, aged 69. He was named 'The father of English Geology'.

❖ *Prehistoric Times: Evidence of Human Presence* ❖

There is much evidence that the countryside around Bath was inhabited and intensively used in the prehistoric period, from about 10000BC onwards. The upland plateaux are densely scattered with flint implements of Stone-Age people, and one such find north-west of South Stoke village provides the earliest direct evidence of a human presence in the parish. These people were semi-nomadic 'hunter-gatherers' in the wildwood (mainly lime, with some hazel, oak and elm) that had come to dominate the landscape after the last Ice Age.

From about 4000BC, probably due to the arrival of Neolithic tribes from the continent, there was a sudden and dramatic change in the practice of farming, with the keeping of cattle and sheep and crop cultivation. Over the ensuing millennia, huge areas of the wildwood throughout the country were cleared for agriculture. People now lived a more settled existence and, although no remains from this time have been found in the parish, their presence is attested by, for example, the Stoney Littleton long barrow in the adjoining parish of Wellow, which is the finest of its kind in Somerset.

The subsequent Bronze Age (from c.2000BC) was a period of relative peace and stability. Agriculture continued to develop and the population increased. The new-found ability to manufacture in bronze was used for ornamental and domestic items and weapons. A fine bronze spearhead found at Midford dates from the middle Bronze Age (c.1200BC). No evidence of a settlement has been found within the parish, but only a little to the west, in the parish of Combe Hay, a late-Bronze-Age settlement (c.800BC) was discovered in 1970, beneath Roman remains.

Two pieces of Iron-Age pottery from Hodshill. (Somerset Archaeology and Natural History Society, Bath Branch, 1914)

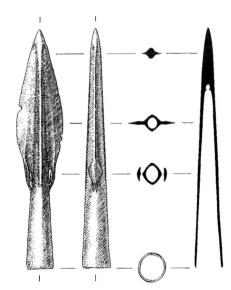

Middle-Bronze-Age socketed spearhead from the foundations of Midford Railway viaduct where it rested 22 feet below the surface of the existing roadway on the course of Midford Brook, 1908. Its actual length is 190mm and it is now in Ulster Museum, Belfast.
(Drawing by Deirdre Crone, courtesy Ulster Museum)

By contrast the Iron Age (from c.750BC) was, in the words of Pevsner, 'a stormy, troubled era, an era of battle and pursuit, when every man's hand was raised against his brother.' Many hill-forts date from this period, such as that on nearby Bathampton Down. This, and many fragments of Iron-Age pottery found in the vicinity of Hodshill, indicate a continuing human presence here during this period.

At the end of the era before Christ, there may have been rather more woodland than there is now and there were probably no hedges, but, apart from the buildings, the landscape may not have differed greatly from that of today. Much of the land within the parish had been cleared of wildwood and was being farmed, with small, scattered, primitive settlements for which the many local springs would have been an asset. Most of the lanes in the parish may have been well-established tracks between settlements. Were the present villages of Midford and South Stoke settlements? There is no evidence that they were, but it is not improbable, as they would have enjoyed advantages similar to those of the small Combe Hay settlement referred to above.

With the beginning of the Christian era, the Iron Age and prehistory were drawing to a close with the arrival of the Romans now imminent.

Roman coffin found at Hodshill early in the 20th century. (Photograph, Rollo Torrance)

Another Roman coffin found at Hodshill early in the 20th century. (Photograph, Rollo Torrance)

CHAPTER 2

From the Romans to the Saxon Charters

❖ *Roman South Stoke* ❖

South Stoke was an important village even in Roman times. It was near the Fosse Way, the main route linking Bath to the trade ports, where goods were imported from and exported to Europe, as well as to the Mendip lead mines. As Bath developed, South Stoke probably became a servicing village for the tourists who came, even in those days, to visit the spa, providing food, pottery and perhaps manpower for the town.

The village of South Stoke was probably the site of at least one, and possibly of more than one Roman villa as well as of a minor industrial complex. Tantalisingly, despite finds of numerous artefacts such as coins, pottery and coffins, there is virtually no documentary evidence for any archaeological work done within the parish boundary, and sites worthy of further investigation have been re-buried beneath rose beds, tennis courts, swimming pools and roadways.

The major finds of the early part of the last century were the discovery of two Roman coffins at Hodshill, the first in 1911, the second in 1914. The 1911 find was made as workmen were laying the terraced lawns south of the house. The coffin was found facing westward and was recorded as being of unusual size. It was thought to contain the remains of two females. In the coffin was found an earthenware vase in good condition and about five inches high. Although there is a photograph of the vase, no one seems to know what has happened to it. A second coffin was found close by, in 1914, this time containing the skeleton of a man about 5 foot 4 inches high. Nails were found around the feet, suggesting that this man was buried in his boots. A considerable quantity of pottery, mainly Samian ware,

Earthenware vase (8½ inches high) from the Hodshill excavations.
(Drawing by Ann Parsons)

was found around both these burials, some of which has recently come to light. One of these pieces is a very fine example of its kind, probably made in Gaul in the 1st or 2nd century AD.

Samian ware from Hodshill.
(Photograph, Rollo Torrance)

Vast quantities of local pottery fragments were found when the gardens of Hodshill were excavated in the 1930s in order to construct the rose garden and croquet lawn. These have generously been given to the village by the Hignett family (in the year 2000) and, at the time of writing, are scheduled soon to become the subject of a major investigation. The pottery includes a great variety of cooking and eating vessel fragments, some patterned with a simple cross-hatch marking or the familiar dimple pattern. There are also a few pieces of colander or draining vessel, as well as an inkwell, and some cup bases.

Evidence for the existence of a Roman villa just outside the parish boundary in Combe Hay, on the site of the fuller's earth workings below Sulis Manor, is much better documented. The site was discovered in June 1968 when work at the mine exposed an intact Roman coffin and a possible pottery kiln. A local archaeologist, Mr Jack Bolwell, undertook exploratory excavations, and a larger scale excavation was organised in 1972 and 1973, funded by the

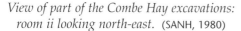

View of part of the Combe Hay excavations: room ii looking north-east. (SANH, 1980)

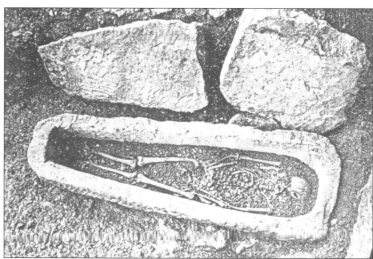

Coffin from the Combe Hay excavations showing the skeleton curved towards the head end. (SANH, 1980)

Department of the Environment and organised by the University of Birmingham. Some of the finds date from the Bronze Age. The majority, however, date from two periods of Roman occupation: the 1st and early-2nd century AD, and the late-3rd and 4th century AD. It is not clear whether the finds from the older Roman period indicate early occupation of the site, or whether they demonstrate that these ancient artefacts, such as jewellery and pottery, were maintained in use over generations before being lost or discarded. What seems to be certain is that the substantial remains of a building found on the site date from the late-3rd century onwards, and that the building was probably abandoned in the early-5th century.

Characteristically, the villa seems to have been the site of some minor industrial activity such as pottery and glass making as well as agriculture. The discovery of ox-shoes suggested that the land below the buildings was ploughed and used for growing corn, and finds from the rubbish tips indicated that sheep and goats were kept for meat as well as their coats. It seems likely, too, that the Romans benefited from the generous local supply of snails by including them in their diet. Red deer and pigs were also eaten and a small number of cattle kept, primarily for milk but also for the table. Sadly, the possible kiln and glass-making works were destroyed in the mining activities, but some of the fragments of pottery found (and there were many of them) were undoubtedly made from local clay.

The footings of the building uncovered were grand in scale – a room about 6 metres by 8 metres, with a paved floor and an elaborate entrance. Contemporary eye-witness accounts of the excavations recall the door sill being very worn and the floor paving being neatly symmetrical in design. It is thought that the low walls surrounding the room provided the foundations for a timbered upper wall and a thatched roof (thatch weights were among the

artefacts found). This room was presumably only a part of a much larger complex that remains to be excavated, stretching to the north (back into the hillside) and west. Because the three coffins were found near the building as well as the evidence of some infant burials, there is a possibility that the room may not have been for habitation but for some religious ceremony and that it actually either stood at some distance from the rest of the complex or was an elaborate entrance to a very much larger structure. It was normal practice for burials to be made away from dwellings, and there were, in fact, strict rules on this type of procedure. The three stone coffins were solidly made and carefully covered with thick stone slabs. One contained shoe nails, like the one found at Hodshill. One of the bodies was curled towards the head end, with the feet not reaching the foot of the coffin, suggesting that the coffin had been put into the ground head first.

There were coins and many other artefacts found on the site. Most of the coin evidence dates the development of the site to the 4th century: other objects give a less clear picture. Although many pottery fragments seem to be made from local clay, others come from pottery factories in the New Forest and a few are of Samian ware from mainland Europe. These are not easily dated with precision, but are likely to be from the 3rd and 4th centuries AD. It does, however, seem certain that the estate was a well-developed and important one, probably benefiting from its proximity to the Fosse Way and other well-trodden routes to the Mendips and the ports of Sea Mills and Poole Harbour.

Further evidence of Roman occupation in South Stoke itself emerged from artefacts (coins, tiles, pottery and part of a wall) dug up in the 1930s in the garden of Southstoke House by Colonel Pitt. The Bath and Camerton Archaeological Society dug the site in 1965 and 1966 and confirmed the existence of a Roman villa, but no records of the work survive

Sketch from the Revd John Skinner's diary of 1828, showing Southstoke Hall with Hodshill in the distance. Roman remains in the bottom right-hand corner. (By kind permission of The British Library)

Remains of a Roman pillar found in South Stoke village.

except a minute quantity of fragments of base pottery kept in Bristol Museum. The major artefacts seem to have been lost from view.

The Revd John Skinner, visiting South Stoke in 1828, was convinced that he had found Roman remains near Southstoke Hall, then the residence of the local vicar, Mr Charles Johnson:

The Roman remains I was brought here to examine are close to Mr Johnson['s] garden wall: the foundations of a Roman residence are here very discernible, having 3 layers of stone, some neatly squared: the ground is dark and abounds in pottery, which the men turned up while digging: they found the blade of a small knife and another article of iron, like a candlestick, but not Roman.

John Skinner left a drawing of where he saw the basis of the villa, between Southstoke Hall and Southstoke House in the field below Packhorse Lane. To date no excavation has been done on this site. Skinner also claims to have found Roman remains in Rowley Meadow to the south of Hodshill.

An impressive collection of column and capital fragments was discovered in a South Stoke village garden and these were identified by the County archaeologist and other experts in 1999 and 2000 as being positively Roman. If they are from a local building, their size and scale would suggest that the villa, if it existed, must have been a splendid one. The same archaeologists recognised stones found in a grass verge off the Midford Road as possibly part of capitals from a Roman site (they are carved in the classic acanthus leaf style) or perhaps of 18th-century origin. Quite how they arrived in the parish is a matter for conjecture.

A stone statue head was dug up in the paddock of Kingsfield in the late-20th century which is Roman in style, and the weight of expert evidence indicates

that it is Roman. Surprisingly, it is relatively unweathered for a Roman artefact.

There are accounts of the existence of a Roman road running through the parish from Bath to Frome. Remnants have been discovered in the field below Midford Castle and continuing below Atcombe. The same road possibly continued through the garden of the property Romain in Midford, where the present inhabitants saw part of it when their neighbour was replacing a boundary wall. On the Tithe Map of 1840 there is a notation 'Fosseway' close to where the house now stands. In 1995, the interim report of a Management Study on the West Wansdyke carried out for English Heritage suggested that the Wansdyke (i.e. the section to the west of South Stoke Lane and in the field known as Thirty Acres) may have been superimposed on a Roman road. John Skinner suggested an extension of the Wansdyke along the Old Midford Road and also described the structure as the 'vallum of Ostorius'.

As far as South Stoke is concerned, it seems that the millennium history project has been merely the starting point for a serious investigation. It has certainly provided an opportunity for a team of well-known experts to come and see what exciting Roman remains we have in the parish. Over the next few years we hope to be able to make many more significant claims for the importance of South Stoke both in Roman times and as an Iron-Age settlement. The studies are to be conducted by the University of Bristol and the Bath and Camerton Archaeological Society.

Roman stone head found in the paddock of Kingsfield.
(Photograph, Rollo Torrance)

❖ *The Saxon Charters* ❖

The immediate post-Roman history of South Stoke is bound up with the fluctuating boundary between Wessex and Mercia and before that with the conflicts of Saxon with Saxon and Saxon with Briton, one of which probably gave rise to the construction of the West Wansdyke.

South Stoke had been a possession of the monastery of Bath before 961, for in that year King Edgar (959–975) restored the land after it had been unlawfully taken from it. The Abbey's Cartulary asserts that the 'parish' had been first granted nearly 100 years before by King Ethelred of Wessex (865–871), King Alfred's elder brother, by whom he was succeeded. South Stoke may have been held by the monastery earlier if North Stoke, granted in 757, was so called to distinguish it from South Stoke in the Church's administration. Because the boundaries of the parish are so straightforward, being defined by simple landscape features, it may even have belonged to the short-lived nunnery established at Bath in 676 by Osric, king or underking of the Hwicce, a people who occupied Gloucestershire and Worcestershire and whose bishopric was at Worcester. The Hwicce were at that time subject to the Mercians whose royal centre was at Tamworth. The nunnery was granted 100 'hides' of land which may have corresponded to the later Hundred of Bath, in which case they will have included South Stoke; alternatively, those lands may have lain entirely north of the River Avon. Bath itself was at that time not in Wessex, but in Mercia. However, South Stoke could well have constituted part of the southern boundary of Mercia. It may be significant that the brook that marks off the lands of South Stoke from those of Combe Hay is called in the charter the maerbroc, that is, 'the boundary brook'. This only makes sense if the brook was part of a pre-existing and important boundary, perhaps the boundary between Wessex and Mercia.

The estate granted in 961 was called Tottanstoc, that is the 'stoc' of a man, probably a Saxon noble, called Totta. The most likely sense of 'stoc' here is that of 'outlying dependency' (as Limpley Stoke was of Bradford on Avon) and the most probable dependency was on the Church at Bath. Totta will have been the name of an early tenant, possibly the man who held it from the Abbey and failed to honour the provisions for returning the estate at the expiry of the lease, thus necessitating the restoration by charter.

The first authenticated appearance of South Stoke in the records is in 961 when King Edgar, who was crowned 'King of all England' in Bath on 11 May 973, restored to St Peter's of Bath five hides of land at Tottanstoc. The hide was the area of land considered enough to support a family or occupy a plough for a year. The relative size of South Stoke can be judged from the fact that, at the time of the Domesday Book (1086), Bathford contained ten hides, Lyncombe ten hides and Bathampton five hides. A near contemporary copy of the charter in the *Registrum Cartarum Abbatiae S. Petri De Bathoniensis* headed, 'De Sudstoca' (concerning South Stoke), survives in the Parker library of Corpus Christi College, Cambridge.

The AD961 charter of King Edgar for South Stoke from Registrum Cartarum Abbatiae S. Petri De Bathoniensis. *(Courtesy of The Master and Fellows of Corpus Christi College, Cambridge)*

The text of the re-grant is in 'monastic Latin' and Old English and has been translated by Mr Michael Edwards thus:

DE SUDSTOCA

In the year of our Lord 961 I Edgar, by divine Grace, King and Chief of the whole land of Albion, bequeath in perpetual right a piece of land consisting of five holdings in the place which is called Tottanstoc to the Church of the Blessed Peter at Bath.

This land which was wickedly and perversely taken from the said Church is to be held free of service save for the maintenance of the fortification and the bridges and the usual service in the militia.

We have solemnly signed the contract of this bequest in the name of our Lord Jesus Christ so that none of our successors shall dare, so long as Christendom endures, to tamper with it in the smallest detail, but if anyone so dare, may he endure the bitter anguish of eternal hell.

The Senators of the whole of Albion are my fellow guarantors of this gift but in particular those whose names are inscribed below:

I, Edgar King, have marked this bequest with the sign of the Cross.

I, Dunstan, Archbishop, have agreed and signed below,

[21 bishops and chiefs also signed]

The piece of land is enclosed within the following boundaries:

First Woden's Dyke bounds it on the north west. Then to the springs at Horse Combe. Along the Brook to the Camelar. Along Camelar against the stream to Boundary Brook. Along the Brook against stream to the Western Seven springs. Then uphill along Boundary Brook. Then due north for some distance. Then bending west round a gore as far as the Old Street (or Made Road). Along the Made Road once more to Woden's Dyke.

❖ The Parish Boundary ❖

The boundary as defined above in the charter endured unaltered for nearly 1000 years, until the Bath City Council, by means of the Bath Extension Act of 1950, annexed some 38 acres in the north-west corner of the parish. (Presumably, in the light of this, the curse in the third paragraph of the charter has been invoked!)

The length of the original parish boundary is some six miles. It is noteworthy that about 80 per cent of it is defined by waterways; a road and the Wansdyke form the rest, so this is a very robust boundary, unlike many created at the same time using non-permanent features, such as trees. Also noteworthy is that when the Somersetshire Coal Canal was built the courses of the Cam and Midford Brooks were in places altered and straightened, but the parish boundary still follows its original course. This is illustrated on the 1840 Tithe Map, pp38–39.

But how much older might that original boundary be? The charter of AD961 was a re-grant of one that may originally have been made 100, 200 or even 300 years earlier. It has been suggested that, because the Wansdyke formed the boundary between South Stoke and Clifton (i.e. Lyncombe and Widcombe), these estates came into being after the construction of the Wansdyke. However, during a recent survey of the Wansdyke, new evidence was noted of a possible southern ditch in the field known as Thirty Acres, immediately west of South Stoke Lane, that could suggest that the Wansdyke might have been superimposed on a Roman road. This hypothesis can only be tested by a full programme of survey, evaluation and excavation.

So the boundary between the South Stoke and Clifton estates could previously have been the Roman road, before Wansdyke was built. The South Stoke estate could, therefore, be much older than the Wansdyke (e.g. as at Marksbury where the Wansdyke cuts across the parish boundary). C.C. Taylor supports this theory:

These (Saxon) charters give the detailed bounds of areas of land which were to become either parishes or the basic agricultural sub-units of parishes in the early medieval period. Again the implication is that these areas of land existed at least in late-Roman times. This means that, in effect, most of the parishes of medieval England and their sub-divisions were in use in the Roman period. Roman rural settlements evolved directly from Iron Age settlements, and exhibited the same features in development. Therefore it is equally possible that some of the estates or land units which existed in Roman times were actually already in being in the late prehistoric period. Indeed there is a little archaeological evidence that certain boundaries used by medieval parochial organisations already existed in pre-Roman times, perhaps as early as the later Bronze Age.

We shall never know for certain; but one can imagine that the 'piece of land' defined in King Edgar's grant in 961, which later became the manor and then the parish, existed as some form of estate or agricultural unit 2000 years ago or more.

The Wansdyke

Wansdyke is cited in King Edgar's charter of 961 as forming the western part of the northern boundary of what is now the parish. What Pevsner calls 'this staggering earthwork' is the longest of its class in the country, one of the few major sites of the Saxon period in Wessex, and an impressive testimony to the former existence of a major political boundary and military frontier across southern central England. It is in two distinct parts.

West Wansdyke runs over the uplands south of the river Avon to the east of Bath. East Wansdyke runs over the downs of Wiltshire and Hampshire, with the Roman road running east from Bath to Mildenhall (Wilts), forming a link between the two parts. The overall length, including gaps, is some 50 miles or more. A number of forts were incorporated along its length.

The dykes consist of a massive bank with a ditch on the north side, the overall width being up to 100 feet or more. In form it is variable and irregular, and it is plausible to suggest that parts of the dyke were built independently and that it was not completed.

Surprisingly, there is no archaeological or documentary evidence to establish conclusively when Wansdyke was built. A traditional date is the late-4th to early-5th century, a period of political and social insecurity near the end of the Roman occupation; or thereafter when Britons were defending against invading Saxons who were in control of the Upper Thames region to the north.

However, in terms of its sheer size and extent it is difficult to see this massive engineering project, for such it was, being carried out during the period of imperial collapse or its immediate aftermath. Moreover, the concept of a full-blown invasion of England by Saxons during the 5th and 6th centuries is now discounted rather in favour of a more gradual infiltration of Germanic people and culture. A later origin is therefore possible.

During the later-8th and early-9th centuries, the Saxon kingdoms of Mercia and Wessex fought a series of battles for control of the border territories between the two kingdoms. The northern boundaries of the counties of Somerset, Wiltshire and Berkshire effectively marked the line of this fluctuating border. Documentary evidence confirms Mercian gains and control during this period in both North Somerset and North Wiltshire, and it is known that Bath was in Mercian hands for short periods. It is in this context that the West Saxons may have built the Wansdyke.

The local part of the dyke, running along the north boundary of Thirty Acres can be seen from the public footpath that runs along it but, regrettably, it has suffered badly on both sides from 20th-century housing development. From the Cross Keys, a spur followed the Midford Road on the north side, while the main dyke ran along the north rim of Horsecombe Vale, past Prior Park and on to Bathampton Down. The Revd John Skinner's suggestion that the dyke (which he also described as the 'vallum of Ostorius') follows the line of the Old Midford Road is unsubstantiated.

The name is Old English: 'Wodnes dic', or 'Woden's Ditch'; Woden, a Scandinavian god, was also the god of tribal boundaries.

Wansdyke, taken in Odd Down Quarry, looking east showing the profile of the ditch.

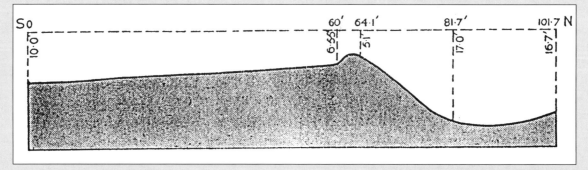

Section through Wansdyke between the Fosse Way and the Cross Keys where it appears largest, looking west. The accompanying illustrations are from Major and Burrow, The Mystery of the Wansdyke (1926).

CHAPTER 3

From Domesday Onwards

❖ South Stoke in the Domesday Book (1086) ❖

The first comprehensive survey of the lands of England is provided in 1086 by the Domesday Book. Those possessions of the 'Church of Bath' (i.e. the Benedictine Abbey of Bath) that can be assigned to Bath Hundred were Weston, Bathford, Monkton Combe, Charlcombe, Lyncombe, Batheaston, Bathampton and 'Woodwick' (in Freshford). Neither North Stoke nor South Stoke is mentioned, although they were held by the 'Church' both before and after this time: for example, in the confirmation of Pope Adrian IV (the Englishman Nicholas Brakespeare 1154–59) Sudstocam appears in the schedule between Lincumbam and Cumbam (Monkton Combe), while Nordstocam appears between Westona quinque hidas and Cherle-cumbam.

A taxation list probably for 1084 assigns 95 hides to Bath Hundred; the list points to the omission of Kelston from the Domesday Book, but in every other respect it can be collated with the Book. Between them the docu-ments account for all the hides that were in Bath Hundred. Not all places are named, but none is omitted. The implication is that just as Lyncombe must have silently included Widcombe, and Batheaston accounted for St Catherine, so North Stoke and South Stoke are included in the Domesday Book under some other entry. North Stoke is no doubt included in Weston's 15 hides (the abbey's holding at Weston itself being only 5 hides).

For South Stoke the candidate is less obvious; it may have been assigned to the 20 hides of Bath, or to Freshford. It is far more likely that its 5 hides lie in the 9 hides allotted by the Domesday Book to Monkton Combe, leaving four hides for Monkton itself. The 13 'ploughs' (though the detail only amounts to 10) counted by the survey suggest a rather larger holding and the estate may have benefited from a generous assessment for tax. Unfortunately, there is no charter relating to Monkton Combe. Clearly, there has not simply been a substitution of names: South Stoke cannot also have stood for Monkton Combe in the Cartulary, since its bounds are given and they do not include Monkton Combe. It is possible that Combe (not yet called Monkton) and South Stoke were among the original possessions of the nunnery and then of the monastery. Alternatively, they were in the 30 hides purchased from the King of Wessex for the monastery. South Stoke was only singled out in the Cartulary because it had been twice alienated and twice restored. Thus it appeared to be a separate entity. Throughout the Middle Ages it was difficult for a church to hold on to its lands and frequent for estates to be alienated in whole or in part. If South Stoke became detached from Monkton Combe, the line of division was along the course of the Horsecombe Brook. The monastery itself may have divided the estate up, letting out one or both portions, and South Stoke did not return to the monastery at the expiry of the agreement. Certainly Monkton Combe and South Stoke were intimately connected: Monkton Combe was a chapelry of South Stoke and the two frequently occur together in documents. Alternatively, Monkton Combe and South Stoke could have been acquired at different times but treated, at least for the Domesday Survey, as a single estate.

The Tithe Barn which dates from, c.1500.
(Photograph, Paul Langham)

❖ *Medieval and Middle Ages* ❖

So long as Bath was in Mercia it was in the Diocese of Worcester. When it came into Wessex, probably towards the end of the 9th century, it was not long before it became subject to the new see (here, the area under the authority of the bishop) that was established at Wells in 909. John de Villula (also known as John of Tours) became Bishop of Wells in 1088. For so worldly a man, Wells was a soggy backwater. Moreover, ecclesiastical thinking was then in favour of establishing cathedrals in major urban centres. Between 1088 and 1091, he was granted by William Rufus the Abbey at Bath, the 20 hides of Bath that had belonged to the king and also permission to transfer his seat from Wells to Bath. The abbacy of Bath was conveniently vacant, so the bishop became de facto the abbot. The day-to-day running of the abbey was left in the hands of a prior; thus Bath Abbey became Bath Priory and remained so until the Dissolution. The lands that had belonged to the abbey were now divided between the bishopric and the priory and as the years passed, the lands were transferred between them as need arose or as power or generosity dictated. For example, in the first year of his episcopacy, Bishop Robert (1136–66) transferred to the monks five hides in Weston, the vill of Monkton Combe, the tithe of the 'Barton' and Lyncombe, and the tithe of the vineyards in Lyncombe and Beckenofna. He also restored South Stoke to them 'to supplement their victuals and Clothing'. Theobald of Bec, Archbishop of Canterbury (1139–61), confirmed these arrangements. South Stoke was now a quasi-independent unit, and no doubt an agricultural entity, though occasionally grouped with other of the priory's estates.

The church of South Stoke, dedicated to St James the Great, probably dates from the mid-12th century. It has Norman, early-English and 13th-century features among its earliest phases, and the first recorded incumbent was in office in 1210. There is no physical evidence of a Saxon church. Before a church was built, the few residents of the Parish could have gone to the church of Bath Abbey for their communion or they could have been visited by a priest. Once built, the church, like the manor, remained in the hands of the Priory until the latter's dissolution on 27 January 1539. Thereafter, for some years, the church came under the patronage of the monarch; later the manor was sold and secularised, a process repeated throughout the kingdom that gave real estate to the newly emergent middle-classes.

The early clergy of the church at South Stoke were invariably associated with the priory. Richard Donekin (also Donekam and Donekar), clerk to Prior Walter, held the living in 1260 and appeared to serve for over 20 years. It is rather curious that in May 1263 he is granted lodgings, with meat and drink in the priory 'so that the said R. may be ordained to the priesthood and serve the priory as chaplain.' Did he hold the living whilst an unordained monk and continue holding it whilst chaplain to the priory? Patronage was also dispensed by way of pensions, for when Thomas de Winson resigned as the prior in 1301 there was 'provision by way of pension viz, the manors of Northstok and Southstok and Staunton and allowance from the common chamber of the monastry.' This may imply that de Winson held the living at South Stoke thus filling a gap in the list of known vicars of the parish. One John de Suthstoke is recorded as being MP for Bath in 1312, 1313, 1318 and 1322.

Another prior, Thomas, during his first year of office in 1332, bestowed his favours on Adam le Smyth, Smyth's wife Isolda and their son John of Midford with a lifetime grant of two plots of land in 'Southstok'. The plots are described as 'two acres of arable land in Harpforlong' and 'two acres of land in Bataylle Forlong by Wodbrok… which Roger de Vox formerly held.' Although the fields directly concerned remain obscure, the field Little Wadbrook is situated immediately south of Midford Castle.

The field Little Wadbrook situated to the south of Midford Castle, c.1920. (Roger Clifford Collection)

Neither Midford nor South Stoke villages would have been isolated in the Middle Ages, both would have experienced a constant flow of travellers on foot and on horse. The route from Bristol and Bath to Salisbury and the south would take traffic over the ford or bridge at Midford, and a major route between Bath and Wells passed over Bisham (Bishop's) Bridge south of South Stoke. Houses would have been constructed from local stone for the more affluent, and wattle and daub for the peasantry. Animals lived cheek by jowl with people, usually being sheltered at one end of a 'long house'. At this time, and for at least another 200 years, rabbits were penned in artificial burrows and farmed in Horsecombe Vale, although the ordinary people lived largely on a diet of grain and vegetables.

THE BLACK DEATH

There are no documents that record the effects of the Black Death on the parish of South Stoke but it is inconceivable, considering the location, that parishioners were untouched by the pestilence. The major thoroughfares of Southern England were well established by the 14th century and South Stoke was close to both the major route between Bristol and Southampton, and the ecclesiastical trail from Bath to Wells.

England in the 14th century was a relatively prosperous place; its architectural legacy is testament to that. However, from 1314 to 1316, harvests failed disastrously, cattle succumbed to disease and there was a widespread decline in population due to starvation and disease. By 1337 the simmering tension with France had erupted into an ill-conceived war – the start of the Hundred Years' War. War brought a brief prosperity that was shattered when the plague (the bacterial disease caused by Pasteurella pestis), having made its way inexorably from the Far East across Asia and Europe, arrived in England. Ports have been established as the major entry routes for fleas bearing bacteria, riding on rats or cargo. At that time Bristol was the wealthiest and busiest port outside London, and must be a principal contender, along with the Dorset ports, as one of the first towns to have experienced the disease.

England was a rural community, 90 per cent of the population living and working in villages; what became known as the Black Death followed the ports and thoroughfares to almost all parts of the South West including Bath and probably South Stoke. Evidence of the effect of the plague on Bath is the decline in the number of monks at Bath Priory from 30 to 15 or 16. The fate of parish clergy is a good indicator of mortality in a parish. It has been estimated that almost half of the clergy in the diocese of Bath and Wells died of the plague and this may be projected to a population mortality of around 40 per cent. Henry de Foxcote had held the vicarage of South Stoke since 1319 but, in April 1349, he was succeeded by Adam Laur of Clyve, of whom nothing is known. Laur's reign was brief as on 11 September 1349 the register of Bishop Ralph de Salopia records: 'The Lord instituted: Robert de Weston priest, to the vicarage of the church of Southstoke.' All three vicars could have perished during the pestilence and the parish could have been left without a vicar. However, because of high mortality amongst clergy, vicars often moved on to a more senior parish.

It is likely that at least one of the incumbents died of plague and a reasonable assumption is that most families in the parish suffered bereavement. There is no evidence that ordinary clergy neglected their duties to save themselves, but the same cannot be said of senior churchmen who isolated themselves in the countryside until late in 1349 when some considered it safe to visit towns once again.

The loss of up to a third of the population of England had an irreversible impact on the nation's economy. Labour was at a premium, wages rose by up to 100 per cent and the structure of the manor was changed forever.

❖ *Local Militia* ❖

Most records from the 14th century to the beginning of the 18th century refer either to the church or to the manor, but there is a scattering of other references to the parish.

From the Conquest onwards there was a national plan for the conscription of local militia. This was particularly important during the reign of Elizabeth I when the country was vulnerable to attack from Spain. To equip conscripted troops with weapons and armour, levies were made and wealthy landowners were required to hold a defined number of horses at the ready. All men over the age of 16 could be conscripted, and a constable, who was an important parish officer, kept appropriate eligibility and armaments records.

A transcript of a Militia Certificate of Musters of 1569 relating to 'Southstoken' exists and reads as opposite:

Perhaps the three Smyths were sons of Thomas and Jane Smyth, who earlier had been tenants of the manor, and perhaps descendants of, or related to, Adam le Smyth of Midford referred to in 1332 (see p20). The name Dagger appeared in South Stoke records over a long period, and some members of the family live just outside the parish to this day.

TITHING OF SOUTHSTOKE

Able Men

Thomas Smyth	pikeman
Anthony Smyth	Archer
Laurence Smyth	billman
Richd. Dymock	gunner
Jno. Browne	Archer
Thos. Love	billman
Jno. Dagger	Archer
Thos. Alberd	billman

Armor

One tethinge corslet furnished
One pair of almaine rivets furnished

❖ Civil War and Rebellion ❖

The Civil War Compensation Claim for South Stoke has not survived, but in spite of this loss it is possible to project the probable effect of the conflict upon the parish based upon the claims of nearby villages.

Hearth Tax returns for the parish in 1664/5 reveal that 14 houses had between them a total of 42 hearths, suggesting that around 70 of the South Stoke population were of above average affluence. The manor (near the present Manor Farm), owned by Richard Cox, was the largest house with 11 hearths. (A tax of 2 shillings (10p) on every hearth or fireplace was imposed in 1662, although very poor cottages were exempt. The tax was finally abolished in 1689).

Before the Civil War, in 1642, the people of North Somerset, many of whom were deeply puritan, rose to support Parliament against the King. Faced with a Royalist force in Wells under the command of the Marquis of Hertford, they marched out to the Mendips and held their first meeting at Shepton Mallet. Many parishes, South Stoke no doubt amongst them, organised food supplies for the uprising. That the vicar of South Stoke, Thomas Hull, was not evicted from the living during the Commonwealth suggests that his sympathies were with the Parliamentary cause.

June/July 1643 saw the campaign of the Battle of Lansdown. Royalists from Cornwall marched over the Mendips to Frome and Bradford before launching an attack on Bath. Three weeks before the battle Sir William Waller's army camped on Claverton Down and the daily rendezvous at Combe Hay would have required some Parliamentarian troops at least to pass through South Stoke.

One compensation claim from Combe Hay was for troops trampling down crops that were ready for harvest, suggesting that similar claims would have been made from the parish. Throughout the region surrounding Bath, troops would have been billeted and fed, and wagons with their teams of oxen and horses commandeered at no small cost to villages and farms. Victuals, etc. were not only requisitioned but were also plundered. Men were drafted into the Parliamentary army and parish constables had the uncomfortable and unpopular task of selecting conscripts from their communities.

In 1645, the first uniformed army, the New Model Army, was formed. Bristol was besieged and once again troops were billeted in and supplied by the local villages. From the compensation claims it is clear that Dunkerton, Camerton and Combe Hay all suffered. South Stoke would have been no different.

Communities took a considerable time to recover once the war ended in 1646. Stock had to be replaced and bridges and roads mended. Smaller farms and farm labourers were impoverished by demands for taxation and supplies. Soldiers returning from the war were sometimes so badly maimed that they were unable to work.

At the time of the Civil War a major route from Bath to Wells passed along South Stoke Lane through the village and up over Hodshill. The strategic high ground overlooking the road from the south is now occupied by Brewery House. In 1917 three cannon balls (some say five) and a candle holder were found in Brewery House garden. Unfortunately the candle holder was stolen and only one cannon ball remains. The 3½ inch cannon ball has been identified by G.M. Hebditch (Bristol Museum) as a 'Saker' ball made for the cannon of the same name of the Civil War period. It is likely that in 1643 Sir William Waller, who was holding Bath, fortified the high ground anticipating the route of Sir Ralph Hopton's Royalist army. Hopton, however, skirted Bath and attacked Waller's Roundheads at Lansdown on 5 July.

As a postscript to the Civil War the following report appeared in the *Bath Chronicle* on 19 November 1808:

> *Yesterday the workmen employed in making the new turnpike-road on Odd-Down, in cutting through an embankment, discovered a heap of human bones and skulls, some of the latter with teeth nearly in perfect state; supposed to be the remains of people slain in the Cromwellian wars.*

Just 40 years after the Battle of Lansdown the parish had another brush with conflict, this time in the form of the Monmouth Rebellion. In the summer of 1685, James, Duke of Monmouth, the illegitimate son of Charles II, landed at Lyme Regis in his attempt to wrest the throne from James II. With his rabble of an 'army' he was repulsed from Bristol and Bath, and made his way to Frome. From the top of Holloway they took the narrow and badly engineered 'Old Warminster Road' entering the parish at the crossroads where the Cross Keys Inn now stands. According to Foxcroft the rebels 'descended its former precipitous course (Old Midford Road below Beeches) now degraded, into roads as far as Midford'. It appears that they avoided the steep hill from Midford and followed an old track via the water meadows to Twinhoe and Wellow and thence to Hinton and Norton St Philip. The retreat ended with a crushing defeat at the Battle of Sedgemoor and savage punishment of the rebels by Judge Jefferies.

❖ *Poverty in the Parish* ❖

After the Dissolution of the Monasteries the loss of the charity that they had given to the poor was soon felt. Voluntary contribution was not successful and so the first poor rate was imposed in 1597. This was followed by the Poor Law Act of 1601 that became the foundation for local poor law administration for over two centuries. The churchwardens were ordered to appoint each year a small number of substantial householders as 'overseers of the poor', whose duties were to levy a rate on all inhabitants of the parish in order to maintain the poor and set them to work. Under the earlier Poor Law Act of 1598 vagrants were required to have passes to move from their parishes. A vagrant found without a pass could be sent to a 'house of correction'. Because paupers were a charge on the poor rate in the parish of their 'settlement', any person without means was legally required to live off their parish. Clearly, in 1680, Jane Attwood was claiming support from South Stoke parish whereas that parish insisted that her place of settlement was Freshford. It was beneficial to South Stoke to shunt Jane into another parish; 'moving on' paupers was common practice. The overseers of Freshford refused to accept her and the matter was thrashed out in the Somerset Quarter Sessions. The Freshford overseers were bound over until the next General Session for contempt of court. A year later,

at the next Sessions, they complained that it was not their fault as Jane insisted on returning to South Stoke and refused to stay in Freshford, which they accepted was her lawful place of settlement. To complicate matters, Jane, who was almost certainly unmarried, had 'delivered of a certaine Child att Southstoake'. The child's settlement was, by definition, South Stoke. Jane Attwood, with her child, was therefore directed by the court:

> ... to repaire to Freshford aforesaid and there remayne as the Lawe directes, On refusall thereof any Justice of the peace of the said County is by the Court ordered and desired to send her to the howse of Correccion by Mittimus as a disorderly person...

The Attwoods had become a well-known local family by the 18th and 19th centuries.

Poverty often resulted in the abandonment of a child who then became the responsibility of the overseers of the poor. The following is from the Quarter Sessions records:

> An order made by John Harrington and William Bassett Esq. For the keeping & relieving of a child born in the parish of South Stocke 26th day of September 1643.

Extracts from South Stoke Churchwardens' Account Book 1663–82

1663	*Widdow Hood at 12s. the month comes to*	£7.16s.0d.
	More for smocks and a blanket for her	11s.2d.
1667	*pd Jo Crump for a fox head* [as bounty for vermin]	1s.0d.
1668	*paid for a child that was left at the Inn* [Pack Horse]	17s.5d.
1678	*paid for a dozen of all* [ale] *at the highwayes*	1s.0d.
	[Paupers were often employed to repair roads receiving ale in lieu of money.]	
1681	*Item paid for several warrants and orders for Jane Attwood*	£2.10s.2d.
	and for our charge at the Sessions at Bath & Welles and for	
	Counsellors fees. [see above]	
1682	*Item paid for Malitha* [Militia]	11s.0d.

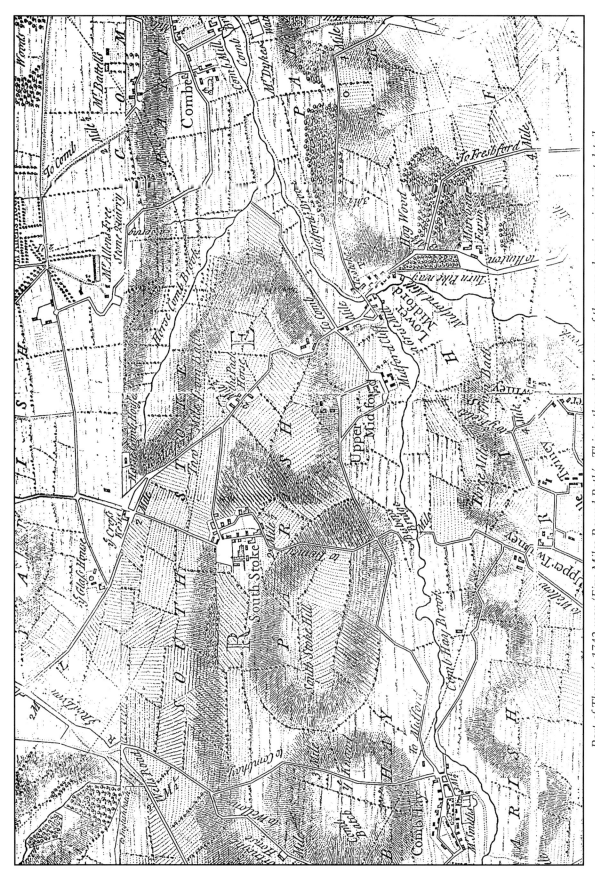

Part of Thorpe's 1742 map 'Five Miles Round Bath'. This is the earliest map of the area showing significant detail, and is interesting in particular for the detail it shows of field boundaries and of the orientation of the field strips.

South Stoke
in the 18th Century

Although some of the parishioners of South Stoke may rarely, if ever, have visited Bath, their fortunes and that of the parish were inextricably bound to the city. At the end of the 17th century, confining medieval walls enclosed a small city of little special distinction other than a fine Abbey church and some 'curative' hot springs. All that changed with Queen Anne's visits to Bath in 1702 and 1703 and again with Richard Nash taking up residence in 1705. Nash took the city in hand and as the 18th century progressed, Bath became a centre of society, elegance and amusement and this brought with it wealth.

Records for much of the century reflect the Church of St James the Great as a focus of South Stoke parish society and governance. The fabric of the church appears to have been severely damaged by terrible storms which hit the South West in 1703, necessitating repairs to the roof and the floor. Clearly this was a holding action as in 1712 extensive rebuilding was undertaken. The churchwardens' accounts record that two loads of sand were purchased from Midford at a cost of 4 shillings (20p). Little new stone was needed so it is likely that old masonry was reused. The cost of labour to rebuild walls to accommodate a new lower pitched roof would have employed three or four men for around three months. Carved stones discovered in the grounds of Homeville in 1963 and identified by G.M. Hebditch (Bristol Museum) as 'decorative work at the tops of pillars in a 13th-century church' suggest that the new roof replaced a more steeply pitched structure of the 13th century. It is also possible that the church register was lost or damaged in the storms as a new one (still in existence) was purchased in 1704 at a cost of 2s.6d. (12½p). During these works and the extensive rebuilding of the 19th century many church monuments were also lost.

To pay for the rebuilding of the church a special parish rate was raised in 1712 and it was notable that the vicar, Robert Crowch (1691–1739), made no contribution. There are hints in the accounts that Crowch was a less than generous man; he had the habit of scoring out the entries for his parish rates in the accounts book. Demonstrating the contempt of at least one parishioner is this entry across a page in the book – 'the first place honest Crowch began to cratch [sic] out his rate 3/2d.' Another entry (27 May 1730)

indicated that the vicar was again in dispute over money. From around 1700 it is likely that Robert Crowch was the recipient of the great tithe.

As the importance of Bath grew so it would appear did the attractiveness of the living of South Stoke Parish Church, in spite of the high level of poverty in the rural community. The appointments of the well-connected and influential Edward Spencer (1769) and Charles Johnson (1792) are examples of this. From 1799 Johnson also held the living at Berrow.

Spencer, it seems, was very much an absentee vicar, exerting his evangelical efforts elsewhere, probably at Oxford, and leaving the day-to-day matters of the church to his curate Robert Graves. John Wesley, a good friend of Spencer, was invited to preach at St James the Great in September 1769, but no record of the event having taken place can be traced. A few years later Wesley was to express disapproval of Spencer's Calvinist leanings.

During the second half of the 18th century some members of the congregation, among them wealthy traders, no doubt attracted by the style of the clergy, made the less than easy journey from Bath to South Stoke village to attend services. The names of some of these devotees are found amongst church monuments and memorials.

As in many churches throughout the country, parishioners for centuries had marked the Dedication Day of their church by a celebration known as 'Revels'. The degeneration of the Revels into unseemly riotous and drunken affairs resulted in most being abandoned by the latter part of the century. Rather later than most places, in 1776, the vicar, John Deere Thomas (1771–80), banned the St James' Day Revels in South Stoke. They were never reintroduced.

For reasons that remain obscure a meeting of the Vestry held on 7 February 1775 resolved to dismiss from his post the Clerk to the Parish, Richard Lansdown, to take effect five days later. The churchwarden was ordered:

... to tender and pay Rich. Lansdown Late Parish Clerk so much money as may be due for his services from the day of his appointment April the 10th 1774 to the day of his dismission from the office Feb. 12th 1775 at the rate of twenty shillings per ann.

The Packhorse. (Drawing by Ann Parsons)

Whatever had happened, such a serious action must have caused tongues to wag around the parish. There was clearly some acrimony and because of the anticipation of legal challenge from Lansdown, the parish officers at a Vestry Meeting on 15 February unanimously agreed to defend their action at parish expense. By 1784 wounds had healed sufficiently for Lansdown to be a signatory on the parish accounts.

A Vestry Meeting of April 1793 approved the partitioning of the north end of the church gallery for the use of 'Miss Aldritts and their scoalers at their expense'. The gallery was erected at the west end of the church some 20 years earlier at a cost of £14.14s.0d. How long a school operated from the church gallery is not known.

An important route for travellers and trade between Bristol, Bath and Southampton and other South Coast ports via Warminster passed through the parish close to the village of South Stoke, down Midford Hill (now part of the Old Midford Road) and through the hamlet of Midford. Keeping this arterial route open was vitally important and when, in 1709, a land slip occurred on Midford Hill a 'hiwayman' was employed for 'throing out the mire'. On the same road a major repair was carried out on 'Mitford' Bridge in 1718. Crossing this road was another important route, an alternative to the Fosse Way out of Bath, through Wellow to Wells. There is also a record of this road being repaired at 'Hodhill way' by one Thomas Savin of Combe Hay. At this crossing the Cross Keys Inn was built early in the century, probably as a coaching inn, and in 1718 was leased to physician

Henry Parker. Although just outside the parish, South Stoke residents were quick to frequent the inn. After the recasting of the church great bell by Thomas Bilbie of Chew Stoke in 1719 the bell founder was entertained in the Cross Keys at a cost of 1s.6d. A more cryptic entry in the churchwardens' accounts for 1727 refers to a Cross Keys account for 3 shillings, perhaps for communion wine.

The inns, of course, were as much a focus of parish life as was the church, but a focus of a very different kind. The 1742 Thorpe map shows the Pack Horse Inn on the Old Midford Road as the only inn in the parish. (There was at least one other inn in Midford.) There is circumstantial evidence, however, that the Pack Horse (now Pack Horse Farm) was an inn long before that. Canvin suggested that an assault on Alexander Morrice of 'Mounten' Combe by John Bowles, a 'waggoner from Keynsome', which occurred at 10p.m. on 23 October 1680 and which was witnessed by Anne and John Smith, must have been at a well-lit location in the parish, perhaps the Pack Horse. There were two John Smiths in the parish, one of Upper 'Mitforde', the other from the mill.

During the latter part of the 18th century the Pack Horse was owned by Ann Grace (see inset) and as newspaper reports illustrated, the inn acquired a high degree of notoriety, particularly as a centre for tea smuggling. After around two centuries as a hostelry the trade and name passed to the present Packhorse Inn in the centre of South Stoke in about 1850.

Ann Grace of the Pack Horse Inn

Long before 20th-century dwellings spread their way along the Old Midford Road (formerly Midford Hill), Pack Horse Inn (now Pack Horse Farm) cared for the needs of travellers and locals. For a time in the latter part of the 18th century the inn was owned by a colourful character, Ann Grace, who conducted business as farmer, innkeeper and carrier. Ann was evidently a woman of parts and resource, for in addition to her lawful pursuits, she had a sideline – tea smuggling. The *Bath Chronicle* of 23 January 1766 includes the following:

Tuesday last about noon, upwards of two cwt of smuggled tea was seized at the sign of the Packhorse on Midford Hill near this City by S. Sykes, an Officer of Excise. The smugglers were dividing it into small parcels which [were] seized but immediately took their horses from the stable and made off.

The East India Company's monopoly in the lucrative tea trade had been resented for decades in Britain and America. Tea prices were inflated and enterprising 'traders' took advantage of the profitable illegal imports from South Coast ports that had a ready market in the salons of Bath and Bristol. The issue came to a head with the Tea Act of 1773, designed to perpetuate the monopoly, leading to the Boston Tea Party.

There is no record of charges being brought against Mrs Grace and her storage and packaging business continued to flourish. However, again, on 27 June 1779, the *Bath Chronicle* made the report that:

On Saturday last, Mr. Hayden, Supervisor of this City, being informed that a large quantity of tea (supposed to be about two tons) was concealed in a barn at the Pack Horse on Midford Hill, he with three of his officers made a seizure of the same but an alarm being directly given, the smugglers attacked the officers with pistols, blunderbusses and bludgeons, when, after combat of half an hour, the smugglers overpowered them (being six to one) who immediately loaded their horses, and proceeded in triumph thro' Comb-Hay and Wellow and, as supposed by way of Old Down to Bristol. The Supervisor and one of the officers are very dangerously wounded. This is the second cargo of tea that has been lodged at the same place within these ten days.

Ann Grace died on 20 March 1786 and is buried at Monkton Combe.

In 1716 the present Packhorse, then a house known as The Breath, was bought by Hanah Charmbury, a member of a long-standing (1594–1840) South Stoke family, who in 1725 shared the office of churchwarden with John Smith.

In addition to the Pack Horse and Cross Keys inns, there were at least two other hostelries in Midford, The White Hart and The Fox (which is just outside the parish). Both buildings still exist, the former having been renamed The Hope and Anchor to identify with a later, flourishing coal canal. In 1782 The White Hart was advertised for sale by Richard Smith as consisting of the inn, two houses and a grist mill. In the same year George Flower became the landlord of The Fox.

The 18th century was not a notably law abiding period and it is therefore surprising that there are not more references to criminal activities. Other than the skulduggery that was focussed on the Pack Horse Inn references are indirect. The village of South Stoke, like most others in the realm, was equipped with stocks for those committing misdemeanours and the location of the stocks is believed to have been just north of the church in the vicinity of the pound. It was usual for stocks, pound, whipping post and lock-up to be clustered together.

In 1757 and 1758 the stocks were repaired first by Richard Fisher and then by Thomas Beady. Whether the first repair was shoddy or the stocks were being excessively used is not recorded. The offer of a reward for information by farmer William Jones in January 1789, when his barn and its contents of corn were burnt out, raises a suspicion of arson. Civil unrest, influenced by the excesses of the French Revolution, was rife throughout Europe at this time and, in microcosm, South Stoke was not immune. James Carter, a coal driver from the parish, probably objected to paying his toll at the Burnt House Gate and his 'abuse' (which could mean cheat in this context) of the gate keeper led to his arrest. He subsequently escaped and had the price of one guinea placed on his head.

When a new gaol was proposed for Bedminster in 1725, the parish officers held a meeting to discuss the matter at the George Inn, Walcot Street (opposite St Michael's Church), and at a cost of 10s.2d. (around 50p) must have entertained themselves royally. The project was abandoned.

For the Manor of South Stoke the beginning of the 18th century was not auspicious. The property was held by John and Winifred Gay, and Thomas Goddard through a lease granted on 12/13 June 1690, which:

> ... did convey the Manor House of Southstoke and other Messuage and Lands in the County of Somerset to Thomas Goddard and Richard Gay intoo the use of John Gay for his Life and then in trust that he might make Leases thereof for payment of his Debts And as to part thereof to Winifred Gay for her Life and then to the said Thomas Goddard and Richard Gay for the term of 99 years upon trust to pay Winifred Gay (if she survived her husband) £20 per Annum for her life and after upon trust to raise the Sale the Summe of £800 to bee distributed among the younger Sonnes and Daughters of the said John Gay & Winifred & after the determination of the said Term then to the wife of Richard Gay their oldest Son & his Heires.

The estate, through John and Goddard Gay (their second son), accumulated considerable debts. John owed a total of £3110.8s.4d. to several people and he and Goddard had mortgaged the property for £500. As a consequence Winifred had to petition the House of Lords for permission to sell the estate. In about 1704 a Bill was passed through Parliament agreeing the sale together with an appropriate distribution of proceeds to the creditors (see page 71).

Ownership of the property passed, in 1711, to Augustine Rock and John Teague of Bristol and John Jones of Dundry. No record has been found to establish whether there was another owner in the meantime. The only other record we have for the period is the 1768 sale of Manor Farm Estate by the Earl of Sandwich to Robert Cooper of Salisbury at a time when farm incomes and values were escalating dramatically.

Throughout the century agriculture was the mainstay of the parish economy with the majority of the population being landowners, lessees or farm workers. This is evidenced by the many extant notices of land and farm sales. Although by the middle of the 18th century much land in the south of England had been enclosed, many villages were still open-field in character. The early-19th-century drawings of Skinner, illustrating Packhorse Lane and Old Midford Road, show that some fields were not enclosed and were probably open sheep runs.

The consternation in the area caused by an outbreak of what is now known as foot and mouth

---

BATH CHRONICLE, 24TH FEBRUARY 1780

To Gardeners and others – Any sober, honest person who is inclined to be in partnership in the Gardening way, may have the opportunity of coming into six acres of good orchard and market garden ground with a lease of fifteen years to come, at the yearly rent of £12. It is pleasantly situated on the south side of an hill in the Parish of Southstoke two miles from the City of Bath good turnpike road and now in occupation of Richard Sadler. Greatest part of ground is well stocked with vegetable crops, gooseberries, currants, raspberries, strawberries, young asparagus beds etc.. Likewise a new built stone house of two tenements built at expense of said Richard Sadler which the owner of the ground agreed to purchase at the end of the term. If it is agreeable to be in partnership may lease with the house, stock and crop at £200 or half the above.

Apply to Richard Sadler on the premises. Letters must be post paid.

---

disease is not hard for us to imagine. The outbreak, first referred to in parish records in 1746, resulted in a meeting of parish officers to be called in Frome (at a cost to this parish of 2s.6d. or 12½p) in an effort to coordinate attempts to fight the disease. South Stoke spent 1s.6d. 'for a prayer book concerning ye cattle' and on 28 December 1746 the churchwardens' accounts record that 6 shillings (30p) was paid 'for Bell Rope for the horned cattle'. At that time a tarred rope was drawn through the hoof cleft as a remedy. Not for over another 100 years was wholesale cattle slaughter used as a drastic but effective means of disease control.

South-facing slopes of the parish were then, as now, ideal for growing fruit and vegetables. There was at least one market garden operating from South Stoke at that time. No doubt the produce was in high demand at the quality market of Bath. Richard Sadler, on 24 February 1780, offered a partnership in a market garden: 'Vegetables and soft fruit grown. House of two tenements. Southside of a hill in the parish of Southstoke.'

Although overall the incomes and living standards of farm labourers had risen steadily during the early part of the century, fortunes were patchy. Parishes, through the parish rate and the overseers of the poor, had a responsibility to support the needy in their communities. In the South Stoke records there are numerous entries illustrating such charity. Poor people not 'resident' in the parish were given temporary help and then efforts were made to return them to their own parish. There are several references in the churchwardens' accounts of 1714 to help given to a pregnant woman (a 'great bellyd woman') passing through the parish, and another (1716) where 1 shilling (5p) was given to a woman 'undon by fire', probably as part of a wider collection. When a baby was found abandoned in 1723 various amounts were spent from parish funds on keep and clothing whilst the mother was sought. 'A poor man took by pyrats', was given 6d. (2½p) in 1733, again probably as part of a wider collection, perhaps a church brief. More macabre is the churchwardens' account of the same year for the burial expenses of the pauper, John Whippy, including the purchase of 'five candels' at 2s.4d. (about 12p). These were to afford light for someone to sit with the corpse overnight, partly for religious reasons and partly as a deterrent to body snatchers.

From the middle of the century the agrarian revolution accelerated with increasing land enclosure and the dominance throughout the country of the capitalist tenant farmer. High food prices, further inflated by war, resulted in widespread deprivation. Grain prices more than doubled in the second half of the century and, when this was compounded by the poor harvest of 1764, civil disturbance occurred. The only evidence we have for this in South Stoke was the report of a 'Waggon load of grain seized at Packhorse, Midford Hill and hauled without aid of horses to Bath Market and there sold at a moderate price.' Another indication of how bad things were in South Stoke 200 years ago was the donation by a General Meadows of 40 quarters of coal and a quantity of beef to 20 poor families. Such a number would have constituted about one fifth of the parish population.

Many of the harmless fauna of the countryside were considered vermin and the bounties placed on their heads supplemented the incomes of the poor and the not so poor. Sparrows, hedgehogs, badgers, moles, polecats, otters and foxes were all hunted and the heads proffered to the churchwardens for reward. In 1759, 1 shilling (5p) was paid for five 'hedgegogs' and in 1750 James Allen earned 4d. (about 1½p) for a 'powlcat'.

Need of quite a different sort arose when refugees in the form of aristocrats and clergy abandoned France during the 'reign of terror' in 1793, at the height of the French Revolution, with many settling destitute in Britain and its Dominions. A churchwardens' accounts entry of April 1793 is for a payment of 1s.6d. (7½p) for the 'french clergy' in response to a national petition or subscription. This was the parish contribution and would have been in addition to individual donations. George III proclaimed that a 'General Fast' was to be observed on 19 April 1793.

The effect of agrarian reform on the rural population was compounded by the less direct impact of the Industrial Revolution. There had been industry of sorts in and near the parish for centuries. The glass works (Glasshouse), probably taking advantage of Midford sand, made glass in the 17th and 18th centuries. By 1746, however, the former works was described as Glasshouse Farm and was advertised to let in the *Bath Chronicle* by Robert Bennett (the Bennett family acquired the Glasshouse in 1702) and Phillip Allen, nephew of Ralph Allen. Within 20 years the buildings, which had been used for storing carts and wagons, had collapsed.

The mining of fuller's earth in the area had been a small industry from the time of the Romans but it

Southstoke brewery before 1920 showing the malting tower at the rear. Brewery House with its crenellation is to the left.

developed into something more extensive from the middle of the 18th century with the increasing fortunes of the woollen industry brought about by advances in spinning technology. Some South Stoke people would inevitably have been involved either directly or indirectly in these industries.

Throughout history, malt production and brewing had been small industries in rural communities. Joseph Burden advertised in 1762 a 'house for sale at South Stoke with brewhouse etc. Also small stable, carriage house, acre or two of good pasture or more.' It is also possible that the Mr Kelson, who paid a church rate of 5 shillings for 'Orchard & Malthouse' in South Stoke from 1815-17, was the same Mr Kelson who was in the brewing trade at the Belvedere Inn in Bath from about 1791. Tragic evidence that brewing was pursued in the area in 1793 was the death of the two-year-old son of Farmer (John) Cox who 'fell into a cooler of boiling wort and scalded to death'. The growth of brewing would

have been in response, at least in part, to the affluent market of Bath as well as to the needs of the local hostelries. Parish accounts record the purchase of beer (and the payment of bell-ringers) to help the festivities celebrating, for example, the coronations of George I (1714) and George III (1761).

Although there was little industry associated with the parish in the 18th century, by 1792 plans for a coal canal were being discussed, and by 1794 the Canal Bill received Royal Assent. The impact of changes in agricultural and industrial practice from the middle of the century transformed forever the character of a community that hitherto had evolved slowly.

By 1775, following the creation of Turnpike Trusts by a 1752 Act of Parliament, the steep and difficult section of Old Midford Road had been by-passed by a new turnpike (B3110), easing the route to Warminster and the south coast.

Extracts from the South Stoke Churchwardens' Account Book 1703–71

1703	Directions for praying for Princess Sophia [Granddaughter of James I]	£1.0s.0d.
1710	For a post for the pound	1s.0d.
1716	Gave a poor woman undon by fire	6d.
1718	Laid out for Mitford Bridg [which suggests a considerable repair on an earlier bridge]	£1.5s.4d.
1723	pd to Edward Weekes for ye parrish childs clothes	13s.6d.
	pd for a cap and a pair of stockings for ye child	9d.
	pd in seeking ye childs mother	6s.0d.
	pd to Thomas Hopkins for keeping ye child	£5.6s.3d.
	pd for ye childs shoons [shoes]	1s.0d.
	[The child had been abandoned in the parish and was a charge on the rates. Thomas Hopkins was probably Overseer of the poor.]	
1725	For sparrows 3½d. and gave a poor man 3d.	6½d.
	[Sparrows being considered a pest, parishioners were paid to do away with them. One Act of 1532 set this sum at 2d. per dozen to be paid for by the landowner.]	
1730	pd Thos Savin for mending Hodhill way	1s.5d.
	[The Savins or Sabins lived at Three Days Cottage, Combe Hay.]	
1751	pd Stephen Dew for six days and a half work in pitching the belfree pointing the Roof of the Tower plastering and whitewashing several parts of the church and mending the church wall.	9s.9d.
1771	pd Edward Blake for the Communion Rails	4s.4d.
	[These were probably replaced by the present ones in 1845.]	

CHAPTER 5

The 19th Century:
A Time of Change

Edmund Marks, South Stoke, near Bath, 1853.
(Courtesy of the Victoria Art Gallery, Bath, and Bath and North East Somerset Council)

The outstanding feature of 19th-century Britain was its dynamism. Great political, social, economic and technical changes were taking place. The century opened in the aftermath of the French and American revolutions, and during the Napoleonic Wars. Having built a national identity, military and technological superiority, and a great overseas empire during the previous centuries, for Britain the 19th century was an era of consolidation. Between 1801 and 1901 the population of England and Wales more than trebled, from 8 to over 30 million people. What implications did these transformations have for South Stoke parish, embedded in the Somerset countryside, yet closely associated with the cosmopolitan city of Bath?

Although the first national census was held in 1801, data from the first four censuses is fragmentary. We know that in 1811 the population of South Stoke stood at 188 with 95 males and 93 females. The parish had 42 households, of which 24 were engaged in agriculture, and there were two uninhabited houses. Other information comes from an extant parish survey of the period. In 1803, in the light of the continuing war with France, all parishes were required to survey residents and resources. Lists of men between the ages of 15 and 60 willing to enlist were categorised as those capable of active service, those willing to act as mounted guides, labourers (mainly woodcutters) and people willing to give 'wagons' and horses. John O'Neal was appointed to lead the local militia and it appears that the two maltsters of the parish chose not to co-operate!

Two major Acts of Parliament, the 1832 Reform Act and the 1834 Poor Law Act, were significant milestones consequent upon increasing industrialisation and urbanisation. A redeployment of workers required political and economic change. Although the traditional small-scale domestic woollen trade was not important to South Stoke, it had been significant in Bath and surrounding areas. The shift of textile manufacture, based largely on cotton, to northern factories led to a decline in population in the South West. It is worth remembering that it was not until 1868 that all male ratepayers were entitled to vote.

At South Stoke the building of the turnpike, coal canal and railway through Midford reflected the rising demand for coal and the increasing need for transport and mobility. Although the restructuring of agriculture followed the Enclosure Acts (1760–1830) and the concentration of landownership and improved husbandry increased productivity, Britain had become a net importer of food from around 1780 and there was a decreased demand for rural labour. As a consequence of these changes and the Napoleonic Wars, vagrancy, poverty and disablement led to increased demands for parish relief.

An examination of the occupations of male South Stoke residents from parish records and decennial censuses provides evidence of a continuous shift out of agriculture (from 49 per cent in 1851 to 19 per cent in 1891) to other manual work such as milling, baking, brewing and work related to transport. In addition there was an increase of those in non-manual occupations such as publicans, victuallers and those holding clerical, professional and managerial posts. These trends continued and accelerated in the 20th century. Female employment in the 19th century was predominantly in domestic service; laundresses, seamstresses and governesses. A comparison with Bath suggests that the parish was a small satellite of the city being clearly focussed on Bath's main industry, the servicing of the wealthy. Surprisingly, there was little evidence of any influence from Bristol, which at the time was one of the most important and prosperous British cities, a flourishing port and a mere 12 miles away.

A more skilled workforce required formal education. In South Stoke, the Church of England School was established by the Revd Henry Calverley in 1840. The school predated by some 30 years the introduction of universal primary education for all five to ten year olds in 1870. The censuses indicate that many South Stoke 'infants' aged three or four were described as pupils or scholars.

The population of South Stoke had grown slowly and erratically up to the beginning of the 19th century from a base of around 150 in the previous 50 years, to 177 according to the 1801 census. Ten years later there had been a further increase of only 11 residents. By 1861, however, the population had reached 355, and by 1891 there were 410 residents. A century on, the 1991 census showed little further change with 419 in residence. Clearly in terms of numbers the population of South Stoke did not reflect the experience of the country generally. It did, however, mirror the national experience in terms of age, sex distribution and household size.

Parish life during the century was dominated by four vicars, each with a powerful personality. At the advent of the century, Prebendary Charles Johnson officiated and continued to do so until 1838. Through the marriage of Johnson's second son Francis to Emma Brooke, a link was forged between the parish and Sir James Brooke and the related White Rajahs of Sarawak. Charles Johnson was also chaplain to the Prince of Wales from 1808–18. In 1826 he and his wife suffered the indignity and, as it turned out, the considerable expense of the elopement of their youngest daughter Lucy (see opposite page).

Parsonage Farm, c.1970.

Henry Calverley succeeded Johnson and was responsible for developing the church to its present form. At his death Calverley owned 75 acres of land in the parish of which 46 constituted the core of Parsonage Farm. For the final quarter of the 19th century William Acworth, and finally, to within living memory, William Samler held sway, introducing more changes. In 1886 William Samler built a parish room and two adjoining cottages. The former essentially took over as schoolroom from Calverley's earlier school and continued in use until 1973.

During much of the century Midford was a hive of industrial activity with fuller's earth processing, stone transportation, coal canal traffic and the railway. Whereas, according to the 1851 census, the coal canal contributed significantly to parish employment, South Stoke brewery, the various fuller's earth works and stone quarries made very little impact. In spite of the industrial surge, agriculture and horticulture dominated the life of the parish. Shops, Post Office, tea rooms and public houses serviced the traffic. So, half-way through the century the villages, and thus the parish, appear still to have been mini-worlds of their own, typical of most villages in England at the time.

However, there were clear signs that the outside world was encroaching. The parish had attracted people born in 18 different counties of England, as well as the half dozen people born elsewhere in the UK and overseas.

Living at Midford Castle was Charles Conolly, a young man of 32 at the census date, born in Bath, and a wealthy landowner. He had an 'exotic' wife, Louisa Brancaccio, born in the Kingdom of Naples, daughter of Prince Ruffano. Midford Castle, under the direction of 'Countess' Conolly, was a focus for

An Elopement

The ruddy and jovial demeanour of the Revd Charles Johnson (vicar 1792–1838) must have been severely shaken by the events of 7 May 1826. On that day, at the age of just 17, his youngest daughter Lucy eloped to Gretna Green with Bryan Stapylton. Lucy's parents had quite different plans for her; at 17 she was to marry Sir Lewen Glyn of Ewell. Clearly, the elopement was well planned. It seems that Lucy had contrived an invitation to stay with friends at Laverton and made some excuse for a brief return home. Instead, at noon, she met Bryan, son of Martin Stapylton of Myton Hall near York, who was in Bath at the end of the winter season, for a headlong dash to Scotland. Several letters relating to the incident have survived.

Martin Stapylton assured Charles Johnson of his prior ignorance of the affair and set off in pursuit of the couple. He arrived in Penrith several hours before the couple and tried to dissuade Lucy:

Whilst I was endeavouring to break kindly to your daughter my determination to retain them, my Son suddenly seized me with great violence, forced your daughter from me in which he was supported by the Waiters, etc.

Then with a deputed constable Martin Stapylton chased the couple with the intention of apprehending his son for assault.

All to no avail, the couple reached the border before their pursuers and were duly wed. During a 'honeymoon' at Myton Hall Lucy wrote to her parents begging forgiveness and acceptance of Bryan, but above all, she made the plea: '... allow your maid to pack up my cloathes and send them direct.' Back in England and being under age Lucy was made a ward of court whilst arrangements were made:

... to have the parties... married according to the rites of the Church of England... that the odium may in some degree be removed which now attaches to their Characters.

Although the couple were reconciled to Lucy's parents, the course of true love did not run smoothly; Bryan was an inveterate gambler and the Johnsons had to intervene repeatedly with financial help to keep the couple from prison for debt.

Right: Lucy Stapylton (née Johnson) who eloped with Bryan Stapylton in 1826. She became Lady President of the RSPCA.

society. They kept a substantial household, including a Catholic priest, a lady's maid, butler, bailiff and gardener, a coachman, a cook and housekeeper and a housemaid. On the night of the 1851 census, they had a visitor from Naples, a young man called Peter Cianelli, staying with them. The Conollys certainly had a wider view of the world than most, but did they mix with others in the parish? They were not living at Midford Castle at the time of the 1861 or 1871 censuses, but Louisa reappears in the 1881 and 1891 censuses, a widow, and by now the Marchioness of Agata, living at the castle with a similar household.

Industrial features such as the Somersetshire Coal Canal (SCC), the railways and fuller's earth processors transformed the landscape of the parish,

at least for a time, but only a few large houses were built. Midford House was converted from two cottages into 'a large desirable house; 40 feet square, nearly finished... situated near Midford Castle' with pasture land adjoining of some 40 acres, and Avonhill, now Midford Place, appeared between 1840 and 1854. In South Stoke village, Thomas Hunt, an enthusiastic landowner and developer built The Priory in 1850 for his own pleasure. Southstoke House (formerly Southstoke Villa) appeared in 1846, starting the easterly infill along Packhorse Lane towards Pack Horse Farm, as it had just become. The Revd Charles Johnson made considerable improvements to what was then the vicarage, now Southstoke Hall, and Calverley, following him, renovated and extended the church.

Louisa Lucy Margaret Catherine Brancaccio, Marchesa di Sant Agata, Mrs Charles Conolly, locally known as Countess Conolly. In this photograph she is dressed for an audience with Pope Pius IX. (Courtesy Bath Central Library)

From the time of Elizabeth I the responsibility for paupers had rested with parishes, but by the early part of the century it was clear that there had been a complete breakdown in the operation of the system. Following the Poor Law Amendment Act of 1834 and the establishment of the Bath Union Workhouse (now St Martin's Hospital, Midford Road) this responsibility shifted to more central authority. A reflection of this is the loss of 'pauper' entries in the church-wardens' accounts book, and, incidentally, coinciding with the growth of the trappings of Empire, an increase in 'patriotic' entries. The censuses from 1841 onwards for the rest of the century record workhouse residents from South Stoke, usually, but by no means always, the elderly poor. A domestic servant recorded as living in South Stoke in 1841, was found in the next four censuses (1851–1881) in the union workhouse.

Crime was not a stranger to the parish as the *Bath Chronicle* records. Isaac Beak took particular exception when, in 'Horscomb' Bottom on an evening in August 1807, someone shot a (his) hound. He placed a notice in the *Bath Chronicle* offering 'Twenty Guineas Reward' for information leading to the conviction of the culprit. Beak appears to have been the tenant of Manor Farm. In the same edition of the paper he warned, in a separate notice, that game was scarce and that there should be no shooting 'over the Manor'. Beak placed a similar notice two years later, warning: 'Unqualified Persons trespassing... will be prosecuted if they were to sport on his lands in Southstoke and Monkton Combe.'

Theft must also have been relatively common. George Matthews, for example, was committed by Bathforum Magistrates for stealing wheat from his employer whilst working in a South Stoke barn. We have no idea whether he was sentenced because the proceedings of the trial are lost. However, we do know that theft of any kind was treated severely by the example of the three women of the parish who, after stealing turnip greens growing at Manor Farm, were sentenced to 14 days' hard labour. Offences against people were also common as illustrated by this account of an attempted highway robbery:

> *A few evenings ago as Mr. Aldritt, of Fortnight, was returning from this City to his home, between the hours of 6 and 7, a daring attempt was made to stop him by two soldiers, and a man in a smock frock with crape over his face. The latter made a blow at the head of Mr. A's horse, which he prevented from taking effect by resolutely striking the fellow's arm with the butt end of his whip. The scoundrels made repeated attempts to catch the reins of the bridle but without effect. The circumstances took place in the new road leading to the Burnthouse turnpike.*

This was the same Mr W.M. Aldritt who had a school at 1, Devonshire Buildings, Bath, and who was no doubt related to the two sisters who rented a gallery in the church at South Stoke for their pupils.

Reports of murder in the parish are rare but, in 1824, just outside the parish boundaries on the hill from Midford to Hinton Charterhouse, Jacob Wilkins was murdered by his nephew James Reynolds who was 'not yet 19'. Reynolds was executed and 'his body conveyed to Taunton for dissection'.

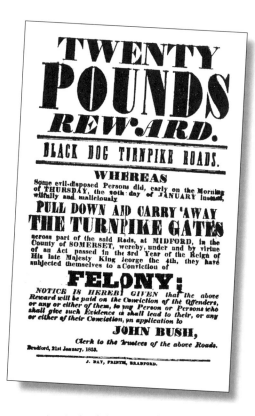

The theft of the turnpike gates in 1853.

There was considerable resentment at the erection of turnpike gates in key locations in settlements, for example, at Midford and near Burnthouse. Families were sometimes divided by turnpike gates, and tolls had to be paid each time one member of a family wanted to visit another. Turnpike gatekeepers were often abused and in extreme cases attacked, and the turnpike gates and toll houses damaged. On 27 January 1853, in the early hours of the morning, the turnpike gates at Midford were 'forcibly removed' after the toll house lamp and back window had been shot out! A reward of £20 was offered for information leading to a conviction. The gates were never recovered.

Early in the last year of the century Countess Conolly of Midford Castle died at the age of 76 and, in April, her belongings were sold in a 'grand auction' that lasted seven days. It would appear that the Countess never owned the castle but, on the death of her husband Charles, the estate had passed back to his mother. Upon the mother's death Midford Castle and the estate were bequeathed to the Catholic Church in the custody of Monsignor Charles Parfitt.

An era was coming to a close and, although the parish was at the turn of the century still a busy but minor industrial focus, the railway had arrived and the internal combustion engine was soon to have its impact on transport and goods distribution. As with many English villages 'gentrification' would continue.

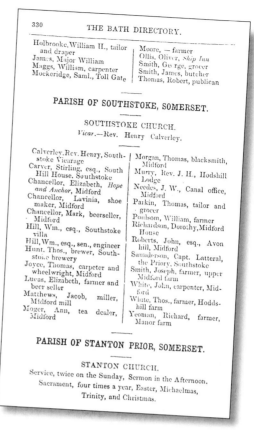

Above: *South Stoke in 1854 – the first year in which villages around Bath were entered in the* Bath Directory.

Outside the church in 1890. (Samler Collection)

❖ *Parish Government* ❖

Even the smallest settlements in medieval times had primitive methods of regulating their communal affairs. In the course of time, these functions were exercised by the lord of the manor through the manorial courts. We know of no records of these courts; but there is a record of a memorandum by the Prior of Bath which refers to 'the hallmote [the manorial court] held at Southstok, Thursday, the Feast of St Alphege, 15 Edward III [19 April 1341].' Gradually, the role of the manor courts declined and by the 15th century they were unimportant. At the same time, the power, wealth and influence of the Church increased and the parish superseded the manor, frequently (as in South Stoke) with the same boundaries. Meetings of parishioners under the parson's direction were a natural outcome, and were often held in the vestry.

These meetings were not established by Act of Parliament; their powers and composition were undefined. There was no rule about who could attend or preside and yet, by the latter part of the 17th century, they had come to be, with the County Magistrates, the rulers of rural England. In addition to maintaining the church and the churchyard, they assumed responsibility for the well-being of the Parish, looked after the poor, the old and the sick and repaired the roads. The appointed churchwardens, overseers of the poor and other officials waged a constant (but usually losing) battle against 'vermin', and of course levied a rate.

The earliest surviving records of such meetings for South Stoke are the churchwardens' accounts from the year 1662 onwards. They were submitted annually for approval of the Vestry, and include occasional Vestry minutes. These account books extend for over 200 years and they well illustrate the diversity of the functions of wardens and Vestry in general parish affairs, and also give a fascinating insight into social conditions and practices of the times.

Family and staff at Clifford's Nurseries, c.1895. Left to right, back row: Mark Barrett, ?, ?, Arthur (Dick) Clifford, Edward Clifford, ?; middle: Annie Maud Clifford (née Plomer, 1862–1950), David William Clifford (1859–1947), Lydia Clifford; seated at the front: William Plomer Clifford (b. 1892) and Neffie (b. 1890).
(Royston Clifford Collection)

A separate minute book for the Vestry exists from 1870. It routinely details the approval of the churchwardens' accounts, the setting of the voluntary rate for the school, and the appointment of the parish officials – churchwardens, overseers and waywarden (who dealt with repair of the highway). Noteworthy also is the nomination until 1872 of 'fit and proper persons to serve the office of Parish Constable', perhaps the most ancient of all parochial positions and in manorial times the most important – the link between the lord and his tenants, the keeper of law and order.

These minutes also show the continuing role of the Vestry in general matters during the last quarter of the 19th century, with references, for example, to:

... a request to the Highways Board expressing the desire of the Vestry that the surveyor should more frequently visit the parish in the discharge of his duty;
*   the additional charge made on the parish to defray the expense of the drainage works...*

and, to notice given:

... that at the next Easter Vestry (Mr A.) will make application for that piece of land commonly called The Pound (now filled with rubbish, broken glass

and earthenware) adjoining my premises 'The Knoll' trusting the ratepayers at the said Vestry will grant me the same that I may improve the entrance to the parish.

During the 19th century there arose a clear need for change. The Church's role was opposed by other religious denominations, and the tasks were outgrowing the Vestry's abilities and resources. New functions had been given to a variety of independently established bodies, adding confusion to inefficiency. The sweeping change came in Gladstone's Local Government Act of 1894 which, in its application to parishes, separated civil and ecclesiastical functions. Civil functions were given to new civil institutions, namely the Parish Meeting and the Parish Council. The first South Stoke Parish Meeting was held in the vicar's Parish Room (later the School, now the Village Hall) on 4 December 1894, and the first Parish Council Meeting on 15 December 1894. The Parish Council marked its centenary in 1994 with an exhibition in the Village Hall entitled '100 years in South Stoke'.

Despite many subsequent local government changes, Parish Councils remain the unit of local government closest to the people, with an enhanced role and powers to serve their communities.

The Parish Tithe Map

Tithes, generally speaking a one-tenth part of the annual produce of land and personal industry taken for support of the clergy and the church, are of very ancient origin. At first voluntary, by the end of the 8th century they were compulsory by law. They were a constant source of grievance and from about 1600 they were increasingly replaced by some form of monetary payment. The Tithe Commutation Act of 1836 had the purpose of replacing tithes in kind by a rent charge. Tithe commissioners were appointed to implement the act. To apportion the rent charge on each plot of land, the commissioners required a detailed large-scale map of each parish. The maps were to be produced by local surveyors under contract, but they caused many difficulties because the landowners had to pay for them and the commissioners' specification was very demanding. The Act was amended in 1837 to allow two classes of maps; first-class maps that met the commissioners' specification, which were signed and sealed by them, certifying their accuracy; and second-class maps which were often adaptations of an existing map or plan. Three copies of the map and accompanying documents were produced, one each for the commissioners, the Diocese and the vicar. They are now a valuable resource. South Stoke produced a first-class map in 1840, duly signed and sealed as such by the commissioners.

The Tithe Map of 1840 is the first map to show the parish on a large scale (26.4 inches = 1 mile). On this greatly reduced facsimile the field names given in the Tithe Apportionment have been added.

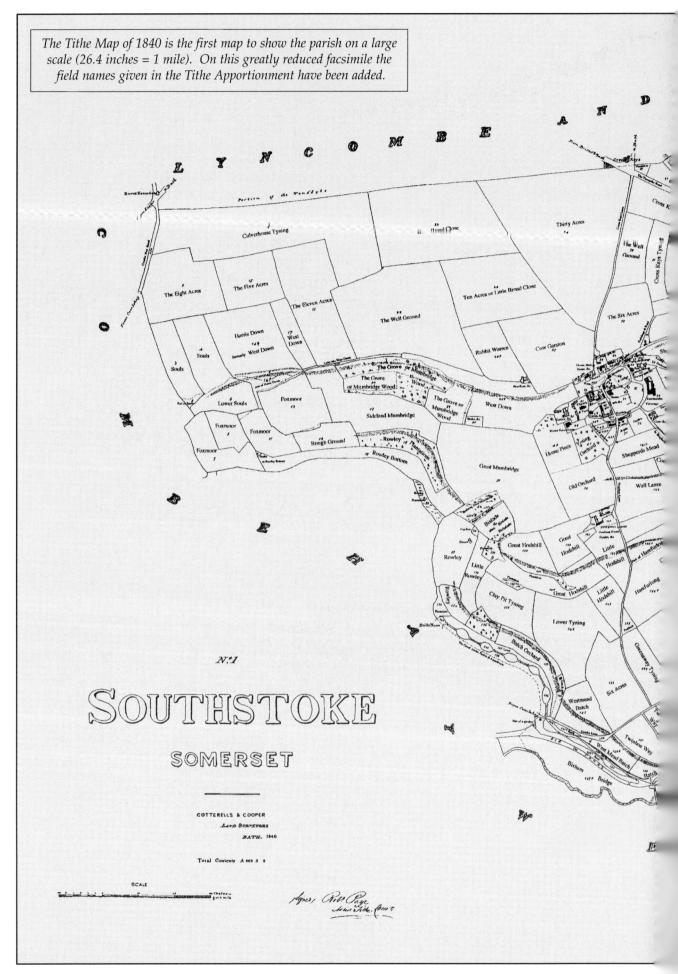

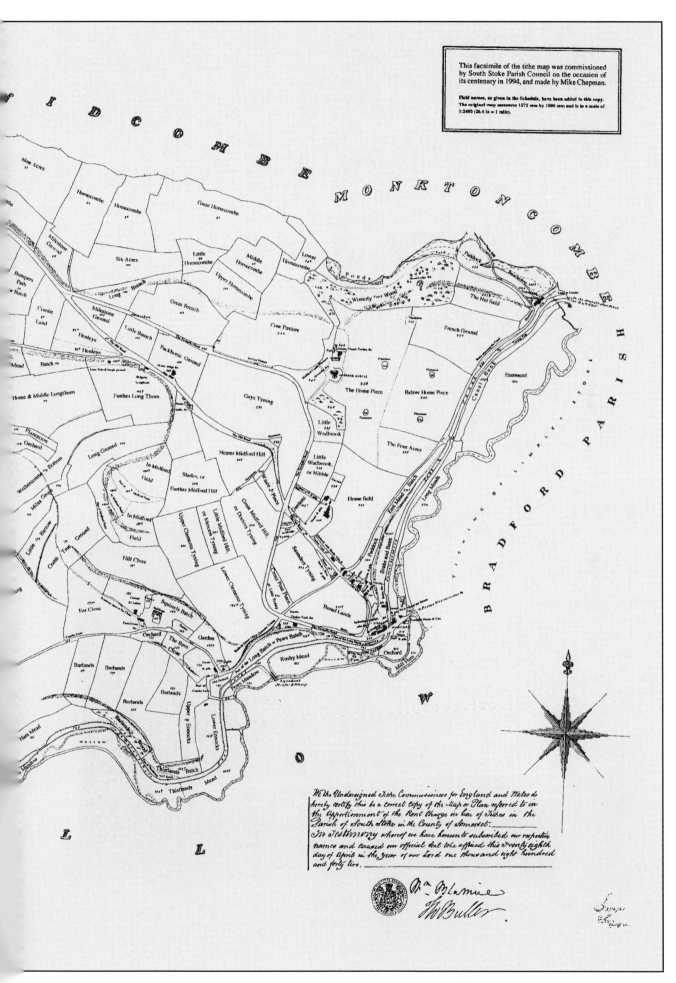

This facsimile of the tithe map was commissioned by South Stoke Parish Council on the occasion of its centenary in 1994, and made by Mike Chapman.

Field names, as given in the Schedule, have been added to this copy. The original map measures 1572 mm by 1000 mm and is to a scale of 1:2400 (26.4 in = 1 mile).

We the Undersigned Tithe Commissioners for England and Wales do hereby certify this to be a correct Copy of the Map or Plan referred to in the Apportionment of the Rent Charge in lieu of Tithes in the Parish of South Stoke in the County of Somerset. In Testimony whereof we have hereunto subscribed our respective names and caused our official seal to be affixed this twenty eighth day of April in the year of our Lord one thousand eight hundred and forty two.

Extracts from South Stoke Churchwardens' Account Book 1812–76

1812	*Pd for a prayer for the victory at Salamanca*	*1s.6d.*
	[Wellington's victory was 22 July 1812.]	
1815	*Pd for a letter of Subscription for Battle of Waterloo*	*2s.6d.*
	[Charitable donation]	
1818	*Pd for instruction for altering the Prayers on the death of Her Majesty*	*2s.6d.*
	Pd the Clerke for ringing the Bell the day Her Majesty was interred	*2s.6d.*
	[Referring to the death of Queen Charlotte, the consort of	
	George III, who died on 17 November 1818.]	
1827	*Pd the Clerke for Tolling the Bell for two days for the Duke of York*	*5s.0d.*
	[Frederick, second son of George III ('he had 10,000 men')!]	
1829	*Paid for 4 stoats at 4d*	*1s.4d.*
1837	*Pd Richard Powell for Tolling the Bell* [King's Funeral]	*5s.0d.*
	Beer for ditto	*6d.*
	[William IV. The ringer was Richard 'Pole'. There had been Poles	
	in South Stoke and Monkton Combe since before the Reformation.]	
	Paid for Proclamation of Queen [Queen Victoria]	*5s.0d.*
	Paid Richard Powell Tolling the Church Bell for Seven Vestries.	*5s.0d.*
1876	*Gas Bill*	*£2.12s.9d.*

St. James' Church, South Stoke in 1821, sketched by the Revd Edward Kilvert.
(Provenance unknown)

CHAPTER 6

The 20th Century:
Modern Times

South Stoke
village centre.
(Drawing by Ann Parsons)

The Vestry Meeting, which had been the focus of parish governance since medieval times, had its authority transferred to the Parish Council in 1894 and, by 1900, many hitherto local functions had been assumed by central government. Although over the decades the scope of Parish Council functions has been enhanced, a drift to central control was the trend throughout the 20th century.

In the course of the 20th century South Stoke changed from being a largely self-contained rural community providing local employment for cottagers living in simple dwellings, to a highly desirable parish of relatively prosperous retired and professional households.

In 1900 the dwellings of South Stoke village clustered largely around the Green, 'a patch of sweet smelling heliotrope with very little grass', and on the southern slope of the hill extending along Hodshill Way (or according to the 1840 Tithe Map 'Twinhoe Lane'). It was not until 1972 that the Commons Commissioners confirmed that the Parish Council owned the Green under the Commons Registration Act of 1965. By a resolution of the Parish Council in 1896, the railings at the entrance to the village were painted white, having been replaced shortly before as they were 'a positive danger to the public'. The telephone box did not make its appearance by the Green until 1936.

Early in the century the village of South Stoke had a school, Post Office and general store and various other small businesses including, in the first decade, a brewery. These have all long since disappeared. The brewery closed in about 1910. The shop was operated from 1898 by George Heal and his family. The butcher's shop, sited in what is now the garage of Slipway, closed in 1953 after George's death, and the Post Office in 1961. Edwin Heal, who took over the businesses from his father George in 1925, died in 1956.

The Green and shops in the 1920s.
(Roger Clifford Collection)

The village school serviced Midford and South Stoke, and children from Midford, who of course had to walk to school, brought sandwiches for lunch. On dark winter afternoons children were allowed to leave half an hour early. Apparently, in those early years, 'a lot of poetry and Church catechism' was taught. South Stoke lost its Church of England primary school in 1973. The school building became the Village Hall in 1975 in the ownership of the Parish Council as trustee.

There was no doctor in the parish and medical advice was sought early in the century from the practitioner in Wellow and later from Dr Cyril Morris of Combe Down who visited patients at South Stoke, Midford and Monkton Combe by bicycle or pony and trap. Later he bought a car that had two outside brake levers. In 1929 Dr Warren Morris, son of Cyril, took over the practice. Although Dr Charles Hagenbach arrived at the Combe Down practice in 1940, he immediately enlisted and Dr Phillips took over until he returned at the end of the war in 1945.

Among the businesses in South Stoke before the First World War was a little haberdasher's shop run by the mother of Miss Shore, a village school teacher, in what is now known as Alderley Cottage. The shop was kept open into the evening and items not in stock were obtained from Bath for customers. On the wall of the shop was an advertisement for Woodbine cigarettes depicting ten women with long tresses and wearing large hats walking one behind the other, with a policeman at the front and one at the rear. It read 'Ten for two coppers' demonstrating the prevailing sexism of the period. Some time before the Second World War, The Priory was a guesthouse owned by Mr and Mrs Fallowfield where Miss Holder, a school teacher, boarded. The cobbler's shop run by David Cairns, situated in what is now the garage below Quoin Cottage, closed in 1939. The blacksmith's shop, long associated with the coaching inn days of the Cross Keys, closed the following year. The smithy was on Midford Road opposite the Cross Keys in what is now Cross Keys Cottage. At the time of its closure it was operated by Will and Mark Barrett. Earlier, Mark Barrett had operated his smithy from what is now the garage of High Combe on Packhorse Lane.

The Mysterious Death of George Hughes Lemon

In South Stoke churchyard there is a grave with a cross, and an inscription which reads: 'In loving memory of George Hughes Lemon aged 25 who met his death on Entry Hill 18th June 1900.' George Hughes Lemon was the son of Charles Henry Lemon, the owner of Southstoke Brewery. He was a single young man who lived with his parents at Brewery House and worked in the business as a brewer. In South Stoke village he was a respected member of the community and captain of the village cricket team.

On the evening of 18 June 1900 he dined at Southstoke Hall with Colonel Bagnall O'Cahan who afterwards drove him into Bath, where he met a friend, Owen Edwards, in Nelson Street at about 9.30p.m. They walked in the park and afterwards went to Wells Road where Edwards lived. They parted company at about 10.30p.m. and after saying 'good-bye', Lemon turned and said that he would drive Edwards to Hinton Charterhouse on the following Saturday to play in a cricket match.

Lemon's way home would have taken him up Entry Hill but he must have taken a path to the left that led across fields to Combe Down and passed the back of a disused quarry. The following morning his dead body was found in the quarry higher up Entry Hill. It was clear that he had crashed through a hedge and barbed wire fence as twigs were broken off. His coat was torn and his face was covered with blood. He had probably been running away from somebody when he crashed into the quarry.

At the inquest it was stated that he had made a bet with a 'Mr C.' living on Combe Down but that the latter had refused to pay and had threatened Lemon. Lemon was also reported as having told a witness that some time earlier he had received a blow on the head from 'some scamp' in Bath and he would take a 'loaded stick' the next time he went into Bath. Yet another witness said that Lemon had asked him if he knew anything about revolvers as he was considering buying one before another winter.

The path from Entry Hill ended not far from Mr C.'s house and it is possible that Lemon had foolishly called on Mr C. to try to collect his bet. The Coroner instructed the jury to return a verdict of 'Accidental Death' but the jury, having serious doubts, insisted on an open verdict. The *Bath Chronicle* in its account of the inquest mentioned that there were 'many stories circulating about the matter'. One such anecdote, handed down from a villager of the time, suggested that George Lemon was in the habit of calling on a married lady living in one of the cottages at the top of Entry Hill!

We shall never know whether he slipped or had a little help.

Smithy at 124 Midford Road in the 1930s. Pictured are Will Barrett, the visiting farmer with his working horse and the blacksmith Mark Barrett. (Roger Clifford Collection)

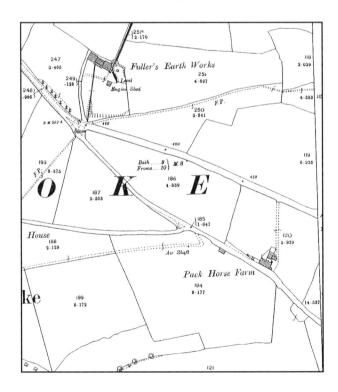

Left: Part of the 1904 OS map. The old Pack Horse was one of the oldest buildings in South Stoke and was situated midway between South Stoke and Midford. A track was made to the Inn from the new turnpike (B3110). Another track (an air shaft is marked to the side of it), also shown in Skinner's sketches, is not evident today.

Right: Clothing and Coal Club balance sheet, 1906.

South Stoke Parish Magazine.

DECEMBER, 1907.

In answer to my application the Becker Fund have given us a grant of £2 for Bibles and Library Books which will mean about 20 new books added to the Sunday School Library.

Clothing and Coal Club Balance Sheet, 1906.

RECEIPTS.	£	s	d	EXPENDITURE.	£	s	d
Balance in hand, 1905	3	3	3	Messrs. Colmer and Co ...	42	13	5
Payments by Club Members	59	17	2	Mr. W. Hamlen	16	7	10
Major and Mrs. Edgell	2	2	0	Mr. C. Stickland	5	0	4
Major and Mrs. Hepworth	2	2	0	Mr. Owen	0	18	0
A. J. Potts, Esq.............	2	2	0	Mr. Willcox	0	17	6
W. Pitt, Esq.	1	1	0	Mr. Heal	0	14	6
Messrs. Colmer and Co. ...	1	1	0	Mr. Quick	0	16	9
Interest	0	15	5	Paid out Members...........	3	16	3
				Balance in hand Dec. 1906.	2	19	3
	£74	3	10		£74	3	10

A gift of 5 cwt. of Coal was given respectively to eleven widows and old people and a Bonus of 3s. added to each Member's Clothing and Coal Card.

The Vicar would be obliged if any who wish to discontinue the Magazine for next year will let him know at once; failing to do so until the New Year has begun occasions extra trouble and expense. He would also be glad to hear of any fresh subscribers. During the last few years the numbers of subscribers have become less each year and quite 25 per cent. less than 8 years ago.

The Magazine is carried on at considerable loss to the Editor, and if it be not appreciated by the majority of the Parishioners it will not be worth the trouble and expense of continuing it.

The Lodge. (Drawing by Ann Parsons)

Four public houses served the parish and surrounding communities. The Packhorse Inn in its present location below the church became a hostelry in about 1845 when the earlier Pack Horse on the Old Midford Road ceased to be an inn. The Old Midford Road ('Midford Hill') Pack Horse continued to operate as a farm until the 1970s. For some years the farm buildings were almost derelict, but in the late 1980s they were extensively renovated as a dwelling and stables, resuming the name Pack Horse Farm. On the turnpike road in Midford was the Hope and Anchor which has been a public house for at least two centuries, and on the opposite side of the road, just before the mill in the direction of Hinton Charterhouse, and outside the parish boundary, was The Fox, now a private house. Also, just over the parish boundary on the corner of Midford Road and South Stoke Road is the early-18th-century coaching inn, the Cross Keys. A fifth hostelry, The Boatman's Arms, was demolished in around 1899 to make way for two cottages that became Hyver Kennels.

Affording core agricultural employment were three working farms, Manor Farm, Parsonage Farm and Pack Horse Farm and, in addition, Clifford's Nurseries (later known as Springfield Nurseries) operated for well over half the century. The 1991 census records no agricultural workers living in the parish.

Manor Farm, bought in 1937 by Gerald Hignett, is doubtless the vestige of the location of the medieval Manor building. The fine Tithe Barn (c.1500) attached to the farm was originally fully tiled in stone but had subsequently been re-tiled in slate. The Hignett family had earlier (September 1910) bought from Dr H. Crook, Hodshill Hall, which is reputed to have Tudor origins, and completely refurbished the front of the property. West View was the chauffeur's cottage. Hodshill remained in the Hignett family until 1979, but in 1940 it was handed over to the Red Cross for the duration of the war for use as a convalescent home for wounded servicemen. During the war village children were always welcome at Hodshill, reminding the patients of their own families. They took full advantage of better-than-wartime rations and a cinema show twice a week. There were also parties and a pantomime at Christmas.

Of Parsonage Farm only fragments remain as grazing pasture for cattle and horses. Farmer Cyril Wilson rented Parsonage Farm from Mrs Bailey of Hinton Charterhouse from the early 1930s and bought the property in about 1950, operating a large dairy herd and offering a daily milk delivery locally. For a period after Cyril's death, the business was continued by his daughter, Sylvia. In the 1980s the farm ceased to work and the remnants of farm buildings situated along Packhorse Lane above Southstoke Hall were converted (1990–91) into dwellings to accompany Beech Cottage and Chestnut Cottage which had been a part of the farm. Before Cyril Wilson bought Parsonage Farm, he rented several plots of land around South Stoke including Close opposite Southstoke House, Plough Field, ground below Hodshill and land behind the Millennium Viewpoint. He grew a mixture of crops including corn, potatoes, swedes and turnips. During the Second World War Land Girls with their children helped tend Wilson's crops.

The advent of easier communications and transport ushered in road improvements. Access to the Somerset and Dorset Railway station in Midford and the start of an electric tram service from Bath to the Glasshouse in 1903 accelerated changes that were already occurring. Although until the 1950s there were few motor vehicles out on the roads, once access to South Stoke and Midford villages had been improved it was inevitable that families would want to reside in such a beautiful location in easy reach of Bath and Bristol. Early in the century housing developments started extending outwards from the Green in a number of directions – along South Stoke Lane, Midford Road, Packhorse Lane and Old Midford Road. During the Second World War no house building was permitted in the parish forcing a number of local families to leave. Since the war only fierce resistance to proposals for damaging widespread housing developments has prevented the villages of Midford and South Stoke becoming contiguous with Bath.

The 'Modernising' of South Stoke

Until the 1970s some parish cottages had slab floors and several shared outside lavatories. In the early 1960s Russell Cottages and Victoria Cottages had neither kitchens nor bathrooms, only lean-to sculleries. Outside there were shared water taps and lavatories just across the yard. Happily conditions in the parish have advanced considerably since then. One of the factors that encouraged ancient people to settle on the slopes of South Stoke was the abundance of spring water. By the 19th century the water was collected in tanks near the Green but by the end of the century the supply was becoming less reliable. In 1896, with the aid of a dowser, a new water source was found and a 1000-gallon tank with pump was installed opposite the school, but by 1911 the pump and tank were proving to be less than adequate. The supply of water to a certain few homes in Midford was a matter of concern to the Parish Council who resolved that it was the responsibility of the owners and not a call on the rate. During the summer months water shortages were common, leading, in 1917, to acrimony between the Parish Council and the Rural District Council (RDC). A comprehensive piped water service was completed in about 1940.

The first record of the use of gas in the parish is an entry in the churchwardens' accounts of 1876 referring to a gas bill of £2.2s.9d. presumably for lighting the church. At Mr F.G. Heal's instigation a gaslight was installed at the top of South Stoke Green in 1903. Although some cottages in South Stoke village were supplied with gas shortly after 1900, it was not until around 1940 that a comprehensive supply was installed. A full electricity supply was available to the parish early in the 1930s but not widely installed until 1946. The telephone box with the number Combe Down 2054 (the same as the Post Office) did not make its appearance on the Green until 1936, although there were some private phones before that.

Refuse disposal was a regular item of Parish Council business. The year 1898 saw environmentalists prevail in the view that 'the tipping of rubbish by the roadside [is] undesirable and objections would probably be raised.' This followed the abandonment of the Pound as a rubbish dump after Mr Andrews, the owner of The Knoll, a property adjacent to the Pound, applied to the Vestry to 'improve the entrance to the parish.' For many years matters were resolved by householders placing rubbish in a collapsed fuller's earth pit, but in 1925 the rubbish problem erupted again because of 'the nuisance occasioned by old tins and other refuse being thrown anywhere to get rid of them.' In 1928 villagers were given permission to tip refuse in the quarry on Barrow Edge. A RDC refuse collection service began in 1939. The Parish Council complained in 1896 that some 'drains [are] in such a state as to be injurious to health', but it was not until 1952 that a full sewerage scheme to feed through Midford into the Tucking Mill plant was proposed. This upgraded the early-1900s inter-connected septic system in South Stoke village. Progress with work on the scheme was reported, as late as 1973, as being impeded by the need to excavate through rock.

There had long been a system of law and order in rural parishes but fire protection was late in arriving. The City of Bath agreed, in 1910, to offer the parish the services of their Fire Brigade at the heavy expense of £40 per annum plus expenses, including for any damage to engines and gear. The charge was dropped in 1929. Water for fire fighting purposes was first supplied by the Waterworks Company from 1914.

Muriel Spear (Beech Cottage) recalls life in South Stoke earlier in the century:

South Stoke was an isolated place in the 1920s. We went to Bath once a year before Christmas to look at the presents and have tea. We walked to the Glasshouse and got the tram from there. My father walked us back to the village from the Glasshouse – one on his back and one holding his hand.

There wasn't a lot to do so we went on errands. Every Saturday the Walls ice-cream man came around on his three-wheeler bicycle… There was a bread man with a trap. There was a rag-and-bone

man with a horse and cart. My grandfather was groom to Colonel Pitt. They had stables then. My grandfather had his own horse which he kept in a field near Southstoke House, and he had his own trap as well.

And Rosemary Taylor remembers moving to South Stoke from Greenford, Middlesex:

We purchased a smallholding called Homehead, just off the Combe Hay Lane. Although South Stoke was a very close-knit community with many of the villagers being related to each other, they were thankfully very warm and welcoming to us. The winter of 1949 was very hard and the coal merchant was unable to deliver to us because of icy roads. However, thanks to some of the villagers who gave my father a bucket of coal we never did run out.

When we first came to the village my father worked as a milk roundsman for Mr Wilson at Parsonage Farm. Mr Wilson was never called by his first name but was always addressed as 'Farmer'. In the summer months my father would help out with the haymaking as well. My favourite occupation was starting up the elevator and riding on it to reach the top of the rick. Below was a crate containing bottles of cider for the men and plenty of lemonade for we kids.

Farmer Wilson's pond was a source of fascination to me. It held a good stock of newts.

There were a couple of characters who were well known in the area. One was Charlie Parker, a tramp with long grey hair and a beard who walked around the lanes in the summer months. The other was 'Skipper Coates', a scoutmaster who lived in Wells but maintained a patch of ground with a wooden scout hut just the other side of the pack-horse track which ran at the top of our land. He was a tall, thickset man with a ruddy complexion who was often seen striding through the villages in his shorts.

A Parish Council committee was established in 1910 to consider whether the building of 'new cottages' was really necessary, but by the time of the First World War houses had been erected on both sides of the Midford Road from the Cross Keys towards Midford. Although as early as 1908 the Parish Council 'strongly disapproved of any alteration being made in extending the boundary of the City of Bath', by 1911 the boundary had been extended (not involving the South Stoke boundary) resulting in a consequent large increase in the rate. In 1950 the sequestration of parish land north of and including Sulis Manor known as Culverhouse Tyning, The Five Acres and The Eleven Acres by the Bath City Council for two schools constituted the greatest threat to the integrity of the village of South Stoke in its history. Clearly the perpetrators were either unaware of, or ignored, the terms of Edgar's 10th-century charter that asserts:

... none of our successors shall dare, so long as Christendom endures, to tamper with it [the parish boundary] *in the smallest detail, but if anyone so dare, may he endure the bitter anguish of eternal hell.*

Motor vehicles have been both the salvation and curse of rural parish life. Although there were few cars in the parish until the 1950s, as early as 1921 representations were being made to the Rural District Council about the dangerous approach at the junction of South Stoke Lane and Midford Road at the Cross Keys. A few years later in 1925 a request was made for warning signs to be placed on each side of Midford (B3110) to warn motorists to drive slowly through the village. Little has changed. The Slipway by the Green was a constant source of potential danger; in 1934 a request was made to prohibit traffic use. Clearly the misuse of the Slipway continued as a further request to the District Council was made in 1939. It was not until 1965 that the County Council made a Traffic Order prohibiting vehicle use and bollards were erected. As the density of traffic continues to increase, the blight of parking and speeding in village lanes has affected rural communities everywhere. Recently (1996) the Midford end of Old Midford Road was made one-way from Beeches to Midford Road to prevent the road's use as a high-speed cut-through.

❖ *In Times of War* ❖

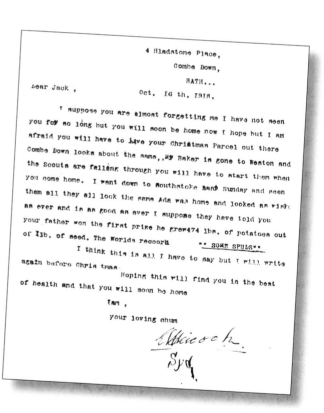

A poignant letter from the First World War sent by Sid Hiscock to his soldier friend, Jack Ainsworth. Jack joined the Army at 16 (under-aged), and spent much of the war in India. His father must have been quite a gardener.

In 1913, the population of South Stoke was at its lowest for many years, with only 348 inhabitants. No village community was spared the tragedy of the First World War, and 57 local men went away to serve, of whom 10 lost their lives. Their names are recorded on the war memorial on the south wall of the church. Some families saw more than one member enlist; from the Marsh family four brothers served. There are very few personal reminiscences recorded, although a few people can remember that fathers and uncles falsified their ages in order to be able to fight. One family can remember a brother who came back so lousy from the trenches that he had to live in the Tithe Barn and wash at the pump. When he needed clean clothes, he would throw stones up to the window of the family home.

Again in 1939 the normal flow of parish life throughout rural England was disrupted by war. During the Second World War 2 women and 49 men enlisted from the parish. Some of the large houses were taken over for the war effort. Brantwood was let to the Army in 1940 and became a British Officers' billet. In 1943, as D Day approached, US forces of all ranks arrived to occupy a tent 'town' that was followed by the erection of Nissen huts. There were field gun placements amongst the trees and in the fields around the property; many of these remaining in place until long after 1945 while the house continued to be occupied by the military until the end of the war. The wartime uses applied to Hodshill are referred to later. Opposite Kapunda, through the hedge of Thirty Acres bordering Southstoke Lane, short trenches were dug for soldiers on guard. Beneath Kapunda Edgar Davis hewed an air-raid shelter out of the solid limestone.

In the Village Hall hangs a certificate presented by the Lords Commissioners of the Admiralty to commemorate the adoption by the Parish of HMS *Beaufort*. She was a Hunt class destroyer of 1050 tons completed in November 1941 and was engaged in many operations in the Mediterranean from 1942 until the end of the war. Commander Alan Cobb of High Combe served on the ship during his early years in the Navy.

The Second World War was a time of rapid change for the parish. Two men were lost out of the many who went away to serve. The departure of so many on active service brought new roles to those remaining and a more complex role for the wives and mothers who stayed behind. Roger Clifford recalls life in South Stoke at that time:

With the outbreak of war came the blackout to all houses and vehicles. All streetlights were turned out and cars only had slits on their headlamps. The ARP (Air Raid Precautions) was formed and the warden used to patrol the village saying 'Put that light out'. The ARP hut was on the village Green. Everyone was issued with gas masks and identity cards.

The Home Guard (Dad's Army) was formed in 1940. They had their headquarters in the wooden cricket pavilion on the Grove. All signposts were taken down so that there was no means of identification of places. In 1941/42 part of the Home Guard formed a separate group which would have been similar to the Resistance groups, should the enemy invade Britain. They had a secret dugout in the woods at Rowley, a store for explosives, grenades and Molotov cocktails, etc. Most of these were disposed of as fireworks in the peace celebrations in May and August 1945 on the Grove.

Captain and Mrs Horton left Brantwood in 1940 and the house was first used as a billet for (Army) officers. Later, when the bombing of Bristol started, there were Ack Ack guns and a searchlight in the grounds. In preparation for D Day, numbers of US forces, both black and white, were billeted in tents all round the grounds. Then in early June 1944, D Day, they all vanished overnight. Every day the sky was filled with planes towing gliders carrying troops to France, Belgium and Holland.

Southstoke House, home of the Pitt family, was used as a children's convalescent home by the Orthopaedic Hospital from Combe Park. It was still in use in 1963.

During 1941 and 1942, Bristol was bombed regularly. The fighters chased bombers back and we often heard stray bombs. Underhill Cottage and Rowley Cottages were damaged and quite a few bombs dropped along the railway line to Camerton Pit.

The ladies of the village formed committees to raise funds for a welcome-home present for servicemen from the village. Dances were held every week either in the school or the WI Room, and [there were] whist drives and sales, all to raise money. There were two separate committees and there was great competition to see who could raise most.

Second World War bunker (the 'secret dugout'), taken in 2000. The bunker has now been filled in.
(Photograph, Charles Swatton)

South Stoke Peace Celebration Sports, 26 July 1919. The photograph includes, on the left: three Hamlen brothers and their father; in the middle: Charlie Green; on the far right: Oliver and Peggy Dobson. (Samler Collection)

Right: *Joan Dyer and one of the Perkins brothers during the May 1935 George V Jubilee celebrations at Combe Path Lawn.* (Roger Clifford Collection)

Above: *Janice Swales and Roger Clifford enjoying the May 1937 Coronation of George VI celebrations at Combe Path Lawn.* (Roger Clifford Collection)

Right: *Coronation celebrations on Combe Path Lawn, 1937. Girls, right to left: Thelma Williams with Joan Dyer and Beryl Lee as two Indians.*

South Stoke parish peace celebration supper for ex-servicemen, 31 July 1919. Left to right, back row: ?, ?, ?, ?, Fred Holley, Sid Owen, Ern Withers, Jack Dobson, ?, Will Spear, ?; middle: Bert Elsworth, ?, ?, Revd Samler, ?, Bill Samler, Charlie Green, Tom Hamlen, Fred Rose; front: George Heal, Tom Townsend, ?, ? Williams, Ted Williams, Robert Pitt, Will Clifford. (Roger Clifford Collection)

Wartime messages were sent by servicemen overseas on official paper to their loved ones. Desmond and Nellie Hawkins were married in June 1942 and Desmond went away to war before their first daughter Natalie was born (on 24 May 1943). He did not see her until she was two years old.

SCHOOL DAYS DURING THE WAR YEARS

The village school took in children from South Stoke and Midford until we reached 11 years and then we had to go to senior schools. The headmistress was Mrs Jessie Clements who was assisted by a pupil teacher at various times. We were taught the basic three Rs very well, and had lessons in history, geography and other subjects besides handicrafts (rug-making and knitting for both boys and girls). Mrs Clements was a very socialising lady and liked organising dances, plays, concerts and whist drives in the school in the evenings. She was a keen pianist and would play all the wartime songs which we children would sing at the tops of our voices. Two sisters used to do a very good version of the Andrews sisters' 'Just Yours'. Most of the children could dance all the dances of the day old and new. The school, now the Village Hall, had no electricity or water. The big room was lit by six gas lamps with mantles, lit by pulling chains with a hooked pole. Water was pumped from a spring to a tank on the flat roof over the cap house leading to the playground. The pump was situated in the corner and the boys had to fill the tank every morning. The boys also had to fetch in coal to stoke the fires.

FOOD RATIONING

Every person was issued with a ration book. Meats, butter, eggs and cheese were the main things, later clothes and other things. When these items were purchased, coupons were taken accordingly. Meat was supplemented with wild rabbits and poultry if obtainable. Fruit from abroad like oranges, all citrus fruits and bananas, were almost non-existent at first. Most people dug up their lawns and grew vegetables as a result of the Dig for Victory Campaign. Coal was very short and petrol only available for necessary trips and work. Petrol was coloured red for vehicles on necessary missions: most private cars were garaged for the duration.

The Glasshouse Garage was a café and shop owned by the Red House (Bath). On Saturday mornings they had a supply of cakes (unrationed). We used to queue for one cake per family.

EVACUEES FROM LONDON

In 1939, evacuees came from London. A whole school came together, complete with their teacher. Billeting officers housed them round the village to anyone with a spare room. Care was taken to house children of the same family together if possible. Two sisters, Winnie and Joan Higgins, stayed with the Walters family at Pack Horse Farm for most of the war. The Women's Institute was used as a school for the evacuees for several months until they gradually went back to London one by one. Those left

used the village school until they were 11 years old. There were also three children called Mills who were later joined by their parents who had been bombed out in London. Underhill Cottage was empty at the time and was requisitioned by the Council for them to be together. Many of the villagers gave them things to help them furnish it. They were quite happy until a German plane being chased back from Bristol dropped two bombs, one in the field behind the cottage and one on the edge of the road in front. (The outline of this crater can still be seen.) The house was damaged so the whole family returned to London saying they were safer sheltering in London's underground stations than here.

HODSHILL DURING THE WAR

In 1940, Mr and Mrs Geoffrey Hignett left Hodshill and allowed the Red Cross to use it as a convalescent home for injured and wounded servicemen discharged from Bath hospitals after treatment. The matron was Miss Janes and the Commandant Miss Bean, who were assisted by Red Cross nurses and staff. The men were of all nationalities; Poles, Australians, Canadians, etc. They all thought Hodshill was a lovely place: the gardens were kept up, but they missed their families. Film shows were put on in the Great Hall twice a week. The children from the village were invited and afterwards food and drinks were provided and the men liked to make a fuss of us. At Christmas the staff put on a pantomime and all children received a present from the Christmas tree. Food was rationed and luxuries of oranges and other foods were always welcomed. The Red Cross left Hodshill early in 1946.

Another personal account comes from Tony Biggs, whose parents worked at Hodshill before the war.

I can recall my parents talking of war with Germany during the summer of 1939 and my father telling me that we were at war with Germany and that things were going to become very hard for all of us. The first real thing I can remember was the issuing of gas masks and I was very proud as I had a 'grown-up one', not a Mickey Mouse one, and that we had to carry them everywhere we went. I also remember the first evacuees coming to the village. We had three to stay for a short time until they were found more permanent homes. My father volunteered as an ARP fireman looking after three villages with two other men (the villages were Midford, Combe Hay and South Stoke). Their meeting-place was the white railings. Their equipment was as follows: one stirrup pump, two five-gallon buckets, one gas cape, one tin hat and a pair of wellingtons. I can still see my father running up the drive when the siren sounded: we were about

South Stoke and Midford Platoon of the Home Guard.
They usually met on Monday evenings in the cricket
pavilion, South Stoke, for instruction and practice.
From the left: Mr Mackway, Mr Woodall, Lieutenant
Edward Cook, Sergeant Dobson, Harry Cross,
Bert Reynolds. The weapon they are inspecting
is a Thompson sub machine-gun.
(Photograph, Sgt Major Tom Webster, courtesy Richard Cook)

half a mile away from the white railings. After a while, they left their equipment in one of the garages under the arches of Brewery House. If my memory serves me right, I think that it was Jack Clifford's wood store.

I can also remember the LDV (Local Defence Volunteers) and it really was like Dad's Army. They used to go on guard with shotguns, pickaxe handles, and I think they only had two 303 Lee Enfield rifles. They soon became more organised with uniforms and equipment. My cousin Bill Scott was in the Air Cadets and his job, with others, was to spend nights at the cricket hut as a look-out in case any German paratroopers landed on the fields between South Stoke and the Cross Keys pub. They also built piles of stones in these fields to stop gliders and planes from landing. In the early days, he had only an airgun which I still have today. There was talk of the South Stoke Commandos, a small breakaway force of the Home Guard, who were to go into hiding should the Germans invade. We youngsters did find some remains of trenches when playing in the woods down towards Miss Moody's farm.

My father went off to war in the early part of 1940: he joined the Royal Air Force and did his basic training at Lytham St Annes close to Blackpool. Then on to Cardington in Bedfordshire for his final training where he joined a mobile barrage balloon unit, which he stayed with throughout the war. He was around on D Day for the landings and travelled right through into Germany. Before he left for the RAF he helped build an air-raid shelter for the families at Hodshill. They blasted it out of solid rock. It had

two entrances with electric light, a portable toilet, canned food, candles and could be sealed against a gas attack. It was situated behind the houses at the bottom of the long drive to the big house. Mr Harry Andrews was the head gardener. He joined the Army in early 1940; he was with the Royal Engineers and spent most of his Army service in the Western Desert.

I remember that when attending the village school every time the air-raid siren sounded, we went off to the Packhorse and went down to the beer cellar and sat on the crates or beer barrels until the all-clear was sounded, always taking our gas masks. The light-brown [gas mask] boxes took quite a bashing from us youngsters. Whether they would have worked or not is another story and I am glad we did not have to find out.

I can also remember seeing a 'dog fight' over Peasedown St John and seeing a plane going down in flames. I can still recall the sound of machine guns on the planes, also the drone of the German bombers flying overhead at night ready to attack Bristol Docks. I can also still see the red glow in the sky over towards Bristol from the fires, when we came out of the shelter after the all clear.

To help the war effort, I can remember my mother taking in three girls from the Land Army. As far as I can recall, one worked on a farm at Midford and the other two worked locally. They stayed for about six months.

The air raids on Bath took place on the nights of 25, 26 and 27 April 1942. I can remember on the second night people coming out into the fields to sleep and that night we had 54 people sleeping in the house and outside in the garden. My mother made food for us all although we had no gas as the gasworks had taken a direct hit. My cousin Bill Scott built an oven by laying a dustbin on its side with earth piled up on each side to stabilise it, with a fire base underneath. Bill built a chimney at the back made with old dried egg cans. We took the shelves from the gas oven in the house to make a platform for the cooking dishes. We used it for a number of months after the gas supply came back on as it made the best rice pudding I have ever tasted, even better than the slow oven in an Aga.

My mother also used to put up the wives and families whose husbands were very ill in St Martin's Hospital. These were very sad times for all concerned. The main time was around the attack by our troops on the Anzio beachhead, which took a considerable number of lives, and the wounded were flown home, many to St Martin's.

I recall hearing machine-gun fire and the noise of a plane. This was an ambulance under attack coming down the long drive, but luckily no-one was hurt. Also, I can remember the bombs being dropped just below the Grove in the woods, and we went to look next day. Some trees had been blown down and we also saw the remains of a bomb.

My mother and I were allowed to visit my father at Weymouth prior to the D Day invasion. We got special passes and I can recall seeing Chesil Beach full of Army lorries, tanks and guns, as far as the eye could see. My father was stationed on a small flat landing craft, with a smaller barrage balloon, which I later learnt from him was to be used on the beaches and just off shore to stop the enemy fighters from strafing the beaches during the first landings, and thereafter to maintain cover for the rest of the equipment to come ashore.

Prior to D Day, last, but not least, I can still see overhead the DC3 planes with bands on their wings and fuselage, each towing a glider. It was a summer's evening with a clear sky and setting sun and the planes had so many colours from the dying rays of the sun. It was so beautiful but very sad as so many soldiers were to die that night and during the next day.

D Day came and I can recall being in a class at St Philip's School in Odd Down and our teacher Miss Down put the radio on at 12 noon and it was announced by the BBC that combined Allied forces had landed in France and the invasion was on. This was followed by the National Anthem, and we were all sent home early that day.

HODSHILL AT THE BEGINNING OF THE WAR

My mother was left in charge by Mr and Mrs Hignett to close down Hodshill for the duration of the war, which was a monumental task for my mother to undertake. She had to oversee the packing of all important items, plus cataloguing and making arrangements for the furniture to go into store, the more important pieces to Hooper and Dark, and the rest to the squash court. My mother also had to arrange for the Red Cross take-over of Hodshill as a convalescent home for St Martin's. St Martin's at that time was a military hospital with little space for soldiers on their recovery programme. Hodshill was close in case of any emergency situations...

Another position my mother had was to collect the rents each week from the houses and cottages that the Hignetts owned in the village and pay the money into a bank on the Bear Flat. This continued for a number of years after the war.

CONVALESCENT HOME

The first matron, Miss Gunn, lived with us until the house was ready to take its first soldiers. I can remember seeing them in their blue suits, white shirts and red ties. Hodshill was changed in many ways. The butler's cottage had four rooms and was made into dormitories sleeping eight nurses, and a new bathroom was built on. The rest of the

nursing staff and other members, such as cooks, slept in the servants' quarters. The dining room became the mess hall, the library became the sitting and reading room, where soldiers could meet their families in private. The great hall was used as a recreation room, where they used to show films and newsreels once a week. The drawing room became a ward, so did the billiard room. Upstairs, Miss Gunn had Mr Gerald's suite, the day/night nursery became the surgery and dispensary, and both Mr and Mrs Hignett's bedrooms became further wards. I cannot recall how many soldiers the home could accommodate but there always seemed to be quite a few about. Miss Gunn stayed for about one year and the new matron, Miss Janes, stayed for the rest of the war. The Commandant was Miss Bean and she was related to the owners of the Bean Car Company. I think her father was the founder.

I used to enjoy visiting soldiers and spent many happy hours with them. I was also their messenger boy, on many occasions going to the village as this was out of bounds for them. I also heard many stories about the war from them. The house came back to the Hignetts in late 1945/early 1946.

THE RESISTANCE MOVEMENT IN SOUTH STOKE

South Stoke was a centre for the 'resistance movement' during the war. Here is an account by Ken Weeks of his part in the construction of the resistance bunker near Rowley Cottages:

Winston Churchill had the idea to develop resistance groups around the country. Lads were chosen from the local Home Guard, mainly people who worked on country jobs. I was only 17 at the time. In South Stoke, those chosen were myself, Fred Holley, Arthur Brown, Mr Joyce, Len Marsh and two lads from Monkton Combe School. Jack Clifford joined us later. The idea was to build a secret underground bunker where we could operate behind enemy lines in case of invasion.

We had several goes at building it. First, we started down by the locks (near the Bull's Nose), then at Tucking Mill, then in Limpley Stoke Quarries. The last one failed because it was discovered by the police who thought it was a German spy's dugout. We started again in South Stoke in 1941, below Rowley Cottages, near the lake.

We could only work at night and not even our parents knew what we were up to. There were always two people on guard. We had to carry the earth we dug out down to the lake or we would have been discovered. Jack Clifford arranged to order the sand and cement that was needed and we

The centre of South Stoke village down to Hodshill taken by the RAF on 23 March 1946. Note the wartime Nissen huts in the grounds of Brantwood (top, left centre). The remains of the derelict house in the field south east of Southstoke Hall are also clearly visible. Cars are conspicuous by their absence!

(© Crown Copyright 1946/MOD)

carried it down at night. The entrance was camouflaged and there was a sort of sprung trap door designed by Jack. We eventually did spend one night there.

We used to train with the Home Guard at Coleshill, and occasionally down at Monkton Combe. We had all the latest equipment – revolvers, sticky bombs, double-sided knives. Jack Clifford and Arthur Brown were the main movers. Roger (Clifford) tried to follow his Dad down once, but got sent back smartly!

The bunker was filled-in in 2000 for safety reasons, but it lasted, solid and strong, for nearly 60 years.

WARTIME IN MIDFORD: RECOLLECTIONS OF JIM SUMMERS

My earliest recollections are from the start of the war in 1939 when I was a boy of five or six. I remember the men being 'called up' and my father volunteering for the RAF. He spent six years in the Middle East before 'demob' in 1946.

In those days we had a Post Office at Hillside House and a little shop run by Nan Bath in the house just past The Moorings on the main road and, of course, two pubs, The Fox, run by the Townsends, and the Hope and Anchor.

At the beginning of the war to me all things started to change. I had to start school at Monkton Combe C of E infants and the railway sidings towards Tucking Mill took on a new importance. 'Automowers' of Norton St Philip were obviously engaged in engineering work for the war effort and their converted tractors, winches, etc were brought to the siding for transport. This caused a great deal of interesting activity past our house. Boxes of ammunition came to the siding to be transported by lorry to the [ammunition] dump in the Bath and Portland quarry at the top of Midford Lane for storage.

During the Bath blitz, the barn, now known as Pipards, was used to give temporary shelter to people bombed out of their homes in the city.

The Case of the Brantwood GI

From 1942 many black soldiers from the USA were stationed in the West Country. One of them, Leroy Henry, a Technician 5th Grade (in the predominantly black 3914th Quartermaster Gasoline Supply Company) was billeted in the grounds of Brantwood. The troops were popular with local people, particularly the children, because they were seen as a steady source of supply of luxuries like chewing gum and chocolate. They were invited into homes and womenfolk enjoyed their company at dances. The Cross Keys became their regular haunt. There was little inherent racism in the West Country at this time and when white American soldiers arrived later on and displayed contempt for their black colleagues, the locals were appalled.

It was not realised by the public that the Visiting Forces Act of 1942 gave the US Army total jurisdiction over its soldiers in Britain for both civil and military offences. One of its laws made rape punishable by death, although in England rape had ceased to be a capital offence in the 1860s.

On the night of 5 May 1944, Leroy Henry had been drinking at the Cross Keys with his Forces friends. At 10.30p.m. they all started to walk back to the camp, but Leroy Henry decided to go 'absent without leave' (AWOL). In his testimony to the court later, he said that he had a date with a girl and was to call at a shop in Combe Down where she lived. She was a young married woman, who was charging Leroy £1 a time for her favours. It was late when Leroy tapped on her window. She told her husband that it was a soldier asking directions to Bristol and he went back to sleep! This time she asked Leroy for £2, at which he balked, so she revealed that she was married and said she would get him into trouble if he did not pay up. Suspicious about her long absence, her husband went looking for her, and when he found her and was told the reason he notified the police. From a patrolling police car the woman identified Leroy on the street and claimed that he had raped her. Leroy was arrested, handed over to the military police and taken to Shepton Mallet Prison where he was charged with rape and AWOL. On court martial he was sentenced to death by hanging. In Britain, up to the year 1945, 169 American soldiers were sentenced to death for rape, 29 were executed and of these 25 were black.

Local people were outraged at the sentence and the style of 'justice' and were not content to let the matter rest. Two of them, Sam Day and Jack Allen, started a petition to free Leroy. The response was remarkable, with 31 000 signatures collected, and the petition was sent to the Commander in Chief of the Allied Forces, General Eisenhower. The *Daily Mirror* took up the campaign and many individuals then wrote both to Eisenhower and the American Judge Advocate General. Finally, Eisenhower ordered a thorough investigation, and eventually the verdict was quashed. There was to be no re-trial. Leroy Henry was freed and was quietly re-deployed. There was a rumour that he had become a priest. He died in St Louis in 1971.

A lone traveller passes in front of Alderley Cottage *and* Russell House *(with creeper).* (Samler Collection)

❖ *South Stoke: To Be or Not To Be?* ❖

Steep-sided valleys among the crumpled green hills south of Bath help village identities to survive in surroundings remarkably rural so close to a city. Physical factors have imposed their own limits on village spread. South Stoke, three miles from the city's heart, retains not only a distinctive village character but a magnificent fifteenth-century barn...

(Geoffrey Wright, *The Stone Villages of Britain*, 1985)

This may have been the case in earlier times and the high, flat plateaux round the city were bleak and inhospitable places to live by choice. But terrain is now less of an impediment to building, and to the modern volume house builder nothing is more desirable than a large, more or less level, green-field site adjacent to services.

Certainly the 1904 edition of the 1:2500 Ordnance Survey map shows how compact and isolated South Stoke village was only 100 years ago. Over the next 40 years sporadic development occurred along South Stoke Lane, Packhorse Lane, Old Midford Road and most notably Midford Road east of the Cross Keys.

The real threat emerged after the Second World War. Bath had sprawled up the slopes to the Odd Down plateau and indeed on to it. The City Council had grandiose plans to expand the population of the city to over the apparently magic figure of 100 000 and, to this end, promoted a parliamentary bill which sought to incorporate within the city boundary extensive surrounding areas, including South Stoke. The bill was opposed by Gerald Hignett on the grounds that Manor Farm would be unviable and that the city's housing targets were unrealistic. The House of Commons committee dealing with the bill accepted his case and amended the bill to exclude any change at South Stoke, except for a small area of 38 acres in the north-west corner of the parish. The committee was persuaded that this area was required for the building of two new schools, for which there was said to be an immediate need, and the land was transferred (with Sulis Manor) to the County Borough of Bath. In the event, only one school was ever built (originally called The Cardinal Newman, now St Gregory's), occupying only about ten acres.

55

But for Gerald Hignett's resolute opposition, South Stoke would long since have become a totally built-up suburb of Bath. However, the threat returned in 1963 when there was a further major review of Local Government areas in the South West. Bath, which had expanded by 1770 acres in 1911 and 1126 acres in 1950, now sought a further 2882 acres, an increase of 46 per cent. The Local Government Commission published some very radical proposals, including for example transferring the whole Limpley Stoke Valley to Wiltshire. In this parish, the Commission proposed transferring to Bath the whole of Horsecombe Vale west of Midford Castle grounds. Also to be transferred was the area north of a boundary zig-zagging roughly from Pack Horse Farm to the Evangelical Church, plus two fields to the west of South Stoke Lane – Thirty Acres, and the next field to the west adjacent to the Wansdyke. Despite strong objections from many quarters, the Commission's recommendations to the Government for this area were unaltered and, in March 1965, they were approved by the Minister. However, in December 1965 the Minister reversed his decision, and resolved that no land should be taken from South Stoke, stating that 'the boundary between Sulis Manor and a point north of Midford Castle [will] be the existing city boundary.' The parish had survived again.

The next threat came not from any proposed boundary changes but through the planning system. It is a long and complex story that ran for a decade from 1980 to 1990, and it can only be summarised briefly here. It is intimately bound up with the Avon County Structure Plan, and more particularly with the Wansdyke Environs of Bath (WEB) Local Plan, mention of which cannot be avoided. The former sets the general strategy for land use, the latter its application to individual plots of land.

Back in the 1960s Somerset County Council produced a new development plan, which included the whole parish within the proposed Green Belt around Bath. However, before approving the plan, the Minister directed that it be modified to leave land on the plateau between South Stoke and the Bath boundary 'unallocated' (known as 'white land'); i.e. it was neither to be committed to the Green Belt nor to be allocated for development, but left for decision in light of needs at some future date. These areas were therefore prime targets for developers during formulation of the WEB Local Plan.

The draft Structure Plan was published in May 1980 and immediately raised concerns about the future use of the 'white land' areas. The Parish Council founded, with interests outside the parish, what became the Bath/Wansdyke Residents Group to mount a strong and unified campaign that all the land south of the Wansdyke between Combe Hay Lane and South Stoke Lane should be formally designated as Green Belt. In September the Group submitted to the Chairman of Avon County Council a carefully argued case to this end, supported by a petition signed by 1630 people. This was 'praised by Avon planners' and undoubtedly influential, but the County Council could only determine general policy, not the detail of the Green Belt. This was the province of the district councils, Wansdyke and Bath.

When Wansdyke Council put the WEB Local Plan 'on deposit' for public comment in July 1986, it proposed putting all the South Stoke 'white land' into the Green Belt. Landowners and developers alike were quick to object to this, and a public inquiry into the Plan was held in 1987. The inspector recommended that none of the 'white land' should be included in the Green Belt, and indeed that some land on the north side of Packhorse Lane should be removed from the Green Belt. This was a seriously flawed report and, to its lasting credit, Wansdyke Council rejected the recommendations early in 1988. Thereupon the Secretary of State instructed Wansdyke Council not to adopt the WEB Local Plan: he only finally released it without modification two years later, and it was eventually adopted by Wansdyke Council in May 1990. The direct consequence of this was that all the previously 'white land' was brought within the Green Belt. However, this decision was a long time coming and by the end of the 1980s there were planning applications on virtually all the open space across the south of Bath, as shown in the plan opposite. It will be evident to the reader that the face of the parish could have been totally transformed almost overnight. The following paragraphs set out as briefly as possible what transpired in each of these cases, as no history of the parish would be complete without this record.

The Hignett family had long been opposed to any development of the land west of South Stoke Lane (1) but in 1984 reversed this stance, as a consequence of which Crest Homes plc, in May 1986, applied for planning permission to develop this site. The application originally referred to 71 acres, but 18 acres in the south west of the site was already Green Belt and was withdrawn. Some 350 houses were envisaged, but that would have been a low density and the number could well have been double that figure. The application was refused by Wansdyke Council in July 1986, against which decision Crest Homes appealed. Both Jack Aspinwall, MP for Wansdyke, and Christopher Patten, MP for Bath, opposed development of these fields. A public inquiry opened at Keynsham Town Hall on 1 March 1988 and lasted seven days instead of the scheduled four days. It attracted much press and public interest; many local residents attended, a number participated and made valuable contributions, and many people had written letters. Shortly before this crucial inquiry, the Parish Council was dismayed to learn that Wansdyke was not intending to be represented by a barrister. A special Parish Meeting had been arranged on 20 February to explain how critical

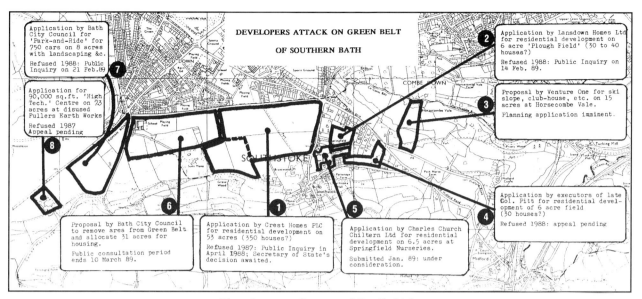

Planning assaults around South Stoke.

this inquiry was to the future of the village, and it attracted a huge attendance. At the meeting an appeal for funds was made which produced £1650 within 72 hours, and this, with £1000 from the Parish Council, persuaded Wansdyke Council to engage a QC, which may have been decisive. It was not until June 1989 that the Inspector reported to the Secretary of State and recommended dismissal of the appeal. Crest Homes continued to fight a rearguard action for a further 18 months, seeking to have the inquiry re-opened; eventually, six months after the site had been formally designated as Green Belt, they withdrew their appeal in November 1990 to avoid having it dismissed.

Plough Field (2) had been acquired by the Bath building firm Beazer (of which Lansdown Homes Ltd was a subsidiary) at the time when it took over the local builder, Wills, after the Second World War. Applications for development of Plough Field for housing or other purposes were refused in 1956, 1966, 1975, 1976, 1977, 1980, 1985 and 1986. Appeals against four of these refusals were heard at public inquiries in 1957, 1976, 1978 and 1986, and in each case the appeal was dismissed. In April 1988, another application was made for residential development, with access off the B3110 via Cranleigh. This was refused by Wansdyke Council: an appeal was lodged and a public inquiry held in February 1989. In June the Inspector dismissed the appeal. Dismissal of all these appeals rested basically on the absolute need to keep this field open, to avoid consolidating a built link between, and the merging of, South Stoke and Bath.

The application for a dry ski slope in Horsecombe Vale (3) was submitted in March 1989. This apparently would have been the largest such facility in the country, catering for regional, national and international events. In addition to the white plastic ski run, ski tows, stainless-steel toboggan run and lighting, there would have been a large building with restaurant, coffee shop, shop, gymnasium, sauna, changing rooms, etc. and a large car park, covering in all 6.5 hectares (16 acres). It received widespread support from many quarters, but equally strong opposition locally. Wansdyke Council was set to refuse planning permission on the grounds that it contravened Green Belt and countryside policies and would generate an unacceptable amount of traffic: however, it failed to do so within the statutory eight weeks, and the applicants appealed. A public inquiry was to be held in March 1989. By this stage the Parish Council had teamed up with others outside the parish to form the Horsecombe Vale Association to fight the proposal. By early January it had already raised some £3500 of its £5000 target, and was about to distribute 2500 leaflets when the promoters withdrew their planning application and appeal. The financial backing for the project was believed to have been withdrawn.

The appeal relating to residential development of Combe Path Lawn (4) was eventually withdrawn when the site was brought within the Green Belt. Springfield Nurseries (5) was already statutory Green Belt and the application for residential development was refused.

Only one school (St Gregory's) having been built on the area transferred under the Bath Extension Act 1950, there remained a surplus of 31 acres (6). Bath City Council resolved in 1973 to treat the surplus land as non-statutory Green Belt, and in 1983 to make it statutory Green Belt. A public inquiry into the Bath City Local Plan was held in April 1988 at which the Green Belt designation was strongly supported by Avon County Council and Wansdyke Council, but opposed by Crest Homes. The Inspector decided that the area served no Green Belt purposes and recommended accordingly: his reasoning was demonstrably seriously flawed, but this was what many city councillors and officers wanted. The City Council accordingly proposed to modify the City Plan to allocate the area for housing. This modification was strongly opposed by the County Council, by Wansdyke Council and Christopher Patten, MP for Bath; and locally also by the Bath/Wansdyke Residents Group which distributed 5000 'Save Bath's Green Belt' leaflets. Resulting from this, over 230 letters of objection were written, and a collective objection was signed by some 3500 people. By contract, the allocation for housing was supported by Crest Homes, landowners and two individuals. However, the City Council was unmoved. The Residents Group in July 1989 asked the Secretary of State to 'call in' the Bath City Plan, which he duly did. In August the County Council did the same; but a month later the full Council over-ruled its Chief Planning Officer and reversed the decision, on the grounds that this site was a unique opportunity to provide low-cost housing for Bath. In the event, the Secretary of State declined to intervene, because this was not a matter of national or regional importance. So this area became formally allocated for housing when the City Council eventually adopted the City Plan in June 1990.

There was, however, to be an ironic end to this saga. Some councillors had been over hasty in accepting Crest Homes' assurances about the provision of low-cost homes, despite warnings that these were unenforceable through the planning process. Crest Homes' subsequent planning application to develop the site went to appeal and, after an inquiry, the Secretary of State ruled in April 1994 that the City Council could not tie Crest Homes to a legal agreement compelling it to include social housing on the site. The press reported councillors feeling angry and betrayed, quoting certain councillors' comments: 'I feel we have been betrayed; I will never trust another developer again' and 'I think we have been taken for a ride.'

The approved Structure Plan policy stated that 'the inner boundary of the Green Belt for Bath will be defined so as to follow generally the limits of existing development.' There could hardly have been a more well-defined limit to existing development at the time than the Wansdyke between Combe Hay Lane and South Stoke Lane. In retrospect it remains astonishing that Sulis Meadows Estate, one of the largest housing developments in Bath, was allowed to intrude into the open countryside south of the Wansdyke and that ministers allowed totally inconsistent planning decisions on the two parts of

this stretch of open plateau, separated only by a wire fence. It is an arbitrary administrative boundary and anomaly of the Bath Extension Act of 1950. Moreover, in July 1980 the two district councils had agreed the development of 500 houses (later increased to over 1000) at Peasedown St John to provide overspill for Bath (especially of lower-cost homes) and to prevent further building on the fringe of Bath.

The other two sites identified in the illustration are rather incidental to the parish: both were already statutory Green Belt. The appeal on the Park-and-Ride site (7) was dismissed because the site was too far out. It was later permitted in its present location closer to the city boundary. The appeal to re-develop the derelict fuller's earth works (8) was withdrawn, probably because of economic recession.

The development of what is now called Sulis Meadows Estate has detracted greatly from the open setting of South Stoke and brought the built-up urban sprawl of Bath too close to the village; but the whole outcome of the situation portrayed in the figure could have been much worse.

Hopefully that situation will not be repeated. The whole parish is now within the statutory Green Belt. However, already in the 1990s, during preparation of the successor Wansdyke Local Plan, objectors have been seeking the removal from the Green Belt of sites (1), (2), (4) and (5). The question therefore remains: South Stoke; to be or not to be – a rural parish? or, to paraphrase the words of Geoffrey Wright which opened this section: 'Will the village identity and distinctive character and its remarkably rural surroundings survive?'

In 1981, South Stoke village was formally designated by Wansdyke Council as a Conservation Area, the purpose of which is to preserve or enhance the special character or appearance of the area, and this positively assists survival of the village identity and distinctive character.

When the Cotswolds Area of Outstanding Natural Beauty (AONB) was designated in 1966, it stopped short at the then Gloucestershire/Somerset boundary, which in landscape terms was artificial. The area around the north, east and south of Bath had long been held to be comparable in terms of landscape quality and natural beauty and, in December 1990, the Secretary of State approved an Order extending the AONB to include these areas. The whole of the parish of South Stoke is now within the AONB, with the exception only of the area of housing along Midford Road east of the Cross Keys. The AONB should assist survival of both the village identity and its rural surroundings.

CHAPTER 7

Church & Manor

(Drawing by
Julia Ponsonby)

❖ *The Church of St James the Great* ❖

The history of the Church of St James the Great in South Stoke is in a very real sense the history of the parish for it embodies the character of each passing generation. In times past it made intense claims on the tithes, labour and materials of every man, woman and child in the parish, requiring a huge diversion of resources from the necessities of life.

Church of St James the Great in the year 2000.
(Photograph, Paul Langham)

Anglo-Saxon Inheritance

During the latter part of the Roman occupation some element of Christian faith had infiltrated into this region and Christian rites practised here would have been performed in secrecy and fear. In any case Roman Christianity had little influence on the local inhabitants. The departure of the Romans brought about the germination of a new spirituality in the lives of the saints and hermits of the Celtic Church and it is thought that Somerset was evangelised by its leaders, notably St Gildas in the 5th and 6th centuries. They founded the Celtic monasteries such as Glastonbury which was already well established when the West Saxons entered Somerset in AD658.

By the end of the 7th century the torch of Christianity was burning brightly in the area. As Osric had endowed a religious community near Bath, so Offa, King of Mercia, is credited a century later with reforming the monastery of St Peter's in Bath and building the Saxon Abbey church, which was to become one of the foremost churches in England. The Christian faith in Bath now had a focus in the monastery, that had come under Benedictine rule, and grew in prestige under the administration of Alphege and the benefaction of King Edgar.

It cannot be said with certainty that a Saxon church ever existed in South Stoke since no evidence for one has been uncovered, but proximity and close association with the monastery make it a strong possibility. Local landlords were urged by monasteries to provide a church for their villagers. The site chosen would have been near the manor, probably on what had once been a pagan place of worship or burial ground, a practice enjoined by St Augustine. The abbot of the monastery would have appointed a priest to serve the church; his duties would have been the cure of all souls.

What was to become the system of dividing England into ecclesiastical parishes with the right of appointment of clergy, supported by tithes and glebe land, was slowly evolving.

Norman Influence

With the arrival of the Normans the Church soon took on a new character which endured until the Reformation. The new Bishop of Somerset, John de Villula, a French priest, moved his see from Wells to Bath in 1088. With his Norman fraternity of architects and masons he built a great Norman church as his cathedral, complete with convent buildings and a collegiate school. Within a century much of this work was complete and the builders could turn their attention to replacing the old Saxon churches on the abbey estates.

At South Stoke the fine Norman portal of the church, which survives today, suggests that a new

A drawing by Ann Parsons of the Norman arch.

The Norman arch (of c.1160) within the porch of the church. (Photograph, Paul Langham)

church was built between 1160 and 1170. This was no mean building, as befitted an episcopal foundation. It must have dominated the humble wooden cottages of the villagers.

The earliest surviving record of an appointment of a vicar is a grant by Robert, Prior of Bath Abbey in 1210, to John de Tusseburi, to the chapels of Siccstoc and Cumba (Monkton Combe) with a saving of 4 shillings yearly to the Infirmary of Bath. The Church had kept a record of bishops in their dioceses for a long time and now began to record the names of priests in their parishes, not with the intention of recording dates but of establishing a line, because a continuous link with the past was now what mattered.

John de Tusseburi was succeeded by Richard Donekin. Donekin may also have been the priest of the same name who was attached to St Catherine's Chantry (cloth makers) in the guild church of St Mary de Stalls in Bath, which was demolished in the latter half of the 17th century. This may explain why, in 1270, he made over the rent from a house to the Commonality of Bath for the maintenance of a sung Mass for the salvation of his soul and the souls of all his ancestors and successors and of all his benefactors and all the faithful deceased. He seems to have held the living of South Stoke for an uncommonly long time.

His successor was one Dr Henry de Foxcote. The doctorate was probably one of law or letters, a high academic distinction in those days. At about the same time a monk, Thomas de Foxcote, had been collated to the important office of Precentor of Bath Priory. It is clear that this family possessed consider-able local influence for, in addition to his office as South Stoke's vicar, Henry was appointed Bailiff of the Manor of South Stoke. It seems that patronage was alive and flourishing and that South Stoke was becoming a desirable living. However, monasteries with the gift of livings were often guilty of appropri-ating most of the rent, to the detriment of the villages and the church.

was all part of the homeliness of medieval religion.

People liked their children to be christened with the name of a saint. Churches were now expected to have a patron saint as a guardian of the community. The dedication of South Stoke to St James probably dates from this period.

The custom of making pilgrimages to the shrines of saints also grew up around this period. Situated as it was on the pilgrim route between the monasteries of Bath, Hinton Charterhouse and Glastonbury, South Stoke would have been well aware of pilgrims passing to and fro.

The church tower. (Drawing by Ann Parsons)

MEDIEVAL CATHOLICISM

In medieval times the church, as the centre of the parish, was of the utmost importance to the commu-nity. In 1215 the Pope decreed that all marriages should take place before a priest and that at least once a year (usually at Easter) every parishioner should confess his or her sins to a priest before receiving communion. In the church every child was baptised, in its churchyard everyone was buried and from it processions went forth to ask God's blessing on the crops. Its festivals were celebrated with the drinking of ale around a bonfire and the church func-tioned as the Village Hall for gatherings and dances, although games in the churchyard were forbidden. It

TUDOR TIMES

The devastation of the Black Death was followed by a period when there was an increased emphasis on prayer and the saying of Masses for the dead. It was now becoming customary for those in high standing in the Church to be buried within its walls. Evidence of these practices is provided from the record of John Sparhawke LLB who, in addition to being Vicar of South Stoke from 1443 to 1467 and the rector at Cold Ashton, was also Advocate to the Consistory of Wells and one of a number of confessors appointed to hear the confessions of the Bishop's subjects in the various deaneries and to absolve them. He died in 1467 carrying many secrets to the grave and bequeathing in his will:

... to the parish church of South Stoke and to the parishioners there a good manual [a psalter containing the daily offices], *a surplice and 40 shillings to the reparation of the missal* [the canon of the Mass] *that they may pray for my soul.*

He also left 20 shillings to the Prior of Bath and bequeathed his body to holy burial in the Cathedral Church of the Blessed Peter before the altar.

The next incumbent, Richard Childe, took his duties less seriously. It seems that he was given leave to absent himself from the parish for other duties in Bristol and appointed a curate, Nicholas Hunt, for pastoral duties.

By 1500 the church needed rebuilding, the Norman building having lasted for three centuries. All over the county new churches with fine perpendicular towers, one of the glories of Somerset, were replacing older churches. When the new Tudor Cathedral in Bath, replacing the earlier Norman one, was completed, the energies of builders and benefactors could now be turned towards the parish churches. It therefore seems more than likely that South Stoke found in John Chaunceler, the vicar from 1501 to 1527, and his family, who were prosperous weavers in Bath, the benefactors responsible for erecting a new parish church. It stood higher than the Norman church with a steeply pitched roof and the fine three-stage tower we see today. The existing bell frame, also dating from the same period, seems to indicate that at least one bell, possibly the Great Bell, referred to in later churchwardens' accounts, hung there in 1525.

THE REFORMATION: YEARS OF STRIFE

By the start of the 16th century the ancient monastic houses and churches dominated the countryside of Somerset with their spectacular buildings and vast estates. Nowhere was more than a few miles from a monastery, yet within a decade these were to be swept away.

Henry VIII wished to marry Anne Boleyn but the Pope refused to declare that his marriage to Catherine of Aragon was invalid. In 1529 the King, in despair of persuading the Pope to comply, dismissed Cardinal Wolsey and embarked on a campaign of controlling the Church with the Pope excluded. A succession of Acts of Parliament required all clergy to take an Oath of Acceptance and a Denial of Papal Authority. Nearly all acquiesced, among them Thomas Boys of South Stoke. None could have seen the consequence of his action. The ease with which the Pope's power was abolished and the clergy subjected to the law of the land encouraged Henry VIII to take further action and the Dissolution of the Monasteries followed. This was not necessary for the destruction of Papal authority but Henry was in sore need of money.

Robert Holloway, Prior of Bath Abbey at that time, clearly sensed trouble ahead for in 1537 he leased the Manor of South Stoke to Thomas Smyth in an attempt, no doubt, to divest the Priory of property. In the lease he makes full provision for South Stoke's vicar to continue to receive the tithe and glebe. Two years later Bath Priory was suppressed and all its assets and property were acquired by the Crown. Most of the buildings and land were immediately sold off to wealthy landowners, but South Stoke remained in the hands of the Crown.

In 1541 Thomas Boys resigned the living and for the next 18 years South Stoke appears to have been without a vicar; understandable, for these were turbulent years. In 1547 Henry VIII died an excommunicated Catholic and the gates were open to the reforming party. Protestantism was in its ascendancy.

The reign of Edward VI witnessed the introduction of the Prayer Book in English, the abolition of vestments and the removal of all images, stone altars and the like. The Holy Days and Fasting Act of 1551, which is still on the statute book, prohibited the Christmas Day churchgoer from travelling to the service in any kind of vehicle. Congregations were expected to participate more actively in the liturgy and the clergy were now officially allowed to marry.

The death of Edward VI in 1553 marked the end of Protestantism for a short time. The Catholic Mass and images in churches were restored by Mary, and about 2000 parish clergy were removed from their livings because they had married, this now being an offence. At an Archdeacon's Visitation in 1555, the churchwardens of South Stoke politely reported that, owing to the neglect of the Crown, they lacked a curate and a service book and that the chancel was in decay. From the accounts kept by other churchwardens during this period we can gain some idea of the turmoil caused by these changes. They paid for craftsmen to remove all the images and hid many of them while selling others. Then they had to pay for them to be replaced under a Catholic queen, only to have to make a third payment for their removal again under Elizabeth – a vexing time for churchwardens.

The accession of Elizabeth in 1558 brought about a less strict form of Protestantism and the appointment of Thomas Vaughan as Vicar of South Stoke. For the first three years he absented himself and appointed a curate in his place, who was probably the first priest in the parish to celebrate Communion in English, using the new *Book of Common Prayer*.

In 1572 the Dean and Chapter of Wells decreed that the ancient chalices should be melted down and, out of the metal thus obtained, new communion cups made. The Elizabethan chalice in

South Stoke dates from this period. Protestant and Catholic passions ran high and purification by fire of prayer books, chalices and clergy was not uncommon. With 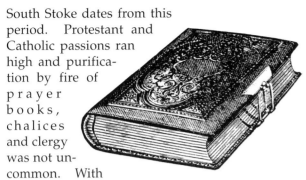 the death of Elizabeth I, the living of South Stoke passed to Anne of Denmark, James I's Queen Consort who, as patron, presented Thomas Hull as vicar in 1618. The Queen visited Bath to take the waters on at least three occasions and it was probably on one of these that Thomas Hull purchased the manor and the living. Reformation theology tended to dominate the universities of Oxford and Cambridge during the reign of James I, and it seems likely that Thomas Hull, who took his degree at Oxford, had strong Protestant sympathies. This may be the reason he was not evicted and the church was spared any damage during the Civil War and Commonwealth. Patronage of the living remained with the Hull family until 1700, during which time five vicars were appointed, all Oxford graduates, who served with varying degrees of distinction. One, an errant schoolmaster, failed to take up his appointment. Another, Andrew Talbot, became one of about 400 non-jurors, priests deprived of their living for refusing to take the Oath of Allegiance to the Protestant monarchs, William and Mary, installed by Parliament after the abdication of James II. In doing so Talbot was following the diocesan Bishop Ken, who would not break his oath of allegiance to James II.

Patronage of the living now passed to Robert Crowch, who installed himself as the incumbent, thus becoming the rector. In this capacity he received the full tithe, although there is no record of his contributing to the rebuilding of the church in 1712.

In 1703 the Great Storm, which rarely escapes mention in the writings of that time, must have severely damaged the old Tudor structure. It left a great swathe 100 miles wide, from the West Country to the Wash, levelling houses in Bristol and killing the Bishop and his wife in Wells. Numerous items appear in the churchwardens' accounts for 1712 dealing with the rebuilding. A sketch by W.W. Wheatly in 1893 shows the church as it must have appeared after the rebuilding, with the height of the walls increased to provide for a new shallow-pitched lead roof in place of the earlier, steeply pitched one. Apart from the small chancel window, there were no windows on the north side of the church and, as yet, no seating arrangements inside.

Vicars of the Parish

1210– ?	John de Tusseburi
1301– ?	Thomas de Winson (?)
1260–(1286?)	R. Donekin
1319–(1349?)	Henry de Foxcote
1349– ?	Adam Laur of Clyve
1349– ?	Robert de Weston
1401– ?	William Plonte
1416– ?	John Lane
1443–67	John Sparhawke
1467–69/70	Richard Childe
1487–93	Thomas Ecklys
1493–1501	Thomas Warrand
1501–27	John Chaunceler
1527–29	Richard Eryngton
1529–41	Thomas Boys
1559–71	Thomas Vaughan
1571–94	Richard Cornelius
1594–1618	John Harris
1618–60	Thomas Hull
1660–62	William Hull
1662–64	Francis Minn
1678–91	Andrew Talbot
1691–1739	Robert Crowch
1739–50	Richard Ford
1750–67	John Taylor
1767–69	Vacant
1769–71	Edward Spencer
1771–80	John Deere Thomas
1780–92	John Wood
1792–1838	Charles Johnson
1839–74	Henry Calverley
1875–84	William Acworth
1884–1944	William Samler
1945–48	Alfred Mulcahy Brown
1948–66	Charles Dicker
1966–74	Kenneth Elphinstone
1974–81	Timothy Forbes Adam [b]

THE UNITED BENEFICE OF THE PARISHES OF COMBE DOWN, MONKTON COMBE AND SOUTH STOKE

1982–95	Jeremy Wordsworth [a]
1983–91	Malcolm Kenworthy [b]
1991–	Frank Brand [b]
1996–	Paul Langham [a]

a	Vicar
b	Licensed by the Bishop to minister in the parish

THE RISE OF METHODISM

After nearly 200 years the dramas of the Reformation were over and the population was growing rapidly. In the countryside the average number of people in a parish was 500, but only four out of ten parishes had resident incumbents. South Stoke was fortunate in this respect and after 1559 the succession of vicars resident in South Stoke was continuous. Nearly all were graduates of Oxford or Cambridge, who by nature of their position and education were expected to be amateur doctors and welfare workers as well as fulfilling their parish duties. The Church was expected to care for the poor and sick, widows and orphans.

Instructions with Royal authority, called 'briefs', were issued to parishes from time to time to make collections in church for specified charitable causes. The churchwardens' account book from 1663 to 1692 contains particulars of such briefs, ranging from the relief of the homeless following fire to the ransoming of captives taken by the Turks. In 1681 Andrew Talbot, vicar, gave £10, a considerable sum in those days, towards the relief of the distressed Reformed Protestant Churches in southern Poland, a remarkable act of charity.

Most people continued to attend church. The normal service was Morning Prayer or Matins, which was not an occasion requiring much involvement except by the village band. Psalms were recited as songs of praise until the first of the great hymn writers, Isaac Watts, followed by Charles Wesley, began the tradition of Anglican hymnody.

In 1773 a gallery was erected at the west end of the church to accommodate an orchestra of cello, clarinet and bassoon with a choir. At the same time pews were installed and a wooden reading desk/pulpit erected. Almost certainly this was to create a 'double-decker' pulpit, where the clerk was seated below to lead the responses. Under the Methodist influence the Bible and the teaching of its doctrines became more prominent, which increased the importance of the sermon. The seating of the congregation in pews was by position in society. Those who could not afford to pay a pew rent could stand.

The Protestant movement was now affecting the Established Church as the Wesleyan and other dissenting sects grew in influence in the surrounding area. South Stoke did not altogether escape this influence. Edward Spencer, who became vicar in 1769, was a close friend of John Wesley and, at Bradford on Avon, where he was also curate, his strong leanings towards Methodism brought him into serious conflict with his flock. After two years he resigned the living at South Stoke to become Rector of Wingfield, where he established a boarding school from whence issued a succession of able, learned and pious ministers.

John Thomas, who succeeded Spencer, was a product of the Oxford Evangelical movement. One of his first acts was to forbid the annual Revels on St James' Day in the parish, followed shortly after by the dismissal of the Parish Clerk for reasons undisclosed.

John Thomas was also responsible for the erection of the double-decker pulpit mentioned earlier and for a new north door and lock, still in position today.

From its monastic roots the Church was now beginning to blaze a trail for education. Church societies encouraged parishes with grants to start their own schools. In 1760 one West-Country layman paid for a few children of the poor to be taught on a Sunday by the women of the parish and, from this beginning, a nationwide Sunday school movement grew up. In South Stoke a Sunday school was still active under Miss Molly Clifford in the 1980s.

The building of the railway brought many Irish labourers to Midford and in 1855 the Roman Catholic Church established a Poor School in that village for their children where a Catholic schoolmaster was employed.

In 1837 an Italian noblewoman, the Marchesa di Sant' Agatha, built a chapel at Midford Castle, the tower of which still stands today. This was served by a resident Roman Catholic priest from 1846 to 1886. Prior to the building of this chapel there are recordings of Mass having been celebrated in Midford House. Also in 1837 a Wesleyan chapel was built in Midford, when South Stoke and Midford became part of the Bath Circuit Preaching Plan, providing for a monthly Sunday service for the Methodists in both communities.

Nationwide, the Church of England was galvanised into realising that it was ill adapted to the needs of the times. So began the reforms of 1835–40 which inaugurated half a century of revival in Anglican worship. New churches were built, one being Holy Trinity, Combe Down, in 1832, and old churches were restored or 'improved', like Monkton Combe in 1814.

Inset: *The Reverend Edward Spencer, Vicar of South Stoke 1769–71.* (Samler Collection)

THE VICTORIAN ERA

'Comes the hour, cometh the man.' Such a man was Henry Calverley who became Vicar of South Stoke in 1839. His first act was to build a school, later to become the base for the WI and now a private house. The following year the tithes were commuted to a tithe rent charge of £168.15s.0d. details of which are recorded in the Tithe apportionment. In 1844 he oversaw the separation of the parish of Monkton Combe from South Stoke to which it had been attached since Norman times. Extensive alterations to the church took place in 1845. A south aisle was added, the chancel rebuilt and the nave re-roofed with new stone tiles. Seating arrangements now provided for 116 seats, 80 of which were declared to be free and unappropriated forever. During his incumbency Henry Calverley probably did more than any other vicar in terms of alterations to this ancient building and it looks today very much as he left it.

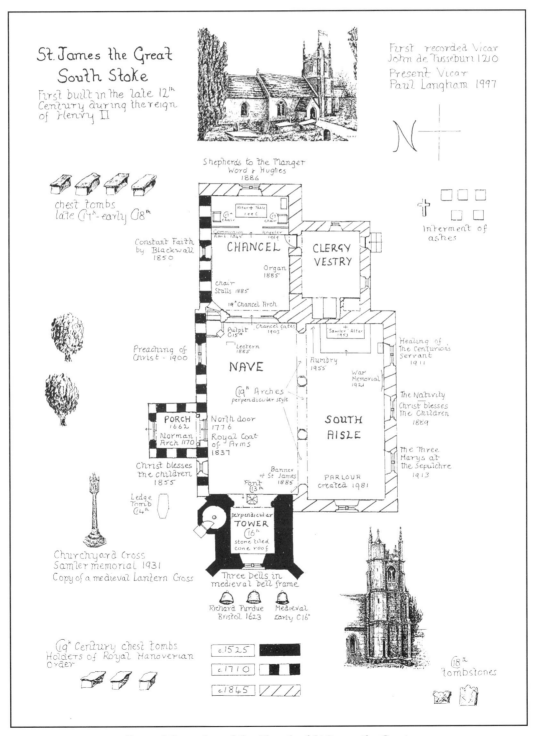

Ground-floor plan of the Church of St James the Great.
(Drawing by Ann Parsons)

The next incumbent, William Acworth, was a very different personality. He married four times and died aged 95. The author of the *Church Rambler* described him as a 'stern prelate of the Norman times' with strong evangelical views, but generously tolerant of the opinions of those who differed from him. He clearly overlooked many things but there is ample evidence to show that Acworth was extremely narrow minded and intolerant. In a published letter to the Archbishop of Canterbury he reported instances of what he considered divergences from the *Book of Common Prayer*. He was horrified to find an altar cross in one church and was particularly severe on a church in Oxford. Following this last outburst he was prohibited by the Church from preaching for a while. After his resignation he offended against clerical etiquette by continuing to reside in the vicarage and claimed the exclusive use of the chancel for his family and household during services.

The visit of the Bishop of Bath and Wells to
South Stoke to dedicate the new Lady Altar,
8 June 1953. From the left: Bishop Dr Bradfield, ?,
Revd C.G. Hamilton Dicker, Mr Swallow.
(Roger Clifford Collection)

Lady Altar, Church of St James the Great, designed by
Joseph Cribb and built by Jack Clifford, and given in
memory of Revd W.S.H. Samler.
(Roger Clifford Collection)

By the late-19th century the Anglo-Catholic or High Church movement in the established Church was growing, largely in response to the strength of Nonconformity that, by 1850, accounted for just under half of the attendance at worship in England. The movement was characterised by an emphasis upon the sacraments, especially that of Holy Communion, and by deep pastoral concern. It was this quiet Catholicism no doubt that led William Samler, and later Charles Dicker, to introduce changes in worship at St James' which have continued to this day. In 1855 the organ was installed and a robed choir, augmented at first by members of St Mary's, Bathwick, was introduced. Vestments were worn and the altar decorated with a cross, candles and a frontal. The stained-glass windows in the chancel and by the font were also given during this period by members of the Calverley family. In 1886 William Samler built a parish room on land adjoining the Packhorse Inn and in 1899/1900 this became the village school, in place of the building erected by Henry Calverley. The churchyard cross, a copy of an old Somerset lantern cross, was erected in 1931 by Samler as a memorial to his eldest son who was killed in action at the Battle of Jutland.

In the last half of the 20th century, changes in the Church had been almost as rapid, though not so violent as in the 1550s. The biggest change in the rural ministry over recent years has been the multiple cure. As the number of clergy declined, benefices could no longer be

South Stoke Church in the last decade
of the 19th century. (Samler Collection)

staffed and had to merge. When the last Vicar of South Stoke, Kenneth Elphinstone, resigned in 1974 to become Chancellor of the Dioceses of York, Hereford and Chester, the right of presentation of a new incumbent was suspended, pending a decision on the future of the parish, and the vicarage was sold. Following the retirement of the Vicar of Combe Down in 1981, a United Benefice of Combe Down with Monkton Combe and South Stoke was created and its first incumbent, Jeremy Wordsworth, appointed.

The creation of united benefices brought about changes in the pattern of ministry and related problems. Non-stipendiary and retired clergy now formed part of collaborative ministry teams to staff united benefices.

South Stoke has been particularly fortunate in this respect. The presence of a 'vicar in the village' and, more importantly, a full pattern of church services, has been preserved by a succession of retired priests who wished to continue their ministry. During the vacancy from 1974 to 1981 Timothy Forbes Adam was licensed by the Bishop to minister to the parish. He was followed by Malcolm Kenworthy, who in turn was succeeded by Frank Brand. In Combe Down a non-stipendiary woman priest, Susan Trickett, was appointed as an assistant curate. She became the first woman to celebrate Holy Communion in St James' in 1995.

Alterations to the fabric of the church continued to reflect changes in the style of worship. A new side altar in memory of William Samler was erected and an aumbry and sanctuary light fitted in 1935. The pews at the west end of the south aisle were removed to provide a communal space for informal gatherings. Maintenance is a continuing burden. After more than 350 years of tolling, the bells were re-hung and the second bell, dated 1623, recast. The chancel, vestry and porch were recently re-roofed and the nave has a new roof to start the new millennium.

The closure of the churchyard in 1986, after 1000 years as a burial site marked the end of a millennium of history but not of the faith that endures.

'Each in his narrow cell forever laid
The rude forefathers of the hamlet sleep.'

Churchwardens' accounts, June 1907.

Above: *The Reverend William S.H. Samler (1854–1944), Vicar of South Stoke, 1884–1944.*
(Courtesy Charles Hignett).

Left: *The Reverend Kenneth and Mrs Felicity Elphinstone.*

South Stoke Evangelical Church recalled by John P. Cross

It is not clear when the church began. A tent mission was held in a field near the present building and, because of the commitment made by several people, a Christian group met for a number of years in what was then the Women's Institute Hall behind Ivy Cottages. Edwin L. Cross, a deacon at Widcombe Baptist Church, was approached by his pastor the Revd John Huntley, who asked if he would be willing to take on the leadership of this work at South Stoke. He agreed and by the early 1920s the fellowship was well established.

The need of premises became more urgent as the years passed. In about 1930 a friend of Edwin Cross, Reginald Biss bought Kapunda Castle in South Stoke Lane. In the grounds of Kapunda was a building used as a garage that seemed to lend itself to alteration to a meeting room. The arrangement they came to was that, if Edwin Cross, a building contractor, would put a garage nearer the house an exchange would take place.

In 1932 there was a grand opening of the newly converted building as a delightful little church, altered by Mr Cross' own staff, several of whom gave of their labour voluntarily, and with a small kitchen added. It was known as South Stoke Gospel Mission and many of the locals became regular worshippers with names that are still recalled such as Granny Francis, Charlie and Mrs Green, Dobson, Marsh, Clifford, Barrett and Heal.

The work grew, with women's meetings, a Sunday school and youth groups, until it was felt that the name was too dated. It was changed to South Stoke Evangelical Church. Over several decades the premises were extended, the church enlarged, a vestry added, a fully equipped kitchen and two fine meeting rooms built at the rear, as well as the addition of a car park to take about 30 cars. Well-known preachers came from afar to preach at special convention meetings and the church was often packed to the doors on these occasions.

Edwin Cross died in 1983 at the age of 95, after giving a lifetime of service to the fellowship, though the work continued with Sunday services and also a very active day centre for the elderly right up to 2000. By now several in the church leadership were becoming quite elderly and felt it wise to consider the future. There were, they felt, many fine churches in the area and in the city and, as over many years the church had supported a number of Christian societies and had made many close friends, it would be a great service to hand over the premises to an organisation that could continue the work but with greater effectiveness.

Trans World Radio, who produce Christian programmes in more than 150 different languages for broadcasting from many transmitting stations to all parts of the world, was the first choice. The team at TWR was delighted at the prospect. The premises could not be more suitable for their purpose, and so in June 2000 the transfer was made and the work of God will now be certain to continue well into the new century at the (now named) South Stoke Christian Centre.

The church and the manor. The position of the ancient manor would have been below and to the left of the church.
(Photograph, Paul Langham)

❖ *The Manor of South Stoke* ❖

In medieval England all land belonged to the King or Monarch. To cover the costs of Army, Government, Church and other expenses he leased his land to tenants-in-chief and these, in turn, sub-granted portions of land (manors) to others in return for various services. The sub-tenants further sub-granted and so on until we come to the 'lord of the manor' who had a few or even only one manor.

The manor was roughly equivalent to the village or parish and in the case of South Stoke the boundaries of manor and parish were the same. The lord granted to his tenants pieces of land in return for, usually, agricultural services and/or produce. If he had several manors he circulated around them 'eating his rents'. His representative was the bailiff or steward; if the lord had many manors, he would appoint a seneschal over the bailiffs. The tenants' representative was the reeve, responsible for them doing their jobs and for safeguarding their rights according to manorial custom.

The first reference we have to the Manor of South Stoke is in 1136, in Bishop Robert's confirmation to the Prior of Bath of his predecessor's earlier gift of the property. This affirmation may have been to clarify ownership, as South Stoke was not specifically referred to in the Domesday Book. South Stoke is included in the Court Rolls of Bath Priory (1309–1502). Bath Abbey Charters of 1301 included this:

This doorway in a cottage in Manor Farm yard is one of two that are older than the present Manor Farm. The archaeologist, Dr R.D. Reid believes the doors to be 15th century and possibly part of the medieval Manor House.

... granted to Robert Brounyng and Joan his wife, certain pieces of land in his Manor of Suthstok, viz: a croft... Curtmede, one acre... Wateley-esacre, together with a certain piece of meadow in Estemede, rent, Twelvepence, and... pieces of meadow called lakes and Overes de Westmede, rent, sixpence. Dated Wednesday next before the Feast of the Nativity of the Blessed Mary, 24 Edward I (Sept. 1296).

Another entry reads:

Grant by Thomas Prior, to Thomas Reynalding of Mere, tanner, of one bushel of corn every week during his life from the Manor of Southstoke next Bath and also one robe.

Clearly, Thomas Reynalding had provided some considerable service to the Abbey.

The benedictines of the great priory of Bath (tenant-in-chief) owned some 14 manors around Bath

of which South Stoke was one. In April 1319 Henry de Foxcote was not only appointed as the parish vicar but also became the bailiff of the monastic Manor of South Stoke. In March of the same year a monk, Thomas de Foxcote, was collated to the important office of Precentor of Bath Priory, suggesting that the de Foxcotes were an important Bath family. In a cartulary of Bath Priory the following entry appears:

Grant by John, Prior to... Sir Henry de Foxcote, Vicar of Southstoke, of one messuage and one virgate of land in their manors of Southstoke and Mydford which John de Acton lately held and also one croft called Courtmede and one acre of land called Wateleyes acre with a piece of meadow in Estmede, certain pieces of meadow called Labes and Overes de Westmede one acre of land at Celereswell, Pasture for cattle with certain exceptions, and grant that the said Henry be quit of certain services.

The field names Court Mead, Wall Leaze, Eastmead and Westmead Batch occur on the 1840 Tithe Map.

In around 1326 de Foxcote was granted a corrody (a pension granted by Royal Foundation) for his work as the bailiff. Many later vicars were probably also bailiffs. It is possible that Henry was a plague victim in 1349.

At about the time the Tithe Barn was built, c.1485, Prior Cantelow accused his predecessor, Prior John Dunster, of destruction of cattle and many other misdeeds and acts of mismanagement on South Stoke Manor. One allegation refers to the vicar of the parish from 1502–27, John Chaunceler, and reads:

Item he (Dunster) received of John Chaunceler of Keynsham in the County of Somerset 100 marks for payment of which the said priory is burdened and on account of this he granted the son of the said John Chaunceler an annual pension of 4 marks until the time when he should promote him to a benefice of 20 marks.

Thus the benefice of South Stoke at this time could have been granted in part repayment of a loan to the Abbot or Priory by John Chaunceler senr. There were Chancellors in the parish until the second half of the 20th century, a tenure of around 500 years.

In 1535 the value of South Stoke Manor, which was still 'owned' by Bath Priory, was £21.9s.6½d.

Apparently in the same valuation the rectory was deemed to be worth nothing. Just two years later, on 12 June 1537, Prior Robert Holloway leased the Manor of South Stoke to Thomas and Jane Smyth. The lease suggests, through an entry in the inventory, that in those days there was an entrance from the manor building to the churchyard on the west side. There is reason to believe that, at the time of the Smyth lease the manor house stood on the site of or adjoining Stable Cottage near the present Manor Farm. Archaeological opinion from Dr R.D. Reid is that, in the open-fronted stable building communicating with the cottage, there are two fine 15th-century doorways and that these were a part of the medieval manor house. It is possible that parts of the Packhorse Inn nearby were also a part of the manor.

These were the troubled times of Henry VIII's Reformation and although Smyth continued as farmer, in around 1540 the manor, flock and other chattels were granted to Elias Wynne for 21 years at £21.0s.2d. Coinciding with this grant Thomas Savage was appointed as the bailiff and collector to several manors in the area, including South Stoke. At the same time the grain rents were granted by Henry VIII to Sir Henry Knevett for 21 years at £6.14s.0d. Knevett sub-let his property to Henry Iseham to whom his tenant, Robert Bradley, paid rent in cash. It appears that the demand of Iseham for a return to payment in kind was refused by Bradley, who, for his temerity, was committed to Fleet Prison. The demand by Iseham may have been because the steep price inflation of grain products at that time would have given him, effectively, a higher value rent, particularly in view of the King's debasement of the coinage. Later, in 1558/9, during the reign of Elizabeth I, Thomas Llewellyn was appointed as bailiff and in 1561 the grain rents went to Geo. Wilcock at £6.19s.4d. If, in granting a lease to the Smyths in 1537, Prior Holloway intended to protect the Church's property from Henry's excesses, then clearly he failed and the Smyths were also losers. However, it seems that in 1577 the Crown lease of the Manor and Advowson of South Stoke returned to the Smyth family, to Thomas Smyth, possibly the son of Jane and Thomas. The reversion of the lease to this Thomas Smyth was short-lived and on 27 November 1583 the Crown granted the lease to John Selwyn. Selwyn died in 1588.

During this period of agrarian upheaval, when tenants were protesting and rioting to maintain their manorial status quo and relative prosperity, landlords were pressing for change in manorial custom. To illustrate the sort of problem that arose, in 1562 eight acres of Wynterly Coppice were sold to tenants of the South Stoke Manor for 11s.6d. an acre. A year later an allowance was made for the fencing of 66 lug (a square pole or perch) and a further eight acres of underwood were sold to the tenants. Clearly the tenants did not look after their purchase as, by 1569, it was described as having been 'spoilt by horses and cattle for want of attention to hedging and ditching.' Consequently the coppice now described as being '25 acres of ash, maple, oak and willow valued at 30s.8d. per annum' was ordered to be sold to George Baker for 21 years at 30s.8d. Baker agreed to incoppice it for seven years to allow the woods to recover. Within five years he had failed to make the rent payments and the area, by then 'Winterly Woods', was leased on 1 March 1574 to William Barnes for 20 years at the same rent.

In the year of Elizabeth I's death (1603) and the end of the Tudor line there is reference to a grant of the Manor's Crown lease but without the lessee's name. A few years later in 1607 the Manor of South Stoke, like many other royal manors, became part of the marriage jointure of Queen Anne (Anne of Denmark), consort of James I, and on 6 October 1608 Gilbert Thatcher completed a survey of the Manor. It continued to change hands regularly and William Baker took a lease on the house, stock and other property in 1610 for a period of 80 years at £12.2s.0d., with a fine (tenancy payment) of £187.2s.8d. His tenancy lasted no more than six years for on 20 September 1616 Queen Anne leased the manor to Dame Susan Caesar for 99 years or three lives at the reduced rent of £12.0s.2d.

However, by 1622 we have a record of the lease being surrendered by John, Lord Dibye (Digby), and three years later (on 24 December 1625) it being sold to Robert Cary, 1st Earl of Monmouth, for 17 years at a value of £24.5s.3½d. Robert Cary was Lord Chamberlain to Charles I when he was Prince of Wales, and when Charles became King, Cary was rewarded with fee farm rents to the value of £600, including South Stoke. In 1635 Cary's eldest son and successor Henry sold the property to Sir Edward Yates.

From the time that Queen Anne, as patron of the living, presented Thomas Hull as the vicar in 1618 until the end of the century, the Hull family held considerable sway in the parish. We know that in 1680 John Hull was the bailiff and it is possible that he had held the post for some years before that. It seems likely that he was either Thomas' son or brother. William Hull succeeded Thomas, his father, as vicar.

South Stoke Manor, together with land to yield an annual income of £4000, was given to Edward Montagu, 1st Earl of Sandwich (*inset*) by Charles II on his restoration in 1660.

Indenture of Lease of the Manor of Southstoke by Prior Holloway

Indenture 12th June, 29 Hen. VIII (1537)

Grant by Prior William to Thomas Smyth of Southstoke with manor house – except rents, services and customary works, waifs and strays courts, advowson, pasture for 50 brace of rabbits with 50 ewes at Horsecombe. Also grant for the whole wetherflock (i.e. sheep for wool only) (280 animals) of Southstoke with all profits and pastures for their lives.

Rents: for manor:- 16d. in cash; 12 quarters of wheat delivered to Priory at stated dates, 16 barley 14 mixed grain 3 oats – with carriage to the Priory, 4 loads wood, they doing the cutting and transport, from Priston Wood and 4 loads hay for said flock (each load to be drawn by 8 oxen). For flock: £5.0s.10d., i.e., 5d. per head, on Feast of St. Margaret in chapel of All Saints in the monastic church. Suit at Lyncombe Halmote Court twice per annum and at Barton Hundred Court twice per annum Housebote etc. (i.e. materials for repair). Tenant to repair – not to sublet without licence. (Recovery clause for arrears of rent and damage). Bond of 100 marks [£66.67p] to return flock intact at end of lease or to pay 8d. per head according to the estimation of the whole homage of Southstoke. MEMORANDUM. The Vicar of Southstoke, Thomas Boys, for the time being shall have going and pasturing freely with the farmers beasts there for three beasts; whereof one shall be a mare, a horse or a gelding the second a kowe; and the third a bullock; which three shall go and pasture in this manner; his mare, horse or gelding, with the farmer's meres, his kowe with the farmer's kyne, and the bullock with the farmer's bullock in certain lesues [sic] and pastures; that is to say in Brode Close, Grove Close and Shepherds Mede, from time to time, as it hath been used and accustomed tyme out of mynde.

De Stauro Vivo (Livestock)
Thomas Smyth and wife Jane have received from the Prior 4 oxen at 7s., a head and 1 cow at 8s., which they will restore at the end of their lease.

De Stauro Mortuo (Deadstock)
They have received: 1 Harpica (Harrow) with iron chain, 2 Yokes, 2 Halters. To be restored as above.

Note: In later leases the halters were replaced by two iron ploughshares.

To this day the Earl of Sandwich collects a fee farm rent, a rent in perpetuity, on the manor (i.e. the parish). An extract from deeds from Hodshill refers to this:

An annual fee farm rent of £24.5s.3d. reserved out of the Manor of Southstoke in the said County of Somerset on the grant thereof made by Letters Patent under the Great Seal of England bearing date 24th December in the first year (1625) of the reign of His late Majesty King Charles the First to Robert Lord Carey Knight his son and heir apparent which said fee farm rent was under or by virtue of another grant made by Letters Patent under the Great Seal of England bearing date 3rd February in the fifteenth year (1675) of His late Majesty King Charles the Second vested in the Earl of Sandwich for an estate of inheritance in fee tail male.

From the 1664/65 Hearth Tax List, Richard Gay gent. appears to have been resident at the manor and to have failed to declare one hearth. In order to minimise his tax liability he either blocked a hearth or it had 'fallen down', or he made a false declaration. At that time the manor, with 11 fireplaces, was by far the largest house in South Stoke. Clearly Richard Gay courted trouble as the churchwardens'

accounts of 1662 have the entry: 'Received of Richard Gay by order of My Lord Bishop for a fine of five shillings for his door through his garden wall into the churchyard it being south of the tower.' The doorway still exists.

The next record we have for South Stoke Manor, in around 1704, is a rather tortuous petition to the House of Lords to enact a bill allowing the sale of the property, to help pay substantial debts incurred by John Gay and his second son Goddard. In June 1690 the manor was in the hands of John Gay, his wife Winifred and one Thomas Goddard. The Gays had four sons, Richard, Goddard, John and Francis, and two daughters, Querina and Mary. John, the father, was clearly not very financially astute and, whether through gambling or speculative business deals, managed to lose a lot of money. The lease conveyed in 1690 appears to have been constructed to remove effective ownership of the manor from John Gay and to safeguard the security of Winifred and the children. The eldest son Richard and Thomas Goddard are parties to the release. At some point after the death of Richard, John senr and Goddard mortgaged the property for £500 and, in addition, John Gay had several mortgages to various people for £3110.8s.4d., a sum far exceeding the value of the estate. At the time of the petition Goddard Gay had been in the East Indies for five years, since 1699, and was presumed dead. Prior to that John senr and John junr had died. Thus, the youngest son Francis was left to pick up the pieces. The petition was presented to the Lords for the passing of a bill to facilitate the sale of South Stoke Manor, pay the debts, and if anything was left, pass it to Francis. Because Goddard was party to an earlier debt it was thought reasonable that he should be barred as a beneficiary.

In 1711 the estate was sold to two 'Stuff Makers' from Bristol, Augustine Rock and John Teague, and their partner Wm John Jones of Dundry and later South Stoke. From 1768, the property, now called Manor Farm, was purchased by Robert Cooper of Salisbury and remained in the hands of the Cooper family until at least the mid-19th century. The following press notice appeared on 20 August 1807 in the *Bath Chronicle*:

MANOR OF SOUTHSTOKE

All qualified persons are requested not to shoot over the Manor, there being a great scarcity of Game in the same – and all unqualified persons trespassing on the said Manor will be prosecuted according to law.

By the time of the Tithe Map of 1840, the estate known as Manor Farm or Manor Farm House (Chapter 9), was owned by another Robert Cooper. According to the 1841 census the farm was leased and worked by Richard Yeoman, aged 35, and his wife Mary. The extent of the land belonging to the farm appears to have been much the same as it is today. Cooper owned over 237 acres within the parish and paid an annual tithe of £20.7s.0d. There is no evidence that Robert Cooper lived in the parish. Yeoman, who was born in Wanstrow, Somerset, spent much of his life in South Stoke village, dying there at the age of 71 in 1872. In 1845 he was a churchwarden. According to the 1851 census Richard Yeoman, described as a widower, employed 13 labourers in farming 225 acres of land; his sister, Jane Porter (47), was live-in housekeeper. The only other resident was Jane Donfrey (or Donprey), a 16-year-old servant from Farmborough. The census returns of 1861 and 1871 show changes in the relatives and servants living at the farm. A Matilda Ward, aged 17, who was born in the village, was a house servant in 1861. Yeoman was married twice; his first wife Mary died aged 46, in 1846. His second wife, Ann, was 59 at the time of her death in 1866. All three are buried against the west wall of the churchyard. It seems there were no children from either marriage. By 1871 the acreage farmed by Yeoman had increased to 258 acres and labour requirements had dropped to five men and three boys.

The severity of landholders, including Richard Yeoman, and the law in the mid-19th century, are illustrated by the following report of 10 March 1853 from the *Bath Chronicle*:

Saturday, Mary Ann Grove, Elizabeth Fowler and ? were charged with stealing turnip greens from a field in the occupation of Mr Yeomans [sic] of Southstoke and in default of paying each 4/- the damage and costs were committed for fourteen days hard labour.

Following Richard Yeoman's death in 1872, we learn from local directories that William Andrews was the farmer from 1874 at the latest, and continued until 1886/7. The 1881 census records that Andrews (57) with wife Sarah (58) and daughter Florence (20) were resident at Manor Farm and farming 260 acres, helped by five men and a boy.

Following Andrews, in about 1888, the name of the farm seems to have been changed to, or perhaps is erroneously recorded as, Southstoke Farm, at which time it was worked by William B. Pease. In the 1891 census William Pease (29), born in Henbury, Glos., is listed as farming Manor Farm with wife Bessie (30) and brother Robert (26). For the next 40 years three families occupied the property which was described by different names:

1894–1902	Col and Mrs A.F. Bingham Wright and son (?) Arthur George, **The Manor.**
1903–21	Mrs Balmain and the Misses Balmain, **Manor House.**
1922–35	Simon R. and Emily J. Kidner and Albert E. Kidner, **Manor Farm.**

Since 1936 Manor Farm has been owned by the Hignett family, although listing in directories does not reappear until 1950, when Geoffrey Hignett is recorded as being of Hodshill Hall and Manor Farm.

Manor Farm today. (Courtesy Charles Hignett)

CHAPTER 8

Schools & Schoolteachers

T he first known mention of education in South Stoke is an entry in the churchwardens' accounts for 1729 when a payment of 2 shillings was made to the schoolmaster for 'feathering ye Church Bible' (i.e. marbling the lining paper of the cover). Another payment, this time for 10s.6d., for the same work, was made in 1746. Tantalisingly, there is no other mention of who the schoolmaster was or of the location of the school. However, John Canvin in his notes makes mention of his belief that the school in question may have been the old school in Monkton Combe, which was possibly the forerunner of the present Combe Down School.

In 1793, the churchwardens' accounts mention that they had agreed to allow the north half of the church gallery to be partitioned off to accommodate the Misses Aldritt and their scholars. The Misses Aldritt were Miss Elizabeth and Miss Anne Aldritt, daughters of William Aldritt, who had been secretary to the novelist Henry Fielding. They had a school at Fortnight Farm, Combe Hay, from 1749–1800. Various members of the family had schools at Stony Littleton, Foxcote, Devonshire Buildings and Bloomfield Place at around this period.

An advertisement for the Misses Aldritt's school appeared in the *Bath Chronicle* on 16 July 1793:

E. Aldritt, many years an assistant teacher at Mrs Wignall's having entered into partnership with her sister, they have taken Mitford Farm, a healthful pleasant situation, near the turnpike road to Salisbury: where they will open their Boarding School for the reception of Young Ladies, after the present recess on Monday the 22nd instant. Miss Aldritts solicit the continuation of the favours of their friends, and assure them every care and attention shall be paid to the Young Ladies' improvement.

Terms 14 guineas a year, one guinea entrance. Bills settled half-yearly.

N.B. Proper masters in the various departments of Polite Education will attend.

The identity of 'Mitford' Farm is uncertain, but it seems likely to have been what is now known as Hyver

Kennels. The school was advertised again in the *Chronicle* in 1794, but there is no evidence as to how long it lasted.

The census returns sometimes record the existence of schoolteachers, but whether they ran schools in their homes or were lodging in the village whilst working elsewhere is not clear. Here, for example, are the entries for 1861:

Catholic School	James Murphy
	Teacher (b. Ireland) Age 36
Day School	James Bryant
	Wharfinger
	Sarah Bryant
	Schoolmistress
National School	Emily Taylor
	Mistress

There had been an 'official' school in South Stoke since 1840, when the Revd Henry Calverley (vicar 1839–74) built the first village school in the building now known as Old School House. Sadly, no records exist of what went on there, other than a note in the Revd William Acworth's parish accounts of 1884 of a teacher (Miss Jones) removing books from the school. Scrutiny of the church records suggests that couples signing the marriage register from about 1860 onwards were able to write their names rather than simply mark the entry with a cross, which may well suggest that the education on offer did at least include practice in making signatures.

Similar parochial schools were founded in other parishes in Bath, such as Bathwick (1828) or Rush Hill, Odd Down (1847), so South Stoke was keeping pace with a common trend. Attendance was not compulsory, and fees had to be paid, ranging from 1d. to 8d. per week. The Education Act of 1870 made primary schooling available to all, and Mundella's Act of 1880 made attendance compulsory for five to ten year olds.

In 1885, the Revd William Samler purchased a plot of land on the site of the ruined malthouse, just below the Packhorse Inn, to provide a parish lecture room. By 1902, this room had already become the new village school. He also purchased adjoining land to build another classroom, a lavatory, and girls' closets. The mortgage document he drew up reveals the use of the building as an Elementary or Sunday School.

The school admission register from 1894 to 1973 is available at the Somerset County Record Office and

Left: *The original school, built by the Revd Henry Calverley in 1840.* (Photograph, Gill Carter)

Below: *The Parish Room, later school, built by the Revd William Samler in 1894 and now used as the South Stoke Village Hall.* (Roger Clifford Collection)

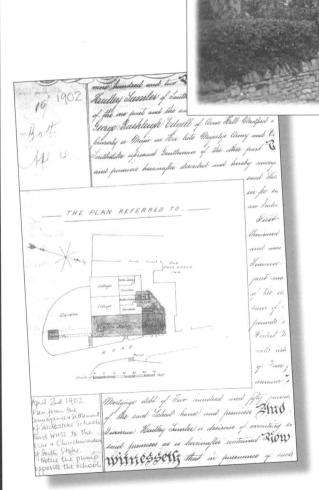

Plan of South Stoke School from 1902 Conveyance and Settlement by William Samler.

Above: *Ellen Heal, assistant schoolmistress, c.1915.* (Courtesy Kathleen Dyer, née Heal)

gives an absorbing account of the names and addresses of the pupils and their parents' occupations. There are many familiar names, such as Sly, Clifford, Marsh, Dyer, Holley, Skrine, Robinson, Heal and Gaylard. Nearly 1000 pupils passed through the school in those years. Many, in the early years, left to go into service. Others went to Odd Down or Combe Down Secondary Schools, where they would have stayed until the age of 13. Many came from the children's home in Odd Down, whose matron, Miss Buckley, was there from 1910–20 and signed the register *in loco parentis*. In the early years of the century, many fathers were agricultural workers, fuller's earth workers, or masons.

In 1903 and 1904 the punishment book records pupils being beaten for lateness and disobedience. In 1911, one pupil was beaten for eating apples. Records were also kept of the sales of goods made by the children, which in 1904 included chemises, nightgowns and pinafores. In 1933, children had made frocks, overalls, woolly balls and raffia-trimmed kettle holders.

The school log gives an interesting account of day-to-day school life. The first infants teacher, Katie Stone, was appointed in November 1894, but there are unfortunately no more entries until 1909, by which time there was an infants' teacher as well as a head teacher. A diocesan inspector visited the school in December 1909 when there were 70 pupils present. He found them very good on repetition of the Old and New Testaments, scripture, hymns and collects, catechism and good on the Prayer Book.

When a government inspector visited in January 1910, he found pupils were doing well generally, but the infants' school was inadequately heated. In fact, the weather that winter was very cold and attendance was low, some pupils finding it difficult to walk from outlying cottages in the snow.

The first head teacher, Sarah Stone, who presumably saw the school through its move from the old building to the new, retired that year after 26 years in the school and her place was taken by Nella Holder. In the autumn of the same year, the school's managers decided to close the school earlier in the afternoons so that pupils could reach their homes in Midford before dark. When teachers were absent their places were taken by older pupils.

Pupils seem to have had frequent interruptions in their education, since the school was closed for numerous events such as the Coronation, Ascension Day, the parish jumble sale, the choir outing, the Red Cross fête and Empire Day. These closures were in addition to a three months' closure for whooping cough, two weeks for German measles and three weeks for diphtheria. Not surprisingly, the managers commented in 1922 that the health of the pupils had been poor for some time.

By 1916, the roll was down to 50, and the lack of playground space was seen as a major issue, since PE lessons had to be taken in classrooms. By 1923, only 23 children remained in the school, but the Revd William Samler purchased a gramophone so that pupils could listen to the King's and Queen's speeches. In 1925, with only 19 children on the roll, May Sly became the head and sole teacher. However, she did have the consolation of being able to use the WI's piano for music lessons.

Muriel Spear remembers the school:

I went to the village school, there was a stove, a round one, where we put coal. There was a guard around and we put our gloves [on it] to dry... Miss Sly was the teacher, she lived with her brother in the house next to the school… There were quite a few of us. The toilet of the school used to be in the yard, a brick place [now a store], at the back of… the playground. It had a notice on the door 'Cleanliness is next to Godliness'.

Numbers were still low when a visiting inspector, Miss Cummings, recognised the difficulties of a single-teacher school, but commented that the younger pupils did not get enough attention, that the premises were gloomy and that older pupils needed training in perseverance and neatness. A pupil at the school from 1930–35 remembers his teacher:

She wasn't strict at all, and we didn't learn all that much. She was mad about cricket, though, and used to play with us every break time. If we couldn't get her out by the end of break time, she'd sometimes keep us out in the playground till lunchtime, trying to bowl her out.

In 1936, Mrs Clements was the head teacher. A former pupil remembers her well:

She was a very good pianist and could play classical, jazz, dance, anything. She taught the children dancing. It was a joy to pass the school at times to hear the music!

In November 1939, the first evacuees, from Hastings, were admitted to the school. Eventually, evacuees, who had brought their own teacher with them, had their school in other premises in the village. Numbers in South Stoke School remained for the most part low throughout the war, and attendance was sometimes poor because of air raids. There was also a period of closure when the school was used as a rest centre. The caretaker in the 1940s, Mrs Harris, who has looked after the school premises ever since, describes how basic the facilities were then:

I used to have to go down to the school at six in the morning to light the stove, get in the coal and pump up the water for the day. The pump was just outside the back door.

Above: *Particulars of the school curriculum in a return made to the Ministry of Education in 1902. All pupils took object lessons, and the girls worked at needlework while the boys studied drawing.*

Above: *School accounts for February 1903*

Left: *Extract from school logbook, 1910, giving an account of the visit of Mr J. Tillard, HMI. Information for February gives details of the pupils' health and their difficulties in getting to school in inclement weather.*

In 1943, Miss Mayes became the head teacher and the school was sometimes closed while she attended professional development courses. The roll began to increase again, and was up to 52 by 1952, when an assistant teacher had to be appointed to cope with the numbers. An HMI visit in 1953 reported work of a high standard, with individual teaching – 'a school where work of distinction is being done.'

Miss Mayes left the school in 1955, her place being taken by Miss Begley. The main event of 1956 was a steam explosion in the water heater, but luckily no children were hurt. Later that year, plans for the installation of electricity in the building were discussed. In 1962, a passing cattle lorry hit the school and did some damage to the building. Frustratingly, the logbook finishes there. The next one saw the school through to its closure in 1973, because of falling numbers, but the record is not yet in the public domain.

Left: *Miss Mayes, the head teacher of the school from 1943–55.*

Class 2, 1912. Left to right, back row: *?, ?, Jack Dobson, Billy Rose, Jack Clifford, Percy Barrett;* middle; *George Morris, ?, ?, ?, Mabel Green, Margery Dobson, ?, Ida Dobson, ?;* front: *?, Charles Heal, Bill Morris, ?, Ida Rose, Enid Bath, ?, ?.*
(Roger Clifford Collection)

Class 3, 1912. Left to right, back row: *Edwin Heal, Walt Barrett, ?, ? Hopkins, Albert Clifford, ?, ?;* middle: *?, Hilda Staddon, Doris Withers (Boulton), Leila Hamlen (Skrine), Kathleen Marsh (Clifford), Winnie Clifford, Lucy Clifford, Rose Hamlen;* front: *no names known.*
(Roger Clifford Collection)

Class of 1918. Left to right, back row: *Ena Clifford, Peggy Dobson, Grace Withers, Celia Hopkins (Gaylard), Grace Williams (Heal), ?, Doris Owen, Mona Staddon;* middle: *?, Coral Clifford, Bob Rose, Ruby Barrett, ? Wilcox, ?, Dora Wilcox, Olive Barrett, Tom Ash, ?;* front: *? Bath, ? Frapwell, Kitty Hopkins, ?, ? Spear, Joyce Spear, ?, Jack Rose, Noel Staddon.*
(Roger Clifford Collection)

Harvest Festival, 1946. Left to right: David Harris, Clifford Robinson, John Wharton, Robert Masters, Christine Lambern, Myrtle Furley, Doreen Perkins, Eileen Heal, Clive Maundrell, Diane Perkins, Catherine Wharton, Mary Wilson, Brian Harris, Rachel Masters.

Harvest Festival, 1946 or 1947. Children standing include: *Robert Masters, John Wharton, David Harris, Christine Lambern, Margaret Perkins, Clifford Robinson, Mary Wilson, Myrtle Furley, ? Wilson (?), Brian (?) Harris, Marian Masters;* kneeling: *Clive Maundrell, Doreen Perkins.*

School photograph of 1948. It was taken in the field below Court Mead where there used to be a see-saw, which remained for many years.

School nativity play, 1951. Mary is played by Elizabeth ?, Joseph by Brian Harris, the Archangel Gabriel by Susan Scott (Dustin), and the angels by Natalie and Valerie Hawkins and Pauline Sparks.

South Stoke School, c.1955. Miss Mayes, the head teacher, is in the centre, and Mrs Beech, her assistant, is centre left.

Above: *Craft display, c.1953.*

Above: *The final class, taken on the day the school closed in 1973, with Mrs Harris, caretaker, left, and Miss Begley, head teacher, right.*

Left: *Continuing education in South Stoke. French class in 2000, with, from the left: Ruth Brand, Frank Brand, Judy and Bob Parfitt, Royston Clifford, Valerie and Jim Summers.* (Photograph, Gill Carter)

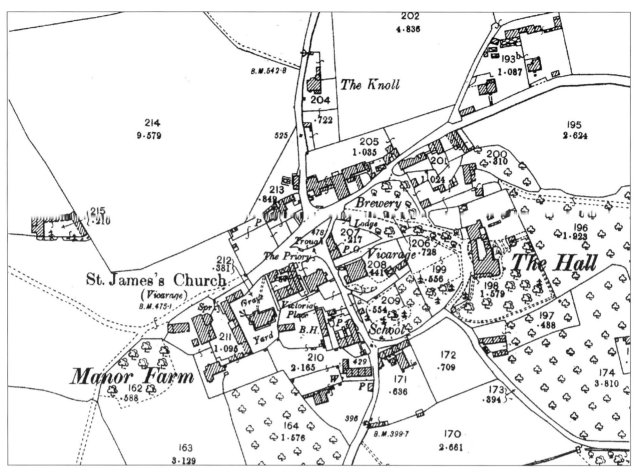

The Centre of South Stoke village in 1904 (from the OS map).

South Knoll with Garage, later Pound Cottage, in the left foreground in the mid-1960s.

CHAPTER 9

Houses & People

❖ South Stoke ❖

South Stoke Lane, the approach to the village from the Cross Keys Inn, would have had fields on both sides 150 years ago. The Thirty Acres would have flanked the west side and on the east side of the lane were Cross Keys Tyning, Well Ground and Six Acres. Thirty Acres still flanks the west side of the lane, but the east side now has properties in a variety of styles of architecture, ranging from substantial eccentricity to the more modest vernacular. Before turnpike roads were built, the lane constituted part of a major early thoroughfare from Bath to Wells via Holloway, Bear Flat, Entry Hill, South Stoke and Wellow.

The first dwelling to be built, in Six Acres to the east of the lane, was Lansdowne Villa in around 1868. Albert Hamilton, carpenter, and his wife Anna, moved up from 1 Victoria Place to occupy the house. In 1871, Hamilton, aged 31, employed two men and two boys in a workshop that can still be seen at the rear of the house, now known as South Knoll. The house has been extensively altered but original features, such as the stone floor, remain. It is the home of Sheila and Sandy Neill; the latter was doctor to many in the parish. A stone garage at the south end of the garden (probably once a stable) was converted to a house in 1981, and is known as Pound Cottage. According to the Vestry Minutes, in 1886 the village pound was moved to the site of Pound Cottage's present-day garage.

Above: *Kapunda, 1937. Edgar Davis (right) and Dorothy Davis (centre) with a friend and their dog, Blanco.*
(Courtesy Michael Davis)

Right: *The construction of an air-raid shelter at Kapunda in 1938 with 'Lardy' Shellard (?).*

The parish's second castle (the first being Midford Castle) was the next dwelling to be built in South Stoke Lane. In 1905, James Owen, a Milsom Street antiques dealer, bought for £400 three acres, two roods and 36 perches of the Well Ground from Bath Stone Firms Ltd who had entertained ideas of quarrying on the site. Because of the aboriginal origins of the name, local folklore suggested that Kapunda Castle was built with a fortune made from copper mining in Kapunda, South Australia, but this was not the case. James Owen quarried the land for stone to build his 'castle', Kapunda, which was completed in 1907. The garage of the property, built so far from the house because of James Owen's fear of the inflammable nature of petrol, was converted to the Evangelical Church (South Stoke Gospel Mission) (see Chapter 7), which became a centre of worship for over 60 years. Owen died in 1924, and left his estate to his wife Louisa and thence to his daughter Daisy Blanche. The two ladies lived in Kapunda for a further seven years. Since the Owens, only two other families have lived in Kapunda, an engineer named Reginald Biss with his family (1931–36) and three generations of the Davis family. Prior to their marriage in South Stoke Church in May 1937, Dorothy and Edgar Davis purchased the 'castle' in October 1936. Dorothy had inherited Longhope in Upper Oldfield Park, Bath, from her father and she exchanged houses with the Bisses. Edgar, an RAF pilot, related how just before the Second World War he and friends excavated an air-raid shelter from the solid stone beneath the floor of the house. Martin and Juliet Davis purchased High Land next door in 1984 and in 1988 exchanged that house for Kapunda. Edgar died at High Land in 1993, and Dorothy in 1998 at the age of 94. In 1933 Reginald Biss sold a southern portion of Kapunda's land, which included an old quarry and the garage, to Henry Cross, building contractor, who built Bushy Leas there. That house was named after a field on Jock Cross' Hill Farm (now Clearbrook), Midford. Bushy Leas is now known as Faith House and the quarry has become its garden. In 1991 a Second World War incendiary bomb was discovered in the garden.

Gradually, the land between Bushy Leas and the South Stoke Gospel Mission was in-filled with houses. St Fillans was built for the Cross family in 1938 by Mr Dobson who lived in Russell House, beside the church. He was ably assisted by the boys of the Cross family whose family home it was until 1980 when the Weavers moved in. Harvington (known formerly as Luill or Lulil) and Somersby were built in the 1930s. In 1965, Horace Brand of Somersby built a house (Tottanstoc) in his garden, into which he moved. In the garden of Tottanstoc there is a large underground rubble-walled chamber of unknown purpose. His great-grandchildren now live in Tottanstoc with their parents. Tucked away

Horace Brand and the building of Tottanstoc in 1965. (Courtesy Gill Carter)

behind the hedge a little closer to the village than the Evangelical Church is Croftlands, a bungalow built by the Clifford family in 1947/8.

Moving south, just before the lane descends to the village, on the west side of the road within the field Cow Garston, is Brantwood, built in Edwardian times for Alderman Bush the proprietor of S.W. Bush & Son, grocers of Kingsmead Square (now a Pizza Hut!) and his wife. They lived in the elegant house from 1910–38. Their son Sydney Bush had the idea of retiring with his two sisters to a new house that he planned to build in the field adjoining the road. The two large round pillars at the entrance were as far as this notion progressed before he died and his sisters moved to South Stoke Road. During the Second World War, Brantwood and its grounds, which were owned by Captain Horton were taken over as a billet first for British troops, then for US Army officers. The Army abandoned their billet overnight for Weymouth and Portland Harbour in early June 1944, to play their part in the D Day landings. Local residents who cleared the garbage from the US billet commented: 'they threw away better food than we were eating!' Captain and Mrs Goodman lived there from the 1950s and Diana is still in residence. They will long be remembered for their hospitality to all and sundry, and for hosting numerous charity functions in the grounds, including, for many years, the church fête.

The Spear family at Hillside in 1916. Proud new grandfather William Spear holds the rein of his horse Molly. In the trap is his wife Matilda, holding Joyce Ellen Louise, born in 1915 at Hillside. Holding Sam the dog is Nellie (aunt) and beside her is Joyce's mother, Louise, also known as Linda.
(Rod Adams Collection)

In the garden at Hillside. Left to right: William James Spear, Nellie (his sister), Mr Church, Mrs Matilda Spear and Mr William Spear (the parents).
(Rod Adams Collection)

Left: *William James Spear (b.1890) and Louise (known as Linda), his bride from Fairfield Park. They raised a family of five children in Parsonage Cottage – now known as Beech Cottage.*
(Rod Adams Collection)

Above: *Three generations of the Spear family all named William, taken in the conservatory at Hillside in 1932. Within ten years the youngest was to die in the Second World War.*
(Rod Adams Collection)

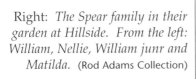

Right: *The Spear family in their garden at Hillside. From the left: William, Nellie, William junr and Matilda.* (Rod Adams Collection)

Left & below: *Mr and Mrs Spear as newly-weds and perhaps 50 years later.* (Courtesy Muriel Wheatley and Rod Adams)

Above & three photographs below: *Matilda Spear and her daughter Nellie* (above left and below left and right), *c.1910.* (Rod Adams Collection)

As South Stoke Lane drops away down to the Green, it passes between the high walls of Brewery House and Hillside Cottage. Outside the front door of Hillside, a small market garden in the 1940s, Miss Spear displayed vegetables for sale. Two original cottages were amalgamated and crenellated to form the gothic villa, Brewery House. During the 1830s this site was developed as a brewery by the Hunt family. By the time Bezin King Reece, from Fairly, Midford, bought the whole brewery site in the 1920s, the business had long since ceased. Reece converted the stables to Longhope and sold it as a house to a Mr Beale, and in 1951 Newstead (now The Linleys) was built in the brewery garden for Mr and Mrs Dent. The 1840 Tithe Map shows that the now fine garden to the rear of Brewery House (formerly known as Belle Vue and The Chalet) had a building on it, but no vestige remains.

In recent years, during the ownership of Ursula and John Brooke, a hidden staircase was uncovered below the floor of the house. Brewery House has a fine garden, developed by the Revd Timmy Forbes Adam and continued by John Brooke; the latter's plant sales and open days have given pleasure to hundreds and raised thousands of pounds for charity.

Elizabeth Cartwright-Hignett, Jack Clifford (who had just restored the carriage), Leslie Cairns (groom) and Judy the horse, passing the brewery garages in 1980.
(Reproduced by kind permission of the *Bath Chronicle*)

Brewery Cottage, c.1920.

Mrs Scott (left) and Miss Prince leave Longhope for the WI party during the hard winter of 1966.

Next door to Brewery House is Brewery Cottage, on the site of brewing vats, and here the Ainsworth family were tenants of Reece for a decade from the 1920s. By this time the western half of the cottage appears to have been derelict and to have collapsed: only the ground floor was later rebuilt. Restoration work on the cottage from 1969 revealed a well under the kitchen suggesting an early, perhaps 17th-century origin for the building.

Across South Stoke Lane, below Hillside Cottage to the west, are Upper Buildings, now known as Upper Cottages, which certainly existed during the mid-18th century. It is believed they were built on land bequeathed by the Manor of South Stoke to 'worthy persons' at the time of Charles II. Deeds refer to 'eleven lugs of ground' adjoining the gardens which 'were formerly part of the capital messuage of the Manor of South Stoke'. This refers to ground where three 1950s bungalows have been built to the west of Upper Cottages. Indenture holders were obliged to contribute 'in equal moiety... the expense of keeping the said Well and Pump in repair.' The well still exists there, behind No. 3 Upper Cottages where for several generations, during the 19th and early-20th centuries, members of the Hamlen family lived. They were a large family to be found also in Midford and Monkton Combe. In 1965 the eastern end of No. 1 Upper Cottages (Burnham Cottage) was divided from the rest, to make a Hamlen son's married home. This grew into Quoin Cottage.

The stone- and timber-fronted building on the corner below Quoin Cottage is on the site of the former pound, and until recently was used as garages. David Cairns is remembered locally as a popular shoe mender who worked in these garages before the Second World War. Prior to that, they were used as stabling for hauliers. Now, in 2000, they have been restored and altered by Gillian Carter as an annexe to Quoin Cottage.

The white railings along the north perimeter of the village Green are a feature of the centre of the village, and 'meet you at the white railings' has long been a familiar phrase. They were erected in 1896 to replace railings that the Parish Council considered dangerous. The Parish Council resolved that they should be painted white, and white they have been ever since. The seat of 1992, replacing the 1953 coronation seat on the Green is a popular public amenity, commanding an attractive view over the village and beyond. The concrete slab on which the seat rests was the base of the ARP/fire watchers' hut during the Second World War. The view from this seat and the appearance of the village were much improved when in 1993 the Parish Council achieved the burying of telephone cables, eliminating a pole at the foot of the Slipway from which a web of 25 wires radiated. Two other poles were also removed. The following year the Council had the lantern and standard of traditional design installed on the village Green to replace an unsightly concrete column and lamp.

Below and facing the Green, the house with the tall chimney stacks is The Priory, built in 1850 by Thomas Hunt, developer of the brewery, for himself and his wife Ann. Their occupancy was very short as

An 1850 lithograph of The Priory.

they both died in 1853 and, curiously, on their death certificates, they are recorded as being of Belle Vue Cottage. In those days, the front door of The Priory was on the east elevation but in 1965 it was moved to the north. This prominent site held an earlier building for it is recorded that 'the said Thomas Hunt the younger did pull down the cottage or tenement and the messuage tenement or dwelling house mentioned'. Two retired servants of Queen Victoria, Miss Holinshead and Mrs Vaughan Jones, are reputed to have lived at The Priory during the 1880s. Between the wars Mr and Mrs Fallowfield ran it as a boarding house. During the Second World War it was let, and a day school for children was held in the house. In 1946 it was bought by Miss Elmira Wade, a notable lady who was awarded an OBE for outstanding services to the Women's Royal Voluntary Service. She later became archivist to Lord Methuen at Corsham Court.

The Priory, Victoria Cottages, Russell Cottages and Alderley Cottage in the 1930s. (Roger Clifford Collection)

Tucked into and adjoining the south-west corner of The Priory is Priory Cottage, previously Victoria Cottage. It has a stone bearing the date 1769, but is likely to be older. During extensive repairs in 2000, it became evident that it had been converted from a barn, probably in the 17th century. Previously much larger, about 40 per cent of the western side was demolished, probably late in the 19th century, for reasons unknown. George Lansdown, a carpenter (and also incidentally census enumerator), lived here in the 1850s and owned most of the land westward to the churchyard.

An 1853 watercolour by Edmund Marks of the village centre shows a familiar view (see page 31). On the left are Nos 1 and 2 Russell Cottages identified on the 1840 Tithe Map as 'Mrs Cleverley'. To their right in the background is a barn which is also shown on the

The lychgate and Russell House. (Drawing by Ann Parsons)

Tithe Map, and it seems likely that this was later converted to form Nos 2 to 5 Victoria Cottages, originally called Victoria Place. A deed of 1853 outlines a cottage where No. 2 now stands. No. 1 Victoria Cottages, built at right angles across the end of No. 2, was probably an addition later in the 19th century. Victoria Cottages were enlarged and modernised around 1980 and at this time an arch was exposed in the wall of the loft between Nos 1 and 2, suggesting that No. 2 had indeed been the end of the barn.

What is now Alderley Cottage (previously Russell Cottage or No. 3 Russell Cottages) does not feature on the 1840 Tithe Map, but is outlined on the 1853 deed. From 1911–15 Mr O'Flaherty kept a draper's shop in the cottage. The car park at the side of the house was once a lean-to wash house for which water was obtained from the spring-fed trough opposite. Numbers 1 and 2 Russell Cottages were a single property until the early 1800s. Alderley Cottage and No. 2 Russell Cottage were linked into a single dwelling when, together with No. 1 Russell Cottage, they were modernised in the 1980s. Unsubstantiated estate agent's details claim that No. 1 dates back to 1640. Russell House, next to the churchyard, was a single-storey building in 1853 and the 1840 Tithe Map records it as a coach house and stable. The conversion to a house occurred at around the turn of the century and it was subsequently occupied by the Heal family and Mr Dobson, a builder. Dobson had his workshop on the opposite side of the road, which was largely garden, until three bungalows were built there in 1955/6.

A view of South Stoke Green in around 1930 with Nos 1 and 2 Russell Cottages in the foreground. (Samler Collection)
And inset as seen today. (Courtesy Jenny John)

Joseph Edwin Heal (1831–1915), his daughter Ellen Heal (1881–1947) and his brother Frederick George Heal (1833–1922) outside Russell House, c.1915. (Courtesy Kathleen Dyer)

The marriage of Mary Pointing and Lionel Williams (Longmynd) in June 1940. Bunty Bartlett was bridesmaid and can be seen to the left of Lionel. The photograph illustrates the tied lychgate, opened only after the offering of a few coins to village children. (Courtesy Lionel Williams)

Buildings in Manor Farm yard viewed from the Grove, c.1935.

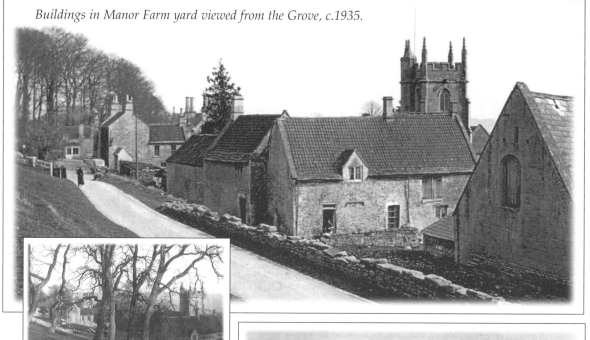

Inset above: *The Walnut Grove, c.1930.*
(Samler Collection)

Right: *Tithe Barn, Parish Church and Manor Farm in 1901.*
(Robert Pitt Collection)

Left: *Arthur and Jack Clifford re-roofing the Tithe Barn, 1938/39.*
(Roger Clifford Collection)

Below: *Tithe Barn in 1937, which was built in c.1500 and the dovecote added in 1660.*
(Samler Collection)

Below: *The butcher's shop and Post Office, c.1908. From the left: Edwin Heal, Mrs Heal, Charles Heal and dog, Miss Parker.*
(Samler Collection)

Below: *Miss Flossie Moody and cow Jenny in the late 1930s. Her three cows were slaughtered during the 1943 foot and mouth epidemic.*
(Roger Clifford Collection)

Left: *Rowley Cottages, a part of the Manor Farm estate, are situated in Rowley Field overlooking the Bull's Nose. They were probably built at the time of the Somersetshire Coal Canal. The Dobson family lived there before 1913. In 1913 the Moody family moved in. The cottages are named after two of the Moody children, Flossies (left) and Edies (right).*
(Courtesy Town & Country Cottages)

Next to Russell House is the lychgate, erected in 1935 by the Wainwright family who left money for 'churchyard adornment'. There is a village tradition associated with the gate. When a newly married couple leave the church, village children tie up the gate, not allowing the couple to pass until a few coins have been thrown by the newly-weds.

Beyond the churchyard to the west can be seen the L-shaped group of cottages in Manor Farm yard. The cottage at the entrance (Gatehouse Cottage) was, until 1999, a store with wooden facing at the east end. Now it has been beautifully restored with Bath stone mullioned windows. Next are Nos 1 and 2 The Grange, which have been occupied over the years by families who have worked at Manor Farm. The blocked-in arch visible in the north wall of No. 2 is believed by Len Marsh to have once been a bakery. After its conversion from cow sheds, Philip Warren, farm manager, was the first person to live in No. 3 The Grange. Stable Cottage has 15th-century arches (identified by R.D. Reid of Wells, archaeologist) incorporated within the stone walls, which may have been part of the original manor house. Earlier it was also a stable, before being converted to a dwelling. The garages between Stable Cottage and today's Manor Farm were formerly the milking parlour.

The eastern end of Manor Farm, as we see it today, is dated 1670–75 by Pevsner. It has relieving arches on the south side and possesses several interesting fireplaces. The house was added to at the east end c.1940 and the west during the 1950s, by the Hignett family, three generations of whom have lived there. Dominating the farmyard is the Tithe Barn (c.1500, listed Grade I). In early times each tenant had to give one tenth of his produce for the support of the clergy and church (tithe). This was delivered to and stored in the Tithe Barn. The size of the South Stoke barn is evidence of the fecundity of the south-facing slopes and the wealth of the manor. Amongst centuries of graffiti on the barn's interior walls is a picture of a sailing ship.

There is a dovecote on the east wall, where young birds known as 'squabs', an important element in the medieval diet, were reared for the pot. The Tithe Barn was re-roofed by Messrs Arthur and Jack Clifford in 1938–39 with stone tiles. The dovecote roof was re-tiled in the 1950s. During the 1990s, the barn was refurbished and is now used for social functions. The village celebrations for the 50th anniversary of VE Day were held there, and a bonfire was lit on the site of the 1945 fire at the top of the hill, close to where the Millennium Viewpoint was constructed. Other national celebrations such as the Silver Jubilee of 1977 and the dawn of the new millennium were enjoyed by many in and around the barn. The farm buildings near the Millennium Viewpoint are 20th-century structures, but the 1840 Tithe Map shows buildings in the vicinity in the corner of an enclosure named Rabbit Warren. Earlier in the 20th century, South Stoke cricket team played matches up on the level field and the remains of the cricket pavilion are still there.

On the east side of the village Green is the Slipway; at its foot in 1900 was the Post Office and grocer's and next door was the butcher's shop. There were buildings marked on this site on the earliest known map of the area, Thorpe's 'Five Miles Round Bath' (1742). George Heal, who was born at the Packhorse Inn in 1871, and his wife Mary ran these shops for around 50 years. Mary Heal died in 1941 and when George died in 1952, their son, Edwin, took over the Post Office and general store until his own death in 1956. The business closed when Edwin's widow left the village in 1961. In 1947 a letterbox bearing the initials VR (Victoria Regina) replaced one that had to be cleared from the living room. The VR box remains in the wall of the Old Post Office, where Carmel Shepherd has lived for many years. The butcher's shop is now a garage.

The Lodge to Southstoke Hall, at the top of the Slipway, is thought to have been built in its present form during the incumbency of Prebendary Charles Johnson (1792–1838). The façade is ornamented with many carved flowers and figures, including a 'green man'. The bellcote on the apex of the porch probably once held a bell, which visitors would have rung from a pull on the pillar. The cast-iron railings were removed for recycling and use during the Second World War. Mrs Lambern, who lived there from her marriage in 1932 until 1994, is well remembered by many villagers, and used to run the village whist drives.

Insets: *George and Mary Jane Heal, c.1900.*
(Courtesy Sylvia Williams, née Heal)

Above: *School's out? South Stoke centre, c.1930.*
(Samler Collection)

Below: *Mr Dobson, a builder who lived at Russell House in the 1930s, at the wheel of his late-1920s bull-nosed Morris. In the front seat are Mr and Mrs Oliver Dobson; in the back are Miss Elizabeth Curry and Mrs Mary Jane Heal; standing is Mrs Agnes Heal and the children of Agnes and Charlie Heal, Kathleen and Rowland are to the front.*
(Courtesy Kathleen Dyer, née Heal)

Above: *The Lodge.*
Insets: *Carved head and a carved 'green man', both from The Lodge.* (Photographs, Jenny John)

Southstoke Hall (the vicarage until 1884), c.1970. The Stable House (inset) (with terracotta roof tiles) at the top was built c.1800 by the Revd Charles Johnson as a stable and coach-house with accommodation above. The overgrown old track leading along the ridge to the Old Midford Road is in the top right of the picture.

The drive down to Southstoke Hall was also made in Johnson's time. Old maps show that prior to that, the house was approached through Parsonage Farm yard. Today there is only a footpath where before a horse and cart could pass with ease. Christmas Cottage was built over part of the track. Southstoke Hall was once the vicarage, but it is unclear whether all vicars, dating back to John de Tusseburi (1210), lived in a house on the site. The oldest, medieval part of the building is recognisable from a terrier (inventory) dated 10 August 1606:

Imprimis. The Mansion House hath a Hall, a Parlour with a chimney and a Loft over it and a Kitchen with a chimney newly built by the said Harris, a Stable for an horse and two Kine built by the said Harris (vicar 1594–1618) a Farme of iiii fildes built by the said Harris a court a Garden the land about the house is about an Acre three young Lime trees in it a Grabbe tree and a young apple Tree.

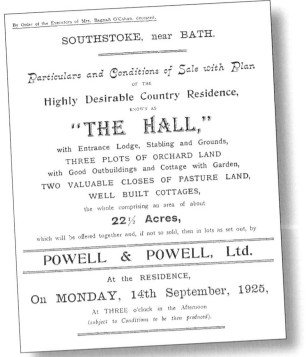

Sale particulars for Southstoke Hall in 1925.
(Courtesy Muriel Moon, née Heal)

Southstoke Hall in 1937. (Pinney Collection)

The vicarage was added to several times over the centuries, to the south in the 18th century, and then most extensively by the Reverend Charles Johnson c.1800. With the help of his architect father, John Johnson (surveyor to Essex 1782–1812) who worked on many country houses, Charles Johnson added an elegant ashlar-fronted coach-house and stables to the north of the original house, and two large rooms to the east. One was a schoolroom providing for Prebendary Johnson's 12 children; the other a drawing room with protruding bay. Above there were bedrooms, below a cellar. All this was built in ashlar, matching the facing of the south elevation of the house, which was converted to a separate residence in 1974 and is now known as The Stable House. To set the seal on these grandiose projects, the Johnson crest was placed above the front door of The Lodge. Charles Johnson was appointed a chaplain to the Prince Regent (1808–18). It is not known whether this was due to their meeting in April 1799, when the Prince visited Combe Hay for a trial of the Caisson Lock on the Coal Canal, or through family influence. His wife, Mary Willes, was granddaughter of a Bishop of Bath and Wells and her uncles and brothers all held ecclesiastical positions.

Charles Stuart Calverley (1831–84). He is remembered for his songs and the verse 'Ode to Tobacco'.

Students of Christ's College, Cambridge, 1859.
Fourth from the left is Charles Stuart Calverley.
(Courtesy Paul Mann)

The Reverend Henry Calverley continued the building tradition, erecting, according to J. Turnstall in his *Rambles about Bath* 'at his own cost, in 1840, a handsome village school, with a dwelling house for the mistress.' Now a private house, Old School House, it served as a Mission Hall (1925), Women's Institute Hall and, during the Second World War, as the Institute's food-preservation centre as well as being used for British and US forces' entertainments. The Calverleys had a celebrated son, Charles Stuart Calverley – athlete, scholar, poet and parodist, who spent his late childhood in South Stoke, where he impressed all with his ability to leap over hedges and ditches with ease. (Ultimately one such leap led to his death!) He was rusticated from Oxford University for 'having climbed into college' and 'persistent infringements of discipline and neglect of his studies'. At this time the family surname of Blayds reverted to the old family name, Calverley, and Charles Stuart was admitted to Christ's College, Cambridge, where he won prizes as a classical scholar. He became a lawyer, published several books of poetry and verse translations and was an accomplished pianist and singer.

The last clergyman to live at Southstoke Hall as vicarage was the Reverend William Acworth. He came to the parish from Pembrokeshire in 1875 aged 72, and his wife died in the village in 1877. In 1881 he married his fourth wife, Sarah Stokes, who was 37 years his junior. When Acworth retired in 1884, he did not, as was customary, vacate the vicarage to make way for the next incumbent. A new vicarage had to be found for the young Reverend William Samler. According to Canvin, two dwellings known then as South Cottages, just over the Acworth 'vicarage' garden wall and opposite Packhorse Inn, were united and enlarged to form what is now known as The Old Vicarage, for many years the home of Drs Paul and Monica Mann.

Continuing the village tradition of clergymen-builders, William Samler embarked on building a 'Parish or Lecture Hall and cottages'. In 1885 he purchased for £100 'all that plot of ground Malthouse (and) garden' immediately below the present car park of Packhorse Inn. He engaged a Mr J.C. Atwell, surveyor, of Bath, and Mr H.S. Brown, builder, and the building was to be completed in stages culminating in March 1886. When, in 1899, the Board of Education condemned the School House, which 'would no longer be recognised unless extensive alterations were carried out', the vicar generously transferred ownership of his lecture hall to enable it to become the new village school. The Revd William Samler, it was recorded in the *Parish Magazine* in 1904:

... wishes it to be clearly understood that the only reasons that led him to hand over his Room to Trustees were: i) that the children of the Parish should be taught definite Church teaching, and ii) to save the Parish a very heavy expense.

The new village school buildings were now in the hands of the vicar and churchwardens as trustees.

The Old Vicarage in 1933. (Samler Collection)

The vicarage garden at the time of the Reverend Samler.
(Samler Collection)

Samler's early years as vicar were marred by a difference of opinion with his predecessor concerning the use of the chancel. Acworth died in 1899 and the former vicarage was then sold and became known as The Hall, and more recently Southstoke Hall. William Samler was vicar for over 60 years and was greatly loved. As well as refurbishing the church, he added a conservatory and tennis court to his garden. Tragically, he was widowed in 1901 and his elder son was killed in the Battle of Jutland (1916), but descendants of his other son, William, still have close connections with South Stoke. When Mr Samler, still in harness, died aged 90 after falling downstairs in an air-raid in 1944, parishioners were shocked and saddened. At the time of his death he had been on the Parish Council for 50 years, since its inception, and Chairman for 44 years. Samlers have been patrons of the Church of St James the Great since 1884, the current patron being Commander H.R. (Tim) Samler RN, of Midford.

One charming story relates how Agnes Parfitt, a young maid at the vicarage, was courted by Charlie Heal from the Post Office 'over the garden wall'. The happy pair married in 1926.

Situated immediately below the Packhorse is the Village Hall that from 1900 until 1973 was the village school. The hall is used regularly for the South Stoke Show and harvest supper, Parish Council meetings, WI meetings, the Art Group, public meetings, the Thursday morning Toddler Group, fund-raising functions and private parties. Mrs Harris, who has lived in the village since 1939, occupies one of the adjacent cottages and has been caretaker and custodian for 60 years.

The oldest rooms in Packhorse Cottage, which lies behind the Packhorse Inn, are one above the other and linked by a spiral wooden staircase that rises over an inglenook fireplace. The cottage has been altered and added to over the centuries, but structural evidence indicates that there had been a building on the site since the 16th century at least. Earlier in the 20th century Packhorse Cottage, now a single dwelling, was two cottages owned, along with the inn, by Georges' Brewery. A new wing was added to the north side of the old cottages in 1987 by the owners at the time of writing, Robert and Jane Hellard.

Tucked away from the road below the hall are Snowdrop Cottage and Rose Cottages which were built by Thomas Hunt the younger in 1829–30 on the site of an orchard named Wisdoms. It is recorded in

Agnes Parfitt

Charles Frederick Heal

deeds that Hunt erected 'five several cottages... and did lay out the residue of the said orchard as and for gardens to the same several cottages.' The gardens are still in their original fan shape today and all five cottages, together with Sunnyside (just beyond the spring), share rights to the spring that flows next to No. 4 Rose Cottages.

John and Mary Clifford once lived nearby at The Nook, a cottage belonging to the Revd William Acworth, bringing up eight children there. Because Acworth failed to maintain the property, the floor was rotten and the sons decided to put in a new wooden one themselves. For their efforts, and for not asking his permission, Acworth turned them out and they had to take lodgings. In around 1892, the sons, who were in the building trade, bought a plot of land and erected 2 Sunnyside. Later, Arthur (Dick) Clifford bought land and built 1 Sunnyside for himself and his wife Georgina in 1901. Their daughter Lucy was born shortly after they moved in. The property remains in the hands of the Clifford family, who can be traced back in South Stoke to 1797. Miss Ena Clifford, who was a mine of information about the village, lived at 1 Sunnyside until her death in 1995.

Opposite Rose Cottages are Ivy Cottages, which are shown on Greenwood's map of 1822. The lower level of these cottages is built into the hillside, so that the front door is at first-floor level. In 1840, the cottages and gardens below belonged to the vicar, Henry Calverley, and at that time may have been known as Lower Buildings. There is still a functional bread oven in the sitting room fireplace of one of the cottages.

Further down the hill is Shepherd's Mead, formerly known as The Nook (already mentioned above), which also has a large bread oven, roofed with enormous stone slabs protruding on the west elevation. The solid oak roof timbers bear Roman numerals suggesting that they were formerly timbers from ships broken up in Bristol. The cottage was extended and modernised in the 1970s.

Along the footpath that passes in front of Shepherd's Mead is a row of six cottages called Courtmead after a nearby field. 'Curtmede' appears in a number of 13th-century references to South Stoke. Mrs Alice Hignett of Hodshill had these cottages built to fulfil the accommodation needs of young families. They were up to date for their time with running water and a bathroom in each. Gordon Dyer has lived in No. 5 Courtmead ever since it was built in 1934.

Left: Packhorse Cottage. It is likely that the earliest part of the building is 16th century in origin.
(Courtesy Robert Hellard)

Above: *The marriage of Winifred Clifford and Archie Allen, November 1930, photographed on the path by the Institute at the rear of Ivy Cottages. From left to right: Archie Allen, Winifred Clifford, ?, Lucy Clifford, Dudley Emmer, Ena Clifford, ?, Coral Clifford.*
(Roger Clifford Collection)

Outside Packhorse Cottage. Above are the Morris children in about 1907, George (two), Gladys (six) and Alec (four).

Below (in c.1910) is Maud Morris (née Staddon), wife of Frederick G. Morris, holding Vera. From the left: Gladys (with doll), Alec, George (top right) and William (in the chair).
(Courtesy Molly Elliott)

Right: *Ivy Cottages had a narrow escape in September 1999 when part of a Thuja tree growing in the garden of The Old Vicarage fell towards the cottages.*
(Courtesy Jenny John)

Above: *South Stoke, c.1900.* (Rod Adams Collection)

Below: *South Stoke, c.1935. When compared with the 1900 view the housing density has increased. The gardens of the new Courtmead extend down into Shepperds Mead. A fine haystack can be seen at the bottom of Wall Leaze.*

Several people can remember the cottage in the middle of the field below Southstoke Hall. The field was once an orchard and the Hall gardener's house stood in the centre. Some time between 1900 and 1925, both the gardener and his wife suffered painful illnesses from which they died. From that time Mrs O'Cahan, of Southstoke Hall, would not allow anyone to live there and the house gradually fell into ruin. On the 1936 OS map it was just a pile of stones but now all that remains is the ridge of the perimeter, outlined by long evening shadows.

Further south on the hilltop to the west of the lane is Hodshill, which was owned and occupied in 1840 by the ubiquitous Thomas Hunt and then called Hodshill Lodge. Hodshill first appears on the 1822 Greenwood map and it features in sketches by the Revd John Skinner, Rector of Camerton, a noted antiquarian who visited the ruins of Roman villas and other artefacts in the village in 1828. The name may be a corruption for the name of the hill shaped like a hog's back upon which the house is located. Towards the end of the 19th century it was a farm, owned by

William Acworth and worked by Charles Stickland, a churchwarden, who later moved to Parsonage Farm. W.H. Handley lived in Hodshill House and Uriah Handley worked the fuller's earth quarry on the south side of the property from around 1886 to 1904 (see Chapter 11). It became known as Hodshill Hall in 1901 and passed through two further owners before Dr Crook purchased it in 1906. Crook, an engineer, may have been responsible for the construction on the site of the 100-foot-deep cavernous well with a gas-engined pump to raise the water. The hall was panelled with finely carved oak from Glastonbury Abbey and the kitchen garden boasted peach and nectarine trees. Geoffrey Hignett, of the tobacco family, bought Hodshill Hall in 1910 and, with his wife Alice, further enlarged and enhanced the house and garden, adding stone balustrading to the front, creating a tennis court, swimming pool and, in 1935, a squash court. Many outbuildings and the houses including South View and Grove View (built in 1935) were part of the estate. In its heyday there were many house servants and a team of gardeners. The family

acquired Manor Farm in 1936/7 and the son Gerald Hignett lived there with his wife Betty and their two sons from 1948. The next generation, Charles Hignett and his family, now lives at Manor Farm. After a spell when Hodshill was a hospital and convalescent home during the Second World War, Vice Admiral Sir Raymond Hawkins, who became 4th Sea Lord, took up residence until 1979, when the property was sold by Mr Hignett.

The steep upper southern slope of Hodshill Lane was stepped with drainage ridges until around 1940. Prior to the building of the GWR branch railway through the valley, the lane continued southwards from Combe Lane (joining Midford and Combe Hay) over the canal to a bridge over the Cam Brook. Thorpe's map of 1742 described the bridge as Bishops Bridge and the brook as Comb Hay Brook, although by the time of the 1840 Tithe Map the bridge had become Bisham Bridge. Sadly the very attractive accommodation bridge that carried the lane over the canal was demolished in 1960, when it was deemed unsafe after years of neglect.

Left: *Hodshill, c.1920.*
(Samler Collection)

Below: *Sale particulars for Hodshill Hall in 1910.*
(Courtesy Angela Calonder)

Left: *Nellie Williams aged about 18 who worked at Hodshill during the 1930s.*
(Courtesy Nellie Hawkins, née Williams)

Underhill Cottage lies near the coal canal in the woods close to the footpath by the locks. The cottage was associated with the processing of fuller's earth, mined in Little Hodshill Field, and it was converted to a dwelling in 1911. During the 1930s the Williams family lived there and at the time of the Second World War evacuees moved in. Ironically they had to move out when two bombs fell and exploded near the cottage. After the war Harry and Marjorie Tanner moved in (1949–53) with their seven children. After the Tanners moved the property became derelict until it underwent complete renovation in the late 1970s.

Deeds relating to Glen Cottage, sited a little further into an area earlier known as Mercombe Bottom, date back to the mid-18th century. The cottage and garden were owned by the Somersetshire Coal Canal Co. in 1840 and tenanted by Moses Gay. When the GWR compulsorily purchased the land in 1904, a financial claim was made for the loss of a walnut tree that yielded 18s.6d. worth of nuts per year! From 1953 until 1980 Bert Ellis occupied the cottage.

The parish boundary passes through the garden of Bridge Farm, on Combe Lane. This may have been the lock-keeper's house beside the 'turnover' bridge, where the towpath changes sides. The *Bath Chronicle* of 14 October 1830 reports an accident here:

> *... a lad, engaged in a barge... was winding a windlass to let the water through the locks... he lost his balance and fell in; he was not missed for a space of 4 or 5 minutes when, in apprehending some accident caused by his absence the bargemen dragged the water and found the body with life extinct.*

The house was painted blue in the 1950s, and is still referred to by many as the 'blue house', but within the last decade of the 20th century the paint was removed, and the house enlarged and renovated.

Vicars of South Stoke once owned extensive property in the parish. In 1840, the recently appointed Revd Henry Blayds (Henry Calverley) owned over 30 acres and Reverend Charles Johnson (son of the previous vicar, who had just died) owned over 46 acres. The latter's holdings included Parsonage Farm and the farmhouse and outbuildings adjoining Packhorse Lane, now known as Beech Cottage, Parsonage Farmhouse, The Parlour, Parsonage Barn and Barley-Brake. These buildings, before conversion, had a variety of uses over the years. Barley-Brake, for example, had a cobbled floor and was used for stabling the brewery's dray horses. It then became a workshop for the Clifford family's building and carpentry trade. During 1990–91, along with other farm outbuildings, it was converted to a dwelling. From between the wars until the 1970s milk for the village was supplied by Cyril and his daughter Sylvia Wilson's cows from Parsonage Farm.

The front door of Beech Cottage, perhaps the oldest in South Stoke.

There was a second 'Farm barton and garden' in 1840, situated immediately below Parsonage Farm above the old former Vicarage. This was owned and occupied by farmer Samuel Baily and later became part of Parsonage Farm. In 1990, all the farm buildings were cleared away except for a stone barn that was converted to a dwelling, Orchard Barn. Two modern houses were also built on the site, Awelon (now Matfen House) and Christmas Cottage.

Between Parsonage Farm outbuildings and Pack Horse Farm in Old Midford Road, no houses are shown on the 1840 Tithe Map. A lime kiln and farm building in Further Long Thorn (the field below the junction of Packhorse Lane with Old Midford Road) are all that would have interrupted the pastoral view. This changed when, in 1846, Charles Thomas Conolly of Midford Castle leased land to William Hill, an engineer of South Stoke, on condition that within 12 months he erected 'on some part of the piece of land (West Mead)... a substantial messuage or dwelling house with suitable offices or outbuildings'. Reference is made to his having to maintain the 'shutters, hinges, casements, staples, etc.' in good order, and to insure the buildings against fire. The agreement led to the construction of Southstoke House in 1848. Between 1854 and 1863 William Hill, who worked on the coal canal like his engineer sons, was listed in the *Bath Directory* as residing at Southstoke Villa, no doubt the first name for the property. Following Hill's death in 1868 a series of tenants occupied the house (now listed as Southstoke House), including Walter Pitt, also an engineer, in 1892.

Left: *Southstoke House, c.1900.*
(Richard Pitt Collection)

Below: *Walter Pitt (1852–1921) and his wife Ruth with their children Dorothy (known as Madge) (1890–1967) and Robert, at Southstoke House during the 1890s.*
(Richard Pitt Collection)

Inset right: *Walter and Ruth Pitt in the garden of Southstoke House which they used as a country cottage in the 1890s.*
(Richard Pitt Collection)

Below: *Some 75 years separate these two views of Southstoke House. Mrs Bull, who lived there during the 1960s and '70s is in the foreground of the lower photograph.*

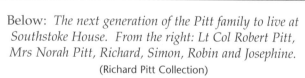

Below: *The next generation of the Pitt family to live at Southstoke House. From the right: Lt Col Robert Pitt, Mrs Norah Pitt, Richard, Simon, Robin and Josephine.*
(Richard Pitt Collection)

*Staff at
Southstoke
House, c.1910.*
(Richard Pitt
Collection)

Left: *Fund-raising auction at Southstoke House
in the late 1940s. Basil Hall (from Whitecroft),
centre, is the auctioneer.* (Photograph, Diana Aldridge)

Below: *Southstoke House as a children's orthopaedic
hospital during and after the Second World War.
Miss L.G. Oldendorff was sister in charge in 1947.*
(Photograph, Ken Weeks)

In 1900 Pitt purchased the house from Charles Parfitt who had inherited it, along with Midford Castle, from the Conolly family. Walter Pitt, his father Robert Pitt, and son Col Robert Pitt were the Pitts of the renowned Bath engineering firm Stothert & Pitt who sold cranes throughout the world during the 19th and 20th centuries. Walter and his son Robert lived in the house for many years through two generations, adding a wing to each side in about 1916. During the Second World War and up until the early 1960s, the house was a children's orthopaedic nursing home. The west wing, having been built in 1916, was extended in the mid-1980s.

Southstoke Cottage, on the opposite side of the road, was built for the gardener of Southstoke House by Col Robert Pitt. The Coach House was converted to a house in 1966 from Southstoke House out-buildings.

The three houses, each a pair, to the west of Southstoke Cottage, all have connections with the Clifford family. The first to be built was Springfield, in 1900–01, by David William Clifford and his younger brother Edward, who were partners in a carpentry business, for David and his wife Annie Maud Plomer. The older brother had learnt his trade from Albert Hamilton of Lansdowne Villa. Next they built just the shell of Summerdale next door, but it was not completed until 1927, when David's son Albert married and needed a home. After Springfield, in around 1901, the brothers built South View for Edward and his wife Lydia. Fairdawn and Highcombe were built in 1921. After he was settled into Springfield, David William, or 'the Guv'nor' as Royston Clifford remembers him, developed an interest in horticulture, built himself a greenhouse, and soon he was more nurseryman than carpenter. The nursery flourished from 1910 until the 1990s, during which time flowers, particularly chrysanthe-mums and bedding plants were grown. The war effort meant a transfer to the growing of vegetables, especially tomatoes. The nursery also supplied the village shop. Water was always a problem as in summer the well often dried up and, although a natural spring was tapped into above the site, pres-sure was poor. When a new main was laid to the village during 1956, a reliable supply was finally avail-able. In 1968 a 210-foot greenhouse was constructed, the largest in the area. At that time the nursery was run by Albert Edward Clifford (younger son of the founder), who lived at Summerdale. Royston Clifford (grandson of the founder) and a staff of between five and thirteen people were employed at its peak. Ralph Whiteman recorded a BBC radio programme with Royston about chrysanthemums for which he was paid a fee of three guineas! Now the large greenhouse has collapsed and beautiful native pyramid orchids grow wild on the nursery land.

South View was added to at the rear and divided into two houses during the 1920s (the east half being called The Haven), but in 1999 it was reinstated as a single home and given a new name, Hay House. There was once a Seventh Day Adventist Chapel, built from corrugated iron, in the garden.

In 1998, in pristine condition, the original architect's plans dated 1920 for Sunshine (known as Fairdawn since the 1960s) and Highcombe were found in an outhouse. The plans show a 21 by 11 foot 'motor house' to be built beneath each front lawn. These were never constructed. A Second World War Anderson air-raid shelter is now a feature in the garden of Highcombe. At the end of the garden is a garage that was once Mark Barrett's workshop. Earlier at the turn of the 20th century he was the village blacksmith with his business, until 1940, in the property opposite the Cross Keys at 124 Midford Road. Mark married Clara Clifford, David's younger sister, and their descendant, John Robinson, lives in Rose Cottages, where they themselves once lived.

Behind the 'Clifford' houses is a lane where there was once a wheelwright, a paintshop, carpenter's workshop and a nursery business, operating in addition to the smithy. This was the industrial heart of the village. Off the lane to the north, just before its junction with Packhorse Lane, is a bungalow, Homeville, built of stone quarried from the now sunken part of the garden by Ted Pearce in 1926/7. Pearce and his wife 'Neffie' Clifford lived there until 1961, when Jim and Valerie Summers replaced them. For many years Jim and Valerie have been mainstays of parish life, with Jim as long-standing church-warden, Parish Councillor and member of the Village Hall Committee, and Valerie a church chorister, staunch member of the WI and long-standing fête organiser. Whilst renewing their driveway in 1967 Jim unearthed three well-worn carved stones, identified by Bristol Museum staff probably as carvings from the medieval church.

No fewer than three family building firms were active in South Stoke during the first half of the last century. The 1938 and 1939 directories list their families living in houses they had originally built for themselves.

1938

Chancellor, A.E.		Kingsfield
Chancellor, W.A.		Hay Tor
Clifford, E.	carpenter	South View
Clifford, Arthur,		
A. Clifford & son		Sunnyside
Clifford, W.	market gardener	Springfield
Cross, Harry E.		Bushy Leas
Cross, Wilfred C.		Wayside

1939

Chancellor, A.E.	Orchardlea
	(from Kingsfield)
Cross, Edwin L.	St Fillians

Left: *The full extent of Clifford's Nurseries half a century after they were started at Springfield House (with the porch lower left in the picture). The greenhouse at the top was 210 feet long, the longest and most hi-tech in the area at the time.*
(Royston Clifford Collection)

Below: *Clifford's Nurseries in the 1890s, looking north, and taken from the east side of Springfield House. David William Clifford and his daughter Neffie are in the centre.*
(Royston Clifford Collection)

Above: *Clifford's Nurseries in 1968.*
(Photograph, Royston Clifford)

Above: *The Ainsworth men of Brewery Cottage, photographed before the First World War at Clifford's Nurseries where they worked. Standing: Tom Ainsworth and son Tom junr; below: Jack and Ted. Young Tom enlisted for the war when aged 16 and sadly was killed.*
(Courtesy Joan Heal, née Ainsworth)

Above: *Royston Clifford and Brian Harris tackle a nursery chimney.*
(Photograph, Alan Cobb)

All of the houses built along Packhorse Lane ridge take advantage of panoramic rural views towards the Mendip Hills and Salisbury Plain. Sites were not always easy to build on, with the land dropping away steeply from the lane, but Wilfred Cross built and lived first in Wayside and then Withycombe until his death in 1955. Wilf Cross did a run across the fields from the 'white railings' to The Viaduct public house at the bottom of Brassknocker Hill in an attempt to beat the time of a car journey by road. Mrs Cross remained at Withycombe until her death in 1965. The house has been added to at both ends since then and is now lived in by a celebrated explorer and climber, Mike Banks and Pat his wife. Mike, a former Major in the Royal Marines, now in his 70s, still leads expeditions to distant parts of the globe. He is also an accomplished writer and photographer and is in the *Guinness Book of Records* as the oldest man to have climbed the Old Man of Hoy. He repeated the climb in May 2000. Longcombe, formerly St Davids, was not built until 1955, and has only had two families living there in almost 50 years. For 30 years it has been the home of Commander Christopher Parsons and his wife Ann; he a long-serving churchwarden and she organiser of the harvest supper for 18 years.

Highclere, known as Penpol when it was built in 1939, was originally a two-roomed bungalow. It was transformed by Joan Carey Jones in 1981. Undaunted by the almost vertical slope to the rear, she took it in hand and constructed a delightful terraced garden. Joan, previously of Kingsfield, has been a pillar of the village community for 45 years.

On the north side of Packhorse Lane and bordered by the Old Midford Road is a triangle of land named Henleys on the 1840 Tithe Map. It was owned by Thomas King, so it was apposite, when Albert Chancellor acquired the land and built a

Mike Banks, climber, explorer and writer.
(Courtesy Mike Banks)

house for himself (c.1923), that the house should be named Kingsfield. The design is based on a house the builder saw in Wales and is said to have been made from stone reclaimed from a demolished Bath church. Soon afterwards, Hay Tor was built by William A. Chancellor who lived there with his family for more than 30 years. It is not known whether the Roman coffin in the garden was dug up on the site or whether it came from elsewhere. The house is now occupied by Aty and Leslie Bell. In 1933 a bungalow, named Orchardlea (now Withdean), was built for Phoebe Chancellor, in the orchard of Kingsfield. Whitecroft, originally called Four Winds when it was built in the late 1920s, was the home of Mr and Mrs Basil Hall. After the Second World War many village fêtes were held in the garden.

At the South Stoke Fête at Whitecroft during the 1960s. From the left: Mrs Bradley, Mrs Harris, Mrs Ellis, Mrs Lambern and Mrs Brand. (Courtesy Diana Aldridge)

Whitecroft, c.1950. (Courtesy Diana Aldridge)

Maypole at the Whitecroft Fête, 1940s.
(Photograph, Diana Aldridge)

The Pack Horse on Old Midford Road is named on Thorpe's 1742 map. It was probably an inn in the 17th century as well as a farm and a carriers. The property was a centre for tea smuggling when owned by Ann Grace in the late-18th century. During the mid-19th century, when it ceased to be an inn, Pack Horse Farm passed through the hands of Thomas Hunt (who leased it in 1840) and later the Conolly family. It was part of the Midford Castle estate of over 392 acres which was auctioned in June 1901:

The Packhorse Farm in the Occupation of Mr Hewlett. The House contains on the Ground Floor – Hall, Parlour, Kitchen, Scullery, Pantry and Dairy; and on the First Floor are five Bedrooms. The Buildings comprise Barn, 2 stall Stable, Cow House and Calf Pen, Waggon Shed and Root House.

(Auction details, June 1901)

For at least 50 years, Pack Horse Farm was worked by the Hewlett family. George Hewlett, aged 29, and his wife Elizabeth, aged 28 from Pembrokeshire, were living there in 1861 with their children Mary, 3, and David, aged 1. Hewlett is listed as a farmer of 38 acres, born in Stogumber, employing himself and one man (probably his younger brother, John), an agricultural labourer who lived with them. The family prospered and the amount of land George farmed increased to 44 acres in 1871 and 100 acres in 1881. Elizabeth, meanwhile, had nine children, seven of whom were boys. Some of them helped on the farm, two became chair makers and one a carpenter's apprentice. Mary, a dressmaker, seems to have remained at home with her parents. In 1900, Elizabeth died, aged 67, and George outlived her by 13 years, dying in 1913 aged 81; a headstone in the church commemorates them. There were Hewletts living at the farm until 1911. The farm was completely restored and extended in 1987 as a residence with stabling.

Opposite the farm is Terrells, built in the 1920s for the Misses Pocock on the site where farm buildings stood in 1840. Originally called Areli, the house was renamed Triscombe (1938–54) by Mrs Groves, and Withdean (1954–88) by Dr Noel and Mrs Ruth Newman. When the Newmans moved from there to the present Withdean nearby, they took the name with them. Next door to Terrells is Longthorne, built in 1949/50 for the Boltons and named after the field in which it is built. The room at the east end of the house was purpose built for the wool spinning activities of Mrs Bolton. The Conifers was the first house to be built (1928) across the road from Pack Horse Farm. Built for Mrs Dupree, it was known as Bella Vista until the mid 1970s. The

Richards family with their ten children lived there from 1965 until 1972. A small segment of land between The Conifers and Larkbarrow did have a 'house, stable, etc.' on it belonging to the Conolly family in 1840, but there is no trace of a dwelling today. A public footpath wide enough to take a horse and cart separates this overgrown plot and The Conifers from Larkbarrow. The latter was built in 1935 for E.H. Gardener as Gales. Its most celebrated occupant was Jack Train, the radio comedian who lived there from 1943–54, and took part in Tommy Handley's show 'It's That Man Again' and in 'Twenty Questions'. The house was acquired, in 1954, by the S.W. Gas Board for its chief engineer, L.F. Ingram, who renamed it The Croft. He was followed by another engineer, Rollo Torrance, previously a director of Stothert & Pitt, and his wife Jenny, a mainstay of the church and friend to everyone. Beeches is the last house along the ridge before Old Midford Road drops down steeply towards Midford. It was built, and originally named Windrush, for Major and Mrs Hilton Light in 1935, on land that was previously arable. Mrs Dorothy Light (née Pitt), sister of Col Robert Pitt, was raised along the lane in Southstoke House. The house was improved and extended, in 1994 and '98, by the present owners Professor Robert Parfitt and his wife Judy. Three varieties of native orchids grow in their garden that has on its south-east boundary a protected old beech plantation, which gives the house its name.

The stretch of Midford Road (B3110) in the parish has been developed entirely during the 20th century. Between the Cross Keys and the junction of Old Midford Road with Midford Road, the 1904 map marks nothing but a 'stone'. At the junction itself, however, as well as another 'stone', was a thriving fuller's earth works below the road on the Horsecombe Vale side, which was not on the map of 1887.

It is interesting to see how the housing development along Midford Road is related to the fields as recorded on the 1840 Tithe Map. Bumper's Batch, for example, now comprises six houses and a road through the middle for access, but the peripheral boundary remains unchanged. Summer Park was built in 1930 as a bungalow called Clouds. An upper storey was added later by Mr and Mrs Woodall, who renamed the house Crich after the village in Derbyshire. Between 1953 and '66, the other five houses were built, each individually commissioned.

The adjacent field to the west known as 'The Land' in 1840 also retains its original peripheral boundary. Now there are nine dwellings within this curtilage. First to be built was Southcote (1919) for the Misses Harvey. They bought the field and had a wooden bungalow built; to the front was an orchard and beside it were allotments. The sisters, who were keen bulldog breeders, started the Bath Folk Dance and Music Society and hosted folk dancing on their tennis court. Whilst Old Wall was being built for the Pointings in 1933 they had a brief stay at Southcote. Stone from the boundary wall of Bumper's Batch (part of which remains) was used in its construction giving Old Wall its name. Since 1933, Southcote has been home to three generations of the Walker family. Walnut House (formerly Longdrive or Longdrive House) was built in 1935, in the southern section of the field. Mintern, occupied now by descendants of the original owners Mr and Mrs Pointing, and Poplars, a pair of semi-detached houses, were raised in around 1937. Just a few years later a ceiling in the latter collapsed from the impact of a Second World War bomb that landed in Clevedale Road near the Admiralty buildings across the valley in Combe Down. In 1940, the Pointings' daughter Mary married Lionel Williams and, to provide for them, Longmynd was built and was their home for almost 60 years. At about the same time, Greenacres was being built for a German gentleman who, on the outbreak of war, disappeared overnight! Sheridan was erected in 1955 for Mr and Mrs MacKelden and, in 1961, the orchard of Longdrive House was sold and Griffins was built on the site.

The southern boundaries of Uplands, High Beeches, High View (formerly Quennells), Cranleigh, Hillcrest, Fosse House, Tunbridge House (now Malvern House) and Glenside follow the line of Cross Keys Tyning, a large rectangular field between The Land and the crossroads at the Cross Keys. With the exception of Tunbridge House built in the 1960s, all these houses were in place by 1936. Meadowland, bordered by Plough Field situated at the top of a rough access road, was rather earlier, probably around 1920, and was erected on land purchased by Wilfred Cross. In its early days it is reputed to have been a 'Dame School'. A feature of the front garden is a Second World War air-raid shelter, used for many years after the war as an apple store. References in the deeds refer to the site 'being a portion of land known as the Southstoke Park Estate'; had the estate been developed, not only would it have destroyed a medieval field structure, but it would have resulted in South Stoke being in danger of engulfment by Bath. Many attempts have been made since the 1970s to develop Plough Field but strong public resistance to these attacks on the integrity of the village has resulted in their being repelled. Cranleigh was built in 1922/3 for the Reverend Moore Piele Butler, who lived in the house with his daughter Grace for many years. Grace died in 1997 aged 97. Opposite Cranleigh on the rough access road is Hillcrest that was in place, like Fosse House, by 1929. Thornton was built earlier in the 1920s by William Burgess of Burgess & Son, Timber Merchants of Bath, and lived in later, for many years, by Roy Fuller of Kingsmead

Motors. Colonel Charles Stewart and his wife Zöe moved to Thornton in 1954; he was a magistrate for many years, Chairman of The Bench and High Sheriff of Avon in 1983/4. Listed in directories as early as 1914 is Mimosa, situated on the corner of South Stoke Lane and Midford Road and occupied then by Mrs Mabel Hope. Geoffrey Fry, who ran the Glasshouse garage, later lived there and his family still owns the house.

On the north side of Midford Road are seven houses that are just inside the parish boundary – in fact the boundary and the line of a branch of Wansdyke pass to the rear of Stokeside House. At one time there was a lane passing behind the sites of these seven houses, linking Southstoke Road and Midford Road, cutting off a corner. The Sundial was the first house of the group to be built, before the First World War, probably for Herbert Jones, quarry master, and his wife Cecilia, who were living in Southstoke Road prior to 1914. They acquired the two plots (one a plantation, the other arable) which comprise the area on which the seven houses were eventually built. The house was fabricated from various sorts of stone, including stone roof tiles, to demonstrate to prospective stone purchasers the quality and versatility of the product. Ravencliffe and Goodwick (the former name of Carron) were occupied by 1927 and Waverley and Avalon appear on the 1936 OS map. Only Symfield and Stokeside House (since 1995 a day nursery named Hickory House) are post-war; the latter was built in 1955 and named Combe Lodge for Reginald Trowbridge, perhaps because he was a freemason. In the back garden there are large old gateposts and stones marking the parish boundary.

THE PACKHORSE INN

The origins of The Packhorse in South Stoke village centre are something of an enigma. From the carved stone above the front door we are led to believe that the building was erected in 1674 although there are unsubstantiated claims for an earlier history. The style of the building is similar to that of Manor Farm (relieving arches over windows), which was tenanted from around 1662 until 1690 by Richard Gay. Clearly, when built, a structure of three floors and a basement would have been the most imposing and important in the parish. Just 22 years after its building, a Window Tax was imposed in England to defray the costs of defaced coinage during the reign of William III and the unfortunate owner filled in less important stone mullioned windows, in order to have fewer than ten and to qualify therefore for a lower tax bracket.

Deeds dated 1716 give the earliest reference to the property, when Mrs Hanah Charmbury of Claverton acquired the house from John Silby the

Left: *The Packhorse, c.1930, showing the effect of the 1695 Window Tax.* (Samler Collection)

Below: *The lane passing the Packhorse in 1912. F.G. Rose was landlord from 1909–50.* (Samler Collection)

Left: *Regulars at the Packhorse in the taproom, c.1951–53. Left to right, back row: Philip Warren, Eddie Weeks, Geoff Evans, Bert Ellis, Jack Clifford, Bob Marsh, Mr Bush, Eric Willcox; front: Ern Sawyer, Bob Rose, Rodney Rose, Fred Rose, Walt Dyer, Arthur Swatton, ?, Claude Freegard.* (Roger Clifford Collection)

Below: *The tenth anniversary of the Over 60s Club at the Packhorse, September 1965. Left to right, standing: Dick Weaver, Harry Skrine, Mrs Skrine, Teddy Hamlen, Godfrey Hamlen, Sarah Holley, Sydney Bourne, Ellen Weaver, Miss M. Prince, Mrs Boulter, Bessie Williams, Mrs Davis, Dora Freegard, Mrs Lambern, Doris Rose; middle: ?, Mr Voss, Mrs Voss, Mrs Ponting, Mrs Goodman, Mrs Royal, Mrs Furley; front: Charlie Heal, Ivy Heal, Gran Badder, Edie Collins.*

Above: *Oldfield School Rugby Team in 1923. Bob Rose is wearing his England Schoolboys cap and Noel Staddon is in the middle row second from the right. Both are from South Stoke.* (Courtesy Jack Rose)

elder, yeoman, and John Silby the younger, a baker of Bradford-on-Avon, for £250. According to the deeds the house had been occupied formerly by John Charmbury, but the relationship between the two Charmburys, a long-standing South Stoke family, is not known. At the time of the sale the property was not referred to as an inn but was described as 'Messuage, Barn, Outhouses, cottages, Ten Acres of Pasture commonly known as The Breath'. Although one could speculate that The Breath is the name of an inn, this is unlikely as in 1719 the churchwardens entertained bell founder Thomas Bilbie of Chew Stoke at the Cross Keys, after the recasting of the church bells. Had there been an inn next door to the church, that would have been a more likely venue. The churchwardens' accounts show other business with the Cross Keys in 1727. In fact there are no references to the Packhorse in the village as a public house until the mid-19th century.

For many years the property disappears from the records to emerge in 1797 in the ownership of Thomas Podger of Bristol. Thos Podger, also called George, died on 20 December 1804, during a voyage on board the *Swift* to Africa and the West Indies. The property was inherited by his sister Ann Podger in trust for his son, also Thomas. In 1804 the house was occupied by Joseph Jefferies. By 1813 it had passed to William Taplin who still owned and farmed 'Part of a Barton', including Packhorse Cottage(s) and 20 acres, at the time of the Tithe Map and audit of 1840–42. For the first time, in 1847, an inn is mentioned obliquely, by James Tunstall in his *Rambles about Bath*: 'The village contains nothing remarkable, except some ancient farmhouses, one of which, bearing the date 1697 (sic), is now a beer house'.

The earlier Pack Horse Inn on Midford Hill (now Old Midford Road) ceased business as a hostelry after the new turnpike road had greatly reduced passing trade (around 1850). At about the same time, possibly under the tenancy of Mrs Elizabeth Lucas (1853–62), the present Packhorse took on the name and no doubt some of the customers. Mrs Lucas is listed in the *Bath Directory* of 1854 as 'farmer & beerseller' and she continued her tenancy until 1862. Early in her tenancy she was summoned in the Magistrates Court for permitting illicit drinking, but the case was dismissed. The event was reported in the *Bath Chronicle* on 24 February 1853:

Saturday – Mrs Lucas, a beerhouse-keeper, of Southstoke was summoned on a charge of allowing beer to be drunk in her house on Sunday 6th instant during Divine Service in the forenoon. Mr Hellings appeared for the Defendant.

The evidence in support of the summons was given by two constables, who stated that they knocked at *the door of the Defendants house several times before being admitted. They had previously looked through the key-hole and had seen persons moving about and on entering saw cups on the table on which were recent marks of liquid, but no beer was in the cups. There was also appearance of smoking having lately been going on.*

In cross-examination, the witnesses said the marks on the table might have been there from the previous night.

The summons was dismissed.

From 1866 to the present day the pub has been in the hands of relatively few families. Joseph Heal (also painter and plasterer) was a tenant of Thomas Taleman and his wife, from 1866–85. Taleman's acquisition deed of 1881 describes the property as a public house, a malthouse and painter's shop. Then came Thomas Quick, under a tenancy from Holloway's Brewery from 1890–1908, and the Rose family from 1909–75. In 1901 Emily Quick(e) married Fred Rose in St James' Church and the couple held the licence from 1909 until about 1950 under a tenancy from Bath Brewery. Frederick Robert Rose (Bob), son of Emily and Fred, took over as landlord until 1975, when the owners were Georges' Brewery. In the 1920s Bob played rugby for England Schools and later captained the South Stoke cricket team. The Rose family connection did not end there as the tenancy passed to Bob's daughter Valerie Wellstead and her husband Ray from 1975–85 by which time Courage Brewery were the owners. Thomas Quick was Valerie Wellstead's great-grandfather. At the time of writing, in the year 2000, the Packhorse is owned by the company 'Innspired' and tenanted by Mr and Mrs Garth Evans.

THE CROSS KEYS INN

Although the Cross Keys lies just outside the parish boundary, from the early part of the 18th century it shared the role of South Stoke village local with the Pack Horse on the Old Midford Road. Hugh Sexey of Bruton acquired the land upon which the inn was built after the dissolution of the Benedictine Priory of Bath. Our first record of the Cross Keys as an inn dates from 4 June 1718 when it was described as 'a new erected tenement or dwelling house called the Cross Keys, now a Public House, on Odwood Down' in a lease to Henry Palmer of Bath, 'Doctor of Physick'. The inn had lands of 80 acres including the Thirty Acres within South Stoke parish. Amongst subsequent lessees was Ralph Allen. The Thorpe 1742 map shows what may be a farmyard on the opposite corner of Southstoke Road on the site where the house Avalon now stands. Some time after 1742 two cottages, associated with the inn, were built on the opposite side of Midford Road in a field called Benbows next to the Thirty Acres. One continued as a smithy until 1940.

The Cross Keys was a coaching inn and a stage for coaches from Bristol to the south of England. In his *Journal of a Somerset Rector* the Revd John Skinner wrote 'Tues. Aug. 5th 1823 Joseph went early in the morning... to meet the Southampton coach at the Cross Keys in order to go to Romsey.' His son Joseph was on his way to school at Winchester. When the turnpike road (B3110) was built in the 1770s, the inn's future was assured. It is interesting to speculate that when the Old Midford Road ceased to be the 'main road', the fate of the old Pack Horse Inn as a hostelry was sealed, the business moving with the name, to the current Packhorse in the centre of South Stoke in around 1850.

Like many inns the Cross Keys has had its moments of notoriety. The *Bath Chronicle* of 9 September 1824 reported that Jacob Wilkins, ostler at the Prince Blucher Inn, Norton St Philip, parted with some female friends at the Cross Keys on the evening of 1 August and was subsequently murdered by his nephew, James Reynolds alias Walters, on the hill between Midford and Hinton Charterhouse.

In November 1896 the Cross Keys was sold by Sexey Hospital to Oakhill Brewery.

The Cross Keys, c.1853.
(Courtesy Mark Palmer)

Above: *Cavalryman outside the Cross Keys, c.1916.*
(Courtesy Mark Palmer)

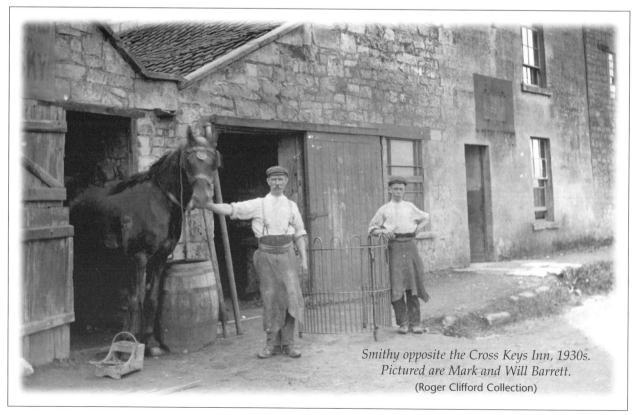

Smithy opposite the Cross Keys Inn, 1930s. Pictured are Mark and Will Barrett.
(Roger Clifford Collection)

❖ *Midford* ❖

Above: This view looking north west shows most of Midford within the parish of South Stoke, c.1920.

Below: Midford in 1904 (from the 25 inch OS map).

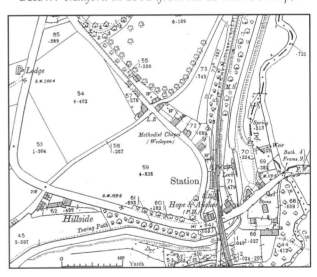

During the past two and a half centuries, Midford has been cut through four times as if by a scythe; first by the turnpike road (Midford Road) towards the end of the 18th century, then the Somersetshire Coal Canal (SCC) from 1795, next the Somerset and Dorset Railway (S & D) in the 1870s and finally the Camerton to Limpley Stoke Branch rail line in 1910. The village has survived this drastic re-landscaping and, away from the main road, tranquility and a strong community spirit prevail.

At the eastern boundary of the parish the now quiet backwater of Tucking Mill was once a hive of activity and it has itself been transformed several times. Built in 1808, the mill for fulling or tucking (removing oils from wool with the aid of local fuller's earth) stood just in front of what is today The Cottage. Nothing above ground remains of the mill or the canal wharf which William Smith built on its ruins. William Smith (1769–1839) (see Chapter 1) has entered posterity as 'The Father of English Geology' on a tablet mistakenly placed on The Cottage! Smith owned land here and lived close by The Cottage in a house called Tucking Mill. By virtue of his profession he lived a peripatetic life: surveying, advising and helping to build the Somersetshire Coal Canal; he was rarely in Midford for long. He is said to have advised the Conollys of Midford Castle on the construction of fishponds in Horsecombe Vale. To the rear of The Cottage, when it was built in around 1815, was a lake. Later this was drained and a huge fuller's earth treatment works developed taking advantage of the proximity of the canal, and later, the railway.

No trace remains of the works and little of the inclined plane built to transfer stone mined in Combe Down to the canal below for distribution.

In 1862, Tucking Mill must have been a lively place. With the enterprise of 'Lusty Alfred, flock and millpuff manufacturer, Tucking Mill' and 'Hooker James Tea gardens, Tucking Mill Cottage' providing employment and leisure for the locality. Now, long after the demise of the fuller's earth works in 1920, the lake has been re-established and, since 1981, has provided facilities for disabled anglers.

Above: *Tucking Mill Cottage shortly after the mill was demolished in 1927. Some of the Morris family are standing in the porch.*

Below: *Morgan's Forge (front door left) and Dorset Cottage (front door right).*

Above & inset: *Broadlands, built in a field of that name by George and Mary Summers.*
(Courtesy Jim Summers)

Below: *Midford in 1870, before the railway and viaduct. The Weigh House is on the far right. Between the cottages (Rose Cottage and Turnpike Cottage) just to the left of the Weigh House, the Turnpike Gate is just visible. The Hope and Anchor is prominent in the centre.*
(Edward Smith Collection)

Westwards towards a quiet little crossroads, the names of houses Morgan's Forge and the Old Post Office reveal something of their origins. In 1840 Morgan's Forge was 'a smith's shop and garden' owned and occupied by Thomas Morgan, who is listed in the *Post Office Directory* until 1868. The 1949 'For Sale' particulars of Court Essington, describe the site as including 'a pair of cottages', though they were not a matching pair. Recently, Dorset Cottage has had a first-floor room added to it. The Post Office has moved around the village over the years. S.H. Hadland ran the Post Office from Hillside between 1902 and 1904 and A.J. Andrews from 1905 until 1933. From 1933 to 1958 Edward (Ted) Hamlen managed the Post Office at Hillside House. The location then moved over the river to Somer Cottage for a while and finally to Ivy Cottage at the crossroads. It is possible that the Joyce family, who are listed in the *Directory* as running the Post Office from 1858–82/3 and Miss Rosa M. Smith (1884–1901) served the community from the Old Post Office.

Ivy Cottage stands on the site of what was, in 1840, a timber yard. At the beginning of the 20th century the property belonged to Midford House and between 1910 and 1940 Mr and Mrs Badder were resident there. Mr Badder was gardener and his wife was cook at the House. When she was widowed, 'Gran' Badder, as she became known, moved up the hill to South Stoke and lived in Alderley Cottage. She was a popular Parish figure.

There has been a collection of structures adjacent to Ivy Cottage since at least 1840. Now bearing the new name of Conifers, these buildings were known locally as The Dairy. Fieldgate Cottage, attached to the Old Post Office, is probably 18th century in origin and appears on a Greenwood map of 1822. Romain, built around 1967 on the site of Hamlen's yard (see Chapter 11), is one of Midford's few 20th-century buildings, its name deriving from a section of Roman road said to have been found in the garden during building excavations. Monk's Barn and Friar's Barn are the north and south halves respectively of a converted early 20th-century barn. Back on the south corner of the crossroads in the enclosure named Broad Lands is another 20th-century dwelling, of the same name. Built in 1926, of wood and asbestos on a stone base for George Milne Summers, the then chauffeur at Court Essington, it now belongs to the son of the original tenants. A second bungalow, Highfield, has since been built within the enclosure.

On the left down Old Road, also known as Station Hill, is a group of three dwellings clearly identifiable on Day and Masters' map of 1782. Fairly, The White Cottage and Hazel Elm have all been altered and enlarged over the course of time with changes such as the replacement of thatch with tiles. Stationmasters, one rather inappropriately named Mr C.F. Hazzard, lived in Hazel Elm. In 1837 a Methodist chapel was built just behind The White Cottage, and here

Above: *The White Cottage in the 1920s.* (Samler Collection)

Below: *White Cottage in 1965.* (Edward Smith Collection)

villagers recall weekly services, conducted by Kingswood School staff, which were held until the 1960s.

The Day and Masters' map is the first upon which Midford Castle appears. The new turnpike (Midford) road passing the original south entrance carves a prominent line through Midford. Midford Castle, high on its hill to the north, was built in about 1775, for Henry Woolhouse Disney Roebuck. Designs for such a gothic mansion are featured in a 1774 edition of *The Builder* magazine. A near contemporary description by Collinson (in 1791) conjures up the atmosphere of the eccentric castle and its elegant Priory:

... with Gothick windows and a circular embattled tower in which is a commodious tea-room, and offices below. A little diftance from this, under a thick mafs of fhade, ftands a ruftick hermitage... The whole furrounding fcenery is highly picturefque and romantick.

Some 150 years later and Nature had reasserted herself, as noted by Christopher Hussey: '... the passage of time has only matured the scene to one of tangled romance.' Local legend has it that Roebuck constructed the castle in the ground plan of the ace of clubs because a win at cards provided the cash to build the property. There is no basis to this story.

Midford Castle, c.1910.
(Samler Collection)

Right: *An unknown gardener at Midford House early in the 1900s.*
(Courtesy Pat and Jack Kingston)

Below: *Major Sir Raymond Menendez and Dame Hetty Tilyou Menendez, residents of Midford House between 1909 and 1952.*

In Chancery.   1802 For Sale particulars

Sir Thomas Hyde Page, Knt. and Others, Plaintiffs,
Between
and
George Leapingwell, and Others,   Defendants.

PARTICULARS
OF A DESIRABLE
FREEHOLD ESTATE,
LATE THE RESIDENCE OF
BENJAMIN PUGH, Esq. M.D. deceased,
CALLED
MIDFORD CASTLE,
CONSISTING OF
A CAPITAL MANSION-HOUSE,
With Stabling for Eight Horses, Coach-houses, Servants Rooms over them,
CONVENIENT OFFICES OF EVERY DESCRIPTION,
PLEASURE-GROUND, WALLED GARDEN, CROPPED AND PLANTED,
AND ABOUT NINETY-FIVE ACRES OF
RICH ARABLE, MEADOW, PASTURE, AND WOOD-LAND,
SITUATE AT
MIDFORD, in the Parish of SOUTHSTOKE,
IN A BEAUTIFUL PART OF THE COUNTRY,
About Two Miles from Bath, on the Road leading to Warminster, Salisbury,
Southampton and Portsmouth;
IN THE COUNTY OF SOMERSET,
To be Sold,
ON THE PREMISES, WITH THE APPROBATION OF
SIR WILLIAM WELLER PEPYS, BARONET, ONE OF THE MASTERS OF
THE HIGH COURT OF CHANCERY,
On *Monday, the 30th Day of August, 1802,*
AT ONE O'CLOCK IN THE AFTERNOON,
PURSUANT TO A DECREE IN THE SAID CAUSE.

Below: *Mowing the lawn at Midford House in the early 1900s. Mr Badder was the coachman and gardener.*
(Courtesy Pat and Jack Kingston)

Midford Castle 'For Sale' notice from 1802.

Midford House and garden, from glass slides found in a cupboard. Dame Hetty's pose is mirrored by Pat.
(Courtesy Pat and Jack Kingston)

Below: *Midford Place in 1970.*
(Courtesy Ann Hopkins-Clark)

Roebuck left his creation after 13 years and around 1810 the Castle and estate entered the hands of the Conolly family, who were to stay there for the remainder of the century, through three generations. The most celebrated family member was Louisa Lucy Margaret Catharine Brancaccio, Marchesa di St Agatha, known locally as Countess Conolly, wife of Charles John Thomas Conolly. During the second half of the 19th century she drew local Roman Catholics to worship at the castle's family chapel. Upon her death much of the widowed and childless Countess' estate, including her valuable art collection, was bequeathed to her spiritual mentor Monsignor Charles Parfitt. In 1900, the collection finally passed to the Victoria Art Gallery in Bath and was an important part of its display in its opening year. The sale of the Marchesa's jewels and other possessions lasted three days and created a frisson of excitement in the local press.

Between 1878 and 1886/7, the Rt Revd Dr Charles Parfitt, Catholic Prelate, is listed as being the occupant of Midford House, situated on the Old Road close to its junction with the B3110. To this day there is a marble stoup set in the thickness of the doorway wall of the upstairs room that he used as a chapel. At this time the house was part of the Midford Castle estate. The stages of development of the house can be seen clearly. Originally it was two small rubble stone cottages, but in the late-18th and early-19th centuries an ashlar-fronted house was added to their southern wall. Two detailed advertisements of 1809 'To be Lett' and 'For Sale' in the *Bath Chronicle* appear to refer to Midford House. In 1901, the Midford Castle estate was sold and split up. An archaeologist, J.A. Potts, lived in Midford House until 1908 and a well-built garden 'shed' lined with shelving may have been where he displayed his artefacts. From 1909, through both world wars, Sir Raymond Menendez and his wife, Dame Hetty Tilyou Menendez, were the residents. When Mr and Mrs Jack Kingston moved there in 1972, to their amazement they discovered a collection of daguerrotypes on glass in the kitchen dresser. These are a marvellous survival from Edwardian times in Midford, showing the occupants and staff against the backdrop of the house and garden.

The house to the west, Atcombe, was formerly the gardener's cottage. Now a paddock, the area south of Atcombe was once a productive walled kitchen garden, lined with fruit trees. Between 1938 and 1949 Atcombe was part of the Court Essington

estate owned by Mr Atcheley. It is thought that 'Atcombe' is derived from his name.

On the other side of the B3110, Midford Place, a 'small country villa in a mixed Gothic and classical style', was built between 1840 and 1854, when John Roberts was listed as residing there. The Edgell family lived there from 1870–75 and, between 1894 and 1920, Major George Rashleigh Edgell was churchwarden and benefactor and a keen member of the Selborne Society. His gardener W. Grant was listed as occupant of Avonhill Lodge from 1905–20. From the time it was built until 1957, the house was known as Avonhill. During the 1960s General Sir Francis and Lady Nosworthy were the residents. The stables, behind Midford Place, were converted to Stable House.

Court Essington in 1949.

Court Essington was built in about 1910 for the Revd R. Moon Perkes, on land which was originally part of the Midford Castle estate. The house has ecclesiastical elements, such as the stone tracery of the windows and the oak panelling. Mr and Mrs E.H. Atcheley (he was a solicitor) lived there from 1930–49, when the property was sold. Its curtilage at that time included Morgan's Forge Cottages and cowsheds which later became Pipards, and all the triangle bounded by the road, except a tiny triangle of green opposite the entrance to Midford House. Curiously, to this day this patch has been retained by Midford House. Together with Atcombe and Broadlands, Mr Atcheley's estate totalled 23¾ acres. As a patriotic gesture after the Second World War, Mrs Atcheley laid out a rose garden in the shape of a Union Jack, a feature that still remains.

To the east of Court Essington is Old Road; to the west is the much later turnpike, now Midford Road. The Turnpike Trust built Turnpike Cottage down beside the river crossing some time between 1742 and 1782 as a dwelling for the toll collector. His job was to charge travellers a toll as they passed 'Midford Gate'. In 1840, Josiah Giddings was toll collector and the trustees of Black Dog Roads then owned the cottage. The last year that toll collectors are listed in the local directories is 1879. The tollgate can just be seen in an early photograph (see page 110).

The Hope and Anchor is certainly a very old inn. Canvin suggested that maybe its name was changed from The White Hart to a boating-related aponym when the Somersetshire Coal Canal was fully opened over the entire length, in November 1801. The inn appears on the 1840 Tithe Map as a dwelling house owned and occupied by Job Chancellor, a surname associated with the parish since the early-16th century.

Left: *Midford Flower Show at Avonhill, now Midford Place, in 1908.* (Roger Clifford Collection)

Above: *The Fox, Midford, in 1913. From the left: Ken Harbutt, Mrs Noel Harbutt, Jeff Harbutt, Mrs Bird; in the car: Mrs Olive Harbutt, Major Noel Harbutt, ?, ?.* (Edward Smith Collection)

Above: *Mr and Mrs George Steger of Canal House, and their son Ernest, c.1900.* (Edward Smith Collection)

Above: *The Hope and Anchor (left) on the B3110 in 1910.* (Samler Collection)

Right: *The Moorings, Midford, possibly built by William Hill when he was a surveyor and engineer with the Somersetshire Coal Canal. It was lived in by the 'toll collector' until the 1890s and purchased by the then collector, Mr G. Steger.* (Edward Smith Collection)

Above: *Turnpike Cottage, built c.1770.* (Courtesy Jenny John)

During the 1850s, Elizabeth Chancellor was listed at the Hope and Anchor and William Chancellor at the Fox Inn, just beyond the turnpike gates and over the river (the parish boundary), a toll charge away. In January 1853 there was a series of incidents here. The turnpike gates were stolen during the night and shots were fired at the tollhouse. Is it possible that the Chancellor family, members of which lived on each side of the tollhouse, objected to the over-zealous collecting of tolls? It seems that the constable was despatched to keep an eye on the locality because, in the following month, the *Bath Chronicle* reported that:

Elizabeth Chancellor, a licensed victualler, was summoned for allowing liquor to be sold in her house before half past 12 o'clock in the afternoon of a Sunday.

The next landlord of the Hope and Anchor, John White, spent almost 20 years there (1858–77) and he was followed by Mrs Emily White from 1878–98, a period of 40 years in the hands of one family. The Whites were followed by another long-standing family, the Creeses, who took the helm of the pub from 1900–34.

On the other side of the bridge over the Somersetshire Coal Canal (although you have to be on foot to appreciate that it is a bridge) is The Moorings, which was built, possibly by William Hill or perhaps by the SCC Company, as the toll clerk's house and office. William Hill junr (he and his father were engineers for the SCC Company) is recorded as the occupier in 1840. George Steger, who was toll clerk and lived there between 1876 and 1906, was followed by his son Ernest at Canal House (as it was known then). Both father and son are remembered on handsome headstones in South Stoke churchyard. When Dr and Mrs Edward Smith lived at The Moorings (c.1965–95), they created a beautiful sunken woodland garden along the canal bed on the opposite side of the road from the house. The garden has now become an extension of the land of The Cottage that has nestled comfortably beside it for two centuries. The Cottage must have witnessed great changes, upheaval and noise – the construction and demise of a canal, two railways and a nearby grist mill.

Across the road is Rose Cottage, tucked into the slope of the ground which is banked up to form the turnpike road. One wonders which was there first. Rose Cottage faces Midford Brook (which forms the eastern parish boundary), and has had much time and attention lavished on it in recent years.

Set right back from the road behind The Moorings is Lynwood, built on the site of the canal Weigh House that had been erected in 1831. At that time the canal was flourishing with around 120 000 tons of coal passing through Midford annually. The Weigh House was a fine sturdy building with a hint of Egyptian features, popular in Regency times, incorporated in its design. In 1914 it was partially dismantled. Each pillar was made from one block of stone; they were purchased by an antique dealer, who had no alternative but to have them sawn up in order to remove them.

The Weigh House is one of several buildings in Midford that no longer exist. A postcard view from around 1870 (see page 110) shows that part of the centre of Midford which falls within the parish of South Stoke. From the right, Rose Cottage, Turnpike Cottage and The Cottage are visible, with the canal toll clerk's house facing the road. The Hope and Anchor – without the leafy covering which has come and gone over the years – adjoins cottages which were demolished to make room for the Somerset and Dorset Railway viaduct (constructed 1872–74). Known as Railway Cottages, the remaining cottages were the homes of railwaymen and their families. Midford Station, behind the Hope and Anchor, was built in 1874 and demolished in 1967, the year after the last train ran. Only vestiges of the platform remain today. The signal box has also gone; the original of 1892 was 'modified' by a train accident in July 1936, and repaired minus its attractive pitched roof.

On the horizon in the 1870 photograph is the ashlar-fronted Hillside House, a late-18th-century Grade II listed house. It has been a farmhouse (Upper Midford Farm on deeds of 1899), timber yard (Tithe Map 1840) and the Post Office in its time. A large barn behind it, hard up to the road junction, that once served as a coach-house/stable for Hillside, was almost entirely demolished in 1960 to improve visibility at the junction. Three former farmworkers' cottages face on to Combe Hay Lane near this crossroads.

Upper Midford Farm, 1961. (Courtesy Babs Honey)

Left: *A view of Midford taken from the Somerset and Dorset Railway viaduct, c.1910. Canal House (now The Moorings) is top left.* (Edward Smith Collection)

Below: *The Spear family in front of Rose Cottage by the canal at Midford, c.1905.* (Edward Smith Collection)

Below: *Upper Midford, c.1900, showing the now neglected Accommodation Bridge and The Boatman's Arms (centre), a watering hole for barges.* (Edward Smith Collection)

Below: *Midford in the 1920s. Avonhill is at the top left of the picture. The steep bank below Hillside at Hillside Cottages (centre) is what is described as 'Midford cliff' on the Thorpe map of 1742.* (Edward Smith Collection)

Behind this little cluster of buildings the ground drops away steeply down Midford Cliff to the Cam Valley.

The terrain here has also been re-landscaped over the years. The course of the Cam Brook was altered so that it did not undermine the canal, leaving the parish boundary on dry land in places, whereas it was once in the middle of the stream. The canal curved round at the foot of the cliff towards the next watering hole, The Boatman's Arms, at Upper Midford – now known as Hyver Kennels. Nicholas Walker, collier, of Midford, was the inn's owner in 1840 and he 'erected three messuages upon some portions of the land'. His tenants were James and Levi Hamilton in 1840, and Joseph Hayden was host at the inn between 1858 and 1871. The year 1889 is the last time The Boatman's Arms is listed in the local directories and by this time transportation of coal was moving from the canal to the railways. We can only presume that it ceased to be an inn with the decline of the canal.

The perfectly proportioned Accommodation Bridge (now listed) remains, but is sadly neglected. Approaching this bridge from the west, the towpath was on the south side of the canal; eastwards from the bridge to Midford there were towpaths on both sides. Through traffic from Paulton to the Kennet and Avon Canal used the northern towpath, while barges crossing the aqueduct used the southern towpath. The lane coming down from Hillside Cottages turned left at this point, to go over the bridge, then crossed the Cam Brook by a ford. An early-20th-century photograph illustrates the then recently built Laura Cottages to the left of The Boatman's Arms, and Honeysuckle Cottage (formerly known as Sunnyside) to the right.

The collection of buildings known as Upper Midford take advantage of being in a small sheltered valley supplied with good spring water, still drunk today. On the Tithe Map (1840) the house now known as Canaan Cottage was the main farmhouse, owned by the Revd C.F. Bampfylde, and then occupied by William Chancellor. Its basic structure has been expertly dated as late-15th century. The remains of a beehive-shaped lime kiln survive in the garden. Part of the farm was the collection of buildings in the field known as Squirrel's Batch; these were cowsheds in 1960 but have since been transformed into a house.

The house now known as Upper Midford Farm was, in 1840, a small cottage and garden. Thomas White, its tenant, farmed four scattered fields. Since 1960, when the Honey family moved in to accommodate their growing family of eight children, the farmhouse has increased in size. Four decades later, descendants of the same family live there.

Skating at Midford in 1908, the Mill centre background. The meadow was deliberately flooded and in later years Miss Cross of Clearbrook Farm collected about 1s.6d. for skating. It cost about 8d. return to travel from Bath to Midford by train.
(Samler Collection)

CHAPTER 10

The Parish at Leisure

At the beginning of the 20th century South Stoke parish life was thriving. Like most traditional English villages, South Stoke and Midford then shared the essential elements of church, school, Post Offices, shops, ancient inns and even a brewery. The church, school and pubs provided the permanent institutions around which community life developed and were the basis for social activities such as fêtes, church suppers and outings, WI and Mothers' Union, children's parties and other gatherings. The Cricket Club held its committee meetings in the Packhorse Inn which also hosted a shove ha'penny club and darts team. Among the many other clubs during the 1900s were Scouts, Girl Guides, the Wiltshire Working Men's Society, South Stoke Association Football Club, the 18+ Club, Over Sixties Club (held in the lounge of the Packhorse) and various thrift clubs. There were the 5 November fireworks and New Year's Eve parties that were held in the Village Hall.

Many social activities were church orientated and organised by the vicar or perhaps some prominent lady of the parish. The Church Choir always played a leading part in village life and, during the time of the Reverend William Samler (1884–1944), the choir of men and boys flourished, ladies not joining until the 1940s. The social activities leading from choir membership were numerous, as an extract from the *Parish Notes* of February 1903 illustrates:

On Wednesday 31st January the Choir Supper was held. Supper ended, the company became considerably augmented when various songs were sung by members of the Choir and others, intermingled with dances and the time passed only too quickly away. At 12.30 Sir Roger and God Save the King brought a very pleasant evening to a termination.

In later *Parish Notes* we read of summer choir outings to Weston super Mare, Weymouth and Bournemouth.

South Stoke Association Football Club, 1920–21. Left to right, back row: *Albert Clifford, Will Clifford, Jack Dobson, Ern Withers, ?;* middle: *Jack Ainsworth, Frank Withers, Norman Dobson;* front: *?, Jack Clifford, Billy Rose, ?, Archie Frankcom.*
(Roger Clifford Collection)

Above: *The Church Choir in the early 1990s. Left to right, back: Rosemary Geake, Tom Geake, Aty Bell, Fred Turner, Philip Wells, Sue Stoneham; front: Peggy Esam, Jenny Torrance, Alfie Walker, Muriel Moon, Freda Hawkins. Alfie Walker (b.1904) received a medal in 1985 for long service after being in the Church Choir for 70 years from 1915. He continued until his death in 1995.*

Above: *Mrs Lambern's wedding at St Mark's Church, Lyncombe, 1932. Cecil Lambern was Captain of the South Stoke Football Team who provided the guard of honour with corner flags.*

Above: *South Stoke Art Group, 20 March 2000. Left to right, back: Jenny Torrance, Patsy Pryce, Bunty Bartlett, Liz Jacobs (tutor), Cecilia Howard-Kyan, Amy Barkshire, Rollo Torrance; front: Judy Parfitt, Alliette Sanville, Aty Bell, Ann Parsons.* (Photograph, Rollo Torrance)

Left: *St James' South Stoke Sunday School, c.1950, taken in the vicarage garden. Left to right, back row: Reverend Dicker, Mollie Clifford, Mr and Mrs Sydney Bourne; 4th row: Myrtle Furley, Meriel Joyce, Eileen Heal, Christine Lambern; 3rd row: ?, Clive Maundrell, ?, ?; 2nd row: Brian Harris, Sylvia Joyce, ?, Natalie Hawkins; front: Valerie Hawkins, ?, Michael Freegard, ?, Marion Furley.*

Above: *South Stoke Choir outing to Cheddar, 1922/23.* Left to right, back row: *?, Miss Morris (Nanny Samler), Mrs M. Barrett, Mrs Green, Mrs Dick Clifford, ?, ?, ?, Mrs Sims (Nell Hancock), Mrs Humphries (Flo Hancock);* middle: *?, Mrs Ern Staddon, ?, ?, ?, Mr Quick, ?, Mrs Hancock, ?, ?, Mrs Withers, driver, ?, Mrs Gibbs, Miss Dorothy Samler;* front: *Bill Samler, Revd W. Samler, Mr Pitt, Charlie Green, Col Gibbs, Ern Staddon, Mr Franklin, Mr Fallowfield, ?, Arthur Humphries, Jack Sims, Alfie Walker, ?.* (Roger Clifford Collection)

Left: *South Stoke Choir outing to Weymouth, 24 July 1923.* From the left the party includes: *Alfie Walker, William Samler, Mr Staddon, Mary Jane Heal (above wing mirror), Mrs Hancock, Eddie Heal, Mrs Withers, Nell Sims.* (Samler Collection)

Right: *South Stoke Sunday School outing, 9 August 1921.* Left to right, front closest to the camera: *?, Nell Sims, Nanny Samler, Revd W. Samler, Dorothy Samler.* (Samler Collection)

Parish children attended Sunday School regularly, dressed in their Sunday best and sitting on tiered forms in an area at the back of the church. Children looked forward to the rewards given for regular attendance. There were Sunday School Christmas parties with a tree, presents, magic lantern slides and gramophone recitals 'which caused some amusement.' We read in the *Parish Notes* of celebrations on 25 July 1907, St James' Day:

> *The enjoyment of the children was considerably marred by the stormy weather. It rained so heavily we were obliged to take shelter in the schoolroom for tea. After tea the rain ceased and all adjourned with the band to Mr Hamlen's field kindly lent to us for the occasion. In spite of the sodden ground and a grey and cheerless sky the children managed to thoroughly enjoy themselves.*

Muriel Walters from Pack Horse Farm and Margaret Canvin taught the Sunday School held in the Village Hall immediately before the Second World War, with Sidney Bourne and his wife of 4 Rose Cottages teaching in the 1950s. During the war years, the Sunday School was closed for lack of leaders and the children were sent for the duration of the war to the Sunday School at the Evangelical Church in South Stoke Lane. After that, Molly Clifford, who had herself attended the Sunday School, continued classes in the village until the late 1980s, a period of about 25 years.

For the ladies of the parish the Mothers' Union afforded some social life and meetings were well attended. The *Parish Notes* of 1904 record:

> *... 30 mothers from the parish attended the evening meeting of the Union held at the Guildhall. Previous to the meeting all assembled at Fisher's Restaurant where a most excellent tea was provided. Most of the mothers used the tram, but several from Midford found the train more convenient.*

Tea parties, sales of work, bazaars and fêtes were held for charities such as the Church Missionary Society and the Society for the Propagation of the Gospel.

For many years groups of singers have sung Christmas carols around the village for various charities. The final stop was Brantwood, where Bill and Diana Goodman plied the gathering with mince pies and sherry (or squash) around a log fire.

The first class of the Art Group was held on 11 January 1985 in the Village Hall, when Ursula Brooke was a volunteer tutor, soon to be joined by Ann Willson. In 1986 Cecily Ford took over until 1992, when professional tutors were found – firstly Victoria Gamberoni and, at the time of writing, Liz Jacobs. Membership is always around 15 to 18 and the class has good fun, works hard and produces some commendable pieces.

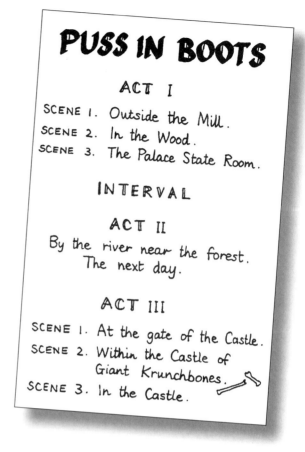

South Stoke Pantomime, 1991, which was Puss in Boots, *produced by Rosemary Geake.*

In the arena of drama and theatre the parish has not been without its successes. An early production by Felicity Elphinstone was a fairy scene from *A Midsummer Night's Dream* and other notable productions included Christmas nativity plays produced by Miss Sly. More recent Village Hall productions were *The Wishing Tree* at Christmas in 1990, directed by Pat Pengilly. The last productions were by Rosemary Geake – of the pantomime *Puss in Boots* at Christmas in 1991 and in 1992 Agatha Christie's *The Hollow* with Christopher Parsons as the lead.

The millennium was celebrated in a number of ways, which are described in the Epilogue.

Royal events are always a good excuse for a party. For the Silver Jubilee of Queen Elizabeth II South Stoke enjoyed a triumphant celebration, under the leadership of Joan Carey Jones. Preparations began in the spring of 1977 with a series of fund-raising events, including an auction, which raised over £1500. The yard of Manor Farm with its Tithe Barn was to be the scene for evening revels on Monday 6 June 1977 and:

> *... all loyal subjects were commanded to assemble by the village Green and church attired in the style and manner of Merrie England for a night of jollification and feasting.*

Right: *Joan Jones and Jack Davison on the day of the Silver Jubilee, 1977.*

Above: *The Pageant, Silver Jubilee, 1977. The centre rider is Alexandra Davison.*

Left: *The town crier, Bill Goodman, Silver Jubilee, 1977.*

Tug of War at Manor Farm, Silver Jubilee, 1977.

South Stoke responded with enthusiasm and 250 tickets were sold. Rollo Torrance remembers highlights of the day:

The weather was unsettled in the run up and a rigging team had to battle with brisk winds to hang their bunting by the Green and in the farmyard. Mike Banks' mountaineering skills were put to good use scaling the walls. But on the day the sun shone and Bill Goodman as town crier, in feathered hat and brocaded coat, led a dazzling procession down past the brewery wall and round the end of the Green. There were mounted knights in armour and wimpled ladies on caparisoned horses, courtiers, monks, priests and friars, soldiers bearing tall standards, pages, jesters and children all filing down the lane with awesome dignity. It seemed to go on and on, extended by a team of Morris Men and finally a huge red dragon, with happy children's faces protruding all along its spine.

Penny Forbes-Adam had revived an ancient mummers' play St George and the Turk *which was brought to spirited life by a cast of village children on the raised grass in front of the bungalows. Penny's daughter Sonia played the villainous Turk, with a huge sabre, and delighted*

the packed audience by dying dramatically and at great length after a stirring fight with the Saint. The Morris Men then performed their ancient rites, including the one where they bang their staves together, at great risk to knuckles. A Hobby Horse cavorted around to add to the confusion, the whole space between the lych gate and The Priory being filled with a colourful throng. A maypole had been erected in the road and Jenny Torrance anxiously watched her trainees creating complicated knitting while the pony of her daughter Judy, hungry after being ridden in the procession, quietly nibbled the floral bouquet of a grand lady standing too close.

In the farmyard Chris Parsons ran a tug-of-war and I remember an intrepid fire eater. At the far side of the barn my son James was cast as a male-factor in stocks, which Joan Jones had instructed me to build, trying to dodge wet sponges thrown at him by the children. And so the evening progressed, with skittles, Punch and Judy, drinking, feasting and country dancing. I also have a final memory of a barber's shop quartet emitting harmonious and other sounds from the Tithe Barn gallery. Jenks Knill was one singer but who were the others? It was a famous South Stoke day to remember and Her Majesty would have been hugely impressed.

The parish Garden Fête, run by the WI, was instituted in 1922 and held at Hodshill House (making a profit of £96.10s.3d.) under the supervision of Mrs Betty Hignett. The WI continued to run the annual fête for many years, although the venue moved to Whitecroft in 1939 and later to The Knoll (now South Knoll) with a gap during the Second World War. Maypole dancing was also at Whitecroft and later The Knoll, followed by a dance at night on the lawn. After the war the Revd Kenneth Elphinstone suggested the reinstitution of the fête and since then successive organisers have been Gilly Harben of Southstoke Hall (where the fêtes were held until 1988), Sheila Cobb, Valerie Summers, who organised six fêtes and latterly Robert Hellard. The event is now held biennially at Brantwood courtesy of Diana Goodman. The 2000 Fête, which raised £4500 for church repairs, took place on an idyllic July day and was a delightful scene, with marquees, stalls of all kinds, children's activities, side shows, vintage cars and the Bath Spa Brass Band.

South Stoke Show, 9 September 2000. Jubilee Cup presentation by Cllr Gitte Dawson to Charlotte Murray for the Murray family. Left to Right: *Cllr Gitte Dawson, Rollo Torrance, Joan Jones, Theodore Murray-Sweetman, Charlotte Murray, Gill Carter.* (Photograph, Judy Parfitt)

The first South Stoke Show was held on 7 September 1974 and was the brainchild of Joan Carey Jones; it has continued in unbroken sequence to the 27th event which was celebrated in 2000. Originally named South Stoke Produce Show, the form is essentially unchanged: trophies are always eagerly sought and the winners recorded, with an auction of exhibits being held at the end. Joan recalls the show's origins and looks forward to its future:

In horticultural terms a seed was sown in 1973, the thought being that South Stoke had a merry band of gardeners who would enjoy showing their produce at a village show. Hence South Stoke Produce Show, as it was then called. Wallace Ford who had experience through the Admiralty Show at Combe

Down became Chairman and Glen Bond Treasurer; Rollo Torrance and I are the only members left of the original committee and I have filled the position of Show Secretary over the whole period with great backing from Carmel Shepherd. Since small beginnings the show has grown and flourished and changed its name, and with experience became more professional. The joy to me is that we ever got it off the ground, and that it brings in a great cross-section of the village. There have been headaches and fun, the nightmare of getting entries into the wrong category or cards getting moved in the classes, at the last moment chasing a lost cup. Then there are late entries that throw out of gear all the staging gang's wonderful calculations of getting a pint into a half pint pot, but that's show business. [There are] lots of lovely memories: Jack Clifford and his beans; Alan Cobb with the longest runner bean he'd spliced together in true Navy fashion; Gordon Dyer's mammoth marrow being brought up to the show on the postman's shoulder; [and] best of all the fun and friendship of it and the great support of a hard-working committee. I don't wear boots so I can't hang those up, but I do pass on the now famous Show Secretary's table knowing it is in good hands.

Any spare funds were often given to support the Village Hall but one special project, to commemorate the Silver Jubilee, was to plant three trees, with commemorative labels, in Victoria Park. The planting was done with a silver spade used by Queen Elizabeth II.

The Harvest Supper was initiated after the Second World War by Babs Honey of Upper Midford Farm. In those days everyone sat on benches and it was a crowded free-for-all, the bill of fare being chicken and ham salad with punch, followed by entertainment. Successive organisers were Gilly Harben, Nancy Bryant and Ann Parsons. Ann planned 18 suppers, retiring in 1999 and handing over to Judy Parfitt. A new format was chosen for the year 2000, with a hot supper and a quiz.

Children's activities were many. A club for children aged 7–11 years named King's Messengers was probably associated with a missionary society and met during the 1940s and '50s under the auspices of Miss Elwell in the vicarage kitchen. Members participated in crafts and read stories of children 'in foreign climes'. After Miss Elwell, Sylvia Heal (now Williams) and Molly Clifford led the club. Older girls joined the Girls Friendly Society ('God first, Friends second, Self last') participating in weekly classes held in the kitchen of The Knoll (now South Knoll). This was another of the redoubtable Miss Rachel Elwell's activities. The GFS meetings were later taken by Mrs Churcher of Southstoke Hall, where the girls were amused by a rather bad-tempered parrot. They sewed collection bags for the church, read aloud serial stories from magazines dating from 1920–30, learnt about dress, make-up and home-made face-packs and had noisy games in the garden, before collecting the hens' eggs, then feeding and shutting them up for the night. Miss Elwell would take the children for local jaunts in her two-seater, open-top car, seriously overcrowded. One trip was to pick lavender at Midford Castle. Miss Rachel Elwell is remembered here by Roger Clifford:

Miss Elwell lived at The Knoll (now South Knoll) with her brother Claude who was the Bath Coroner. Both worshipped regularly at South Stoke Church and did a lot for the church. She also did a great deal for the children of the parish, running the Girl Guides, Girls Friendly Society and Brownies. She took the boys for fretwork once a week in her kitchen. The Elwells owned an Austin 16 car with a hood and a 'dicky' seat at the back. It was a common sight to see Miss Elwell with the hood down, driving off to functions with the car loaded with Guides or GFS.

Miss Elwell was always having small sales of work and held a fête in her garden every year. She used to hold a play and a party in the school at Christmas. Most people remember Miss Elwell for the maypole outside the church on Maydays, with a portable gramophone on a stand which she had to wind up constantly.

Miss Elwell was a shy, retiring lady who should be remembered.

Southstoke Youth Club, formed in May 1979 by Shan Parfitt and Kathryn Eastham at the suggestion of the Revd Forbes-Adam, attracted about 20 members mainly from the village of South Stoke. The Club held regular meetings in the Village Hall and also in members' houses, enjoying themselves with spring fayres, Christmas parties, Valentine's Day discos, a 'bad-taste' party and coffee mornings; funds were raised and donated to charity. Memorable summer camps were held at Combe Hay, by the Cam Brook near Bridge Farm and at Monkton Combe beside the Midford Brook. A special 'T' shirt was adopted in yellow, with blue lettering: SOUTHSTOKE YOUTH CLUB. The club closed about 1982.

In the 1950s, Eileen Heal and Geoff Trimby, later her husband, organised a new Youth Club. At one time there was a billiards table in the Institute, probably for a Men's Club. In addition a Boys' Club met in the present Village Hall. In the late 1940–50s, dances were held in the wooden hut situated in Twinhoe Lane (the site of which is now marked by steps still visible in the bank) and at the Institute at South Stoke, where old-time dancing was taught by Mr Vincent.

The Toddler Group meets regularly in the Village Hall on Thursday mornings for craft, play and singing.

All ages of pre-school children attend regularly, with about 20 children and 12 adults from South Stoke and the surrounding areas. The group was started in the early 1980s by Helen Knill, supported by a grant of £10 from the Mothers' Union to buy the first toys. It has continued to flourish, with Helen Self running it since 1995 and a rota of parents organising the weekly activities.

The South Stoke Women's Institute was inaugurated in 1921. Meetings were held in the Institute, now known as Old School House, which was managed by the committee of the WI and was in effect the Village Hall. (*Pictured is Mrs Ruby Harris on her 80th birthday, the WI's most long-standing active member who was on the WI Committee for 50 years.*) In fact, the WI ran most of the parish social activities, for example the Fête, which they started in 1922. The earliest recorded WI minutes available are for the meeting on 29 July 1937, which include an account of the Coronation trip to London. After the meeting :

Mrs Ruby Harris

... the remainder of the evening was spent in the beautiful garden at Hodshill by kind permission of Mrs Hignett and in the woods a fire was lighted and we all partook of a hot dog supper followed by cheese dreams and coffee.

In December 1937 a Christmas party was held. The minutes give a picture of happy, home-made entertainment typical of life in the 1930s:

The evening started at 7 o'clock with games and dancing alternately until supper was served at 9 o'clock. This was followed by an entertainment given by Mrs Hill on her accordion and Miss Mary Pointing sang 'Little Old Lady'. The Misses Chancellor gave a demonstration on how NOT to keep fit. Games and dancing followed until 11 o'clock. Mrs Pitt acted as MC and presented the prizes. The crackers were a gift from Mrs Pitt who we were pleased to have with us for the evening.

In September 1939, with the outbreak of war, a meeting was held in the Institute to discuss what activities could be arranged for the winter under wartime conditions. It was agreed to discontinue meetings for the present but to continue with social life and anything that could be done to help in the crisis. Members were requested to welcome evacuees wherever possible. Mrs Hignett spoke on arranging classes for sewing and knitting, in conjunction with the WVS, to start as soon as materials were available; the first meeting was to be held at Hodshill. It was agreed to have fortnightly whist drives and it was suggested that, if electricity were laid on, it might be possible to have a small cinema. Thus the WI prepared for its part in the war effort.

Below: *South Stoke Toddler Group, Autumn 2000. Left to right, back row: Seymour and Theodore Murray-Sweetman with grandmother Beryl Murray, Laura and Alexander Nettle with mother Diana Hopkins, Rebecca Reid with Sebastian and Freya, Rachel Stewart-Harris with Isabel and George, Jane Shearn with Ceri; front: Catherine Clements (Nanny) with Madeleine Awan, Cameron Self with mother Helen, Oliver Marchant (in front), Kirsty Banwell with Alfie, Rosie Russell with Jocelyn, Chui Chek with son Brendan Baker, Claire Atkins with Charlotte.*

Above: *Miss Rachel Elwell (top left) and members of the Girls Friendly Society in the early 1940s. The girls include: Doreen Ellis, Rita Furley, Joan and June Gaylard, Muriel Heal, Sheila Holley, Gwen Marsh and several evacuees.*

Left: *South Stoke WI outing, 10 July 1924. Left to right, back row (standing): Mabel Green, Mrs Green, ?, Mrs Adams, Joyce Ainsworth, ?, ?, Mrs Heal, ?, Mrs Badder, Miss Pocock, Miss Pocock, Mrs Fallowfield, Milly Badder, Mrs Reece, Mrs G. Dobson, ?, ?; middle: Mrs Ainsworth, Mrs Staddon, ?, ?, ?, Jack Rose, Bertie Spital, Edith Spital, ?, Coral Clifford; front: Mrs Chancellor, Mrs J. Walters, Mrs Dainton, ?, Muriel Walters, Joyce Walters, Beryl Chancellor, ?, Stella Chancellor, ?.*

Women's Institute, 1955. Left to right, back row: *Mrs Irene Taylor, Mrs Skrine, Mrs Chambers, Mrs Pointing (Mary Williams' mother), Mrs Yaxley, Mrs Edie Hamlen, Mrs Glanfield, ?, Mrs Langley, ?, Mrs Atkins;* front: *Mrs Furley, Mrs Ellis, Mrs Weaver, Mrs Bartlett, Mrs Frost, Mrs Hall, Mrs Chancellor, Mrs Hambleton, Mrs Biss, Mrs Gagg.*

Left: *The last WI AGM of the 20th century.* Left to right, back row: *Monica Mann, Val Germain, Jan Brigden, Betty Cavanagh, Sylvia Williams, Lillian Daniels, Hazel James;* middle: *Dora Freegard, Pat Mason, Muriel Moon, Sheila Neill, Philippa Judd;* front: *Carol Oakes (Chairman), Valerie Summers, Rita Morris, Vera Brigden, Jeanne Clifford.*

Right: *South Stoke Cricket Club, c.1936.* Left to right, back row: *David Cairns, Jack Clifford, L. Roy, ?, ?, Percy Stride, Noel Staddon, Charles Weaver, D. Adams, ? Humphries, Bob Rose;* middle: *Mr Evans, Jack Dobson, Fred Weeks, Len Weaver, ?, Archie Frankcom, ?, J. Tilley, ?, ?;* front: *Donny (dog), Gerald Hignett, ?.*
(Roger Clifford Collection)

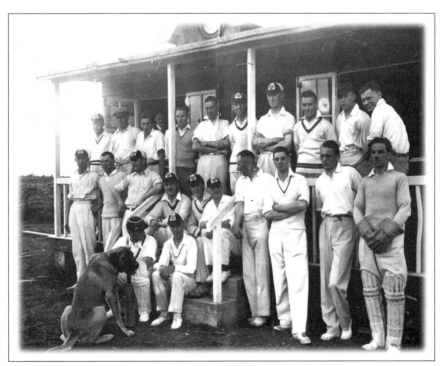

Allotments

The Parish Council has provided allotment gardens, to give them their proper title, ever since its inception in 1894. They were in great demand and an important asset for the community in earlier years, and particularly during the two world wars. There may have been some earlier allotments, but of these there is no record.

In March 1895, the Council rented an area of five acres in what was then called The Lands (now part of Plough Field). A further two acres were taken into this site in 1897. There is no register for the early years, but many of the original tenancy agreements dating from Lady Day 1895, and some more from 1898, are extant. From these it appears that there may have been perhaps three dozen or so separate plots of varying sizes. The Lands at some stage was evidently combined with the two fields known as Cross Keys Tyning, to form a single field of over 13 acres, and the Council considered taking over the remainder of this field, but records do not indicate whether or not it did so. There may also have been a site at Midford in 1895, but if there was, its location is not known.

In 1907, the Council leased a further 4½ acres in the fields called Nearer and Further Midford Hill; this area was divided into nine (later eleven) plots of varying sizes, some of which were considerable. The site was given up in September 1928.

Ownership of The Lands field eventually changed and two plots bordering the Midford Road were sold off for development. What remained is the area now known as Plough Field, and in March 1912 the Parish Council rented this from the new owners for one year subject to notice of only one month. This was evidently a temporary arrangement, because in that year the Council considered no fewer than four other sites; but none of them was taken up at the time.

However, in April 1915 the Council reverted to one of these sites and arranged a lease of the field known as Barrow Edge, although the County Council land agent had previously considered it 'not at all adapted for the purposes of allotments'. (This, incidentally, cancelled an agreement made the previous year to take the field of about eleven acres known as Little Broad Close.) Barrow Edge, of some five acres, was split into two very large plots, accounting for 3½ acres, with 17 plots in the remainder.

In March 1929, no doubt to replace the Midford Hill site, the Council took one acre on the south side of the Midford Road. This was divided into eight plots, and was known as the Chilworthy allotments (from the name of the landowner's house in Midford Road). Another plot was added in 1933. The Council received notice to surrender this site in 1935, probably for development.

Thereafter, Barrow Edge remained the council's only allotment holding for the rest of the century. In 1938, the Council made the existing agreement with Mr Geoffrey Hignett of Hodshill, who had purchased the field as part of the Manor Farm. The two very large plots were surrendered, reducing the holding to 1¾ acres, which was divided into 16 plots of varying size. The annual rent for these plots remained at 3d. per perch from 1915 to 1976, when it was increased to £1 per plot regardless of size: and in 1991 it was increased to the present 40p. per perch. There were very few vacant plots until about 1990, since when demand has declined steadily. In 1993, the holding was further reduced to about two thirds of an acre: this is split into eight more or less equal plots of ten perches, of which only five are now let. After over a century, it seems the days of the allotment garden in the parish are drawing to an inevitable close.

In 1945 WI members were able to return to the Institute having met during the war at Mrs Foster's house. The membership had diminished to 17 but in 1948 had reached 55. In 2000 Carol Oakes handed over as Chairman to Valerie Summers, the membership being about 30, with one lady, Mrs Harris, having been a member for 56 years. Monthly meetings are held in the Village Hall with talks on a wide range of subjects. A popular Christmas fair/coffee morning is held in November.

The South Stoke Cricket Club is one of the oldest clubs in the Bath area; indeed a South Stoke cricket game was reported in the *Bath Evening Chronicle* of 1877, and, even earlier, in 1871, the *Chronicle* mentions a cricket match, Stoke and Combe versus Claverton. One of the present club trophies is a Victorian cricket cap worn by a player in the 1890s. The team originally played on a field at Bumpers Batch but moved to The Warren, a field adjacent to Brantwood, after the war when the club was re-formed in 1953. At that time £100 was raised by residents of the village by subscription to shares in order to build a cricket pavilion. The remains of this building still exist.

In 1965 the club amalgamated with the Old West Hillians and the name was changed to Old West

Hillians and South Stoke. Home matches were then played at West Hill, though now the matches are played at the Civil Service Club on North Road (now Sulis Club, University of Bath). The Club continues to thrive, but sadly there are no playing members from the Parish, although two ladies of South Stoke, Diana Goodman and Joan Carey Jones, are honorary members.

In its time at South Stoke the Cricket Club contributed a great deal to the social life of the village. Apart from the Sunday afternoon matches, which no doubt provided some lively sport and entertainment for the locals, the Club organised fêtes, whist drives, skittle competitions and other fund-raising events. An annual Cricket Club supper is still held.

South Stoke Cricket Club trophy, 1890s. The Victorian cricket cap is worn by player, Albert Townsend.

The Tapestry was completed in 1994, with 34 stitchers taking part in a satisfying community project. It comprises 46 panels each depicting some aspect of South Stoke and is now permanently hung in the Village Hall. *The South Stoke Tapestry Book* was researched and written by Ann Parsons, with Rosemary Geake contributing the beautiful calligraphy.

VE Day 1945 was celebrated with a bonfire on the site of the new millennium seat and all the Molotov cocktails from the Special Home Guard store were let off. VE Day 50th Anniversary celebrations were held in the Tithe Barn, with people dressing up in 1950s outfits: the ladies wore headcloths and pinnies. Roger Clifford fitted into his RAF outfit, Rollo Torrance squeezed into his Army uniform, while Christopher Parsons became a spiv with a black Homberg hat. A dance was held after the meal of mushy peas and Woolton Pie and a beacon was lit to follow the chain around the country.

The WRVS had several members from South Stoke. From 1968 the ladies performed emergency tasks such as deliveries of supplies to farmers during foot and mouth outbreaks and meals to flood victims, as well as the manning of the Police catering van during incidents. They also took library and food trolleys around hospital wards, delivered books to the housebound and also 'meals on wheels'. Of course many of these activities are now the responsibility of Social Services.

Today the South Stoke parish community is as strong as ever and very conscious of a clear identity which is separate and distinct from the city of Bath. The Village Hall is the venue for the annual Harvest Supper, South Stoke Show, Toddlers' Group, Art Group, lectures, concerts and exhibitions, and also functions as the polling station. The winter is enlivened by monthly whist drives held in private houses, with the proceeds going to the hostess' choice of charity. We still assemble at the white railings for

the 'Summers' Tours' and holidays. Jim Summers recalls how 'Summers' Tours' started:

After taking early retirement in the mid 1990s Valerie and I were looking for a challenge. Motoring and driving vehicles of all classes had always been a passion of mine. I decided to take my PSV test. Having passed I was soon in great demand from local coach companies. I found I really enjoyed driving a coach and after gaining some experience decided to use my new skill for local benefit. We realised that for one reason or another there were a number of people who no longer enjoyed long-distance driving and some who did not want to join groups of unknown people. Our first village trip was to Rosemoor NHS garden in the summer of 1994. This was followed in May 1995 with our first venture into France. Since then we have organised two or three holidays each year to France, The Lakes and Scotland, Cornwall and the South East and a number of day trips to London and other places of interest. We hope we have given as much pleasure to those who come with us as we have had ourselves in the planning and organising of each trip.

South Stoke Tapestry, 1993.

A South Stoke outing in the 1920s. The party includes: Fred Rose, George Dobson, Ern Staddon, Amy Barrett, Flo Humphries, Mrs Ainsworth, Mrs Withers and Dolly Hamlen. (Samler Collection)

A South Stoke outing on 15 August 1922. The party includes: W.H.G. Samler (left front with cap), Mrs Clifford, Lou Green, Dorothy Samler and W.S.H. Samler (rear front with moustache). (Samler Collection)

Left: *Parish outing to Burnham, 1946.* Left to right, back row: *Mrs Furley (hidden), Mrs Green, Mrs King, Mrs Perkins, Mrs Clifford, Mrs Heal, Mrs Lambern, Mrs Harris, Mrs Maundrell, Gran Badder, Miss Mayes (schoolmistress), Mrs Wilson, Mrs Hamlen, Mrs Lambern's sister;* middle: *Dora Clifford, Sylvia Heal, Muriel Heal, Margaret Perkins, Joan Moores, Rosemary Summers, Janet King, Hazel Leeson, David Harris, Clifford Robinson (Green), Sylvia Wilson;* front: *Rita Furley with Marion Furley, Doreen Perkins (Christine's cousin), Christine Lambern, Billy Hamlen, Diane Perkins, Eileen Heal, Clive Maundrell, Mary Wilson, Myrtle Furley, Brian Harris, Andrew Wilson.*

Summers' Tour to the Loire Valley, Sancerre, September 1999. The photograph includes, at the back: *Bob Parfitt;* in the middle: *winery guide, Philip Bliss, Pat Potter, John Potter, Beryl Elliott, ?, Ron Elliott;* in front: *Bob Harries, Sandy Neill, Sheila Neill, Pam Harries, Valerie Summers, Carmel Shepherd, Pat Satow, Derek Satow, Ben Rogers.* (Photograph, Jim Summers)

CHAPTER 11

The Parish at Work

❖ Agriculture ❖

There can be no doubt that farming was the dominant activity in the parish from prehistoric times until well into the 19th, even perhaps the 20th century; but there is no specific archaeological evidence in the parish and there are few relevant medieval documentary sources. In many places, the Domesday Book throws the first light on landholding and agriculture, but South Stoke is not separately mentioned in it. The first useful documentary source comes over 500 years later.

After the dissolution of the Bath monastery in 1539, the Manor of South Stoke remained for some years in the hands of the Crown, eventually passing to Queen Anne, consort of James I, and as such it was surveyed in 1610. The record of the survey from H.L. Gray, *English Field Systems*, 1915, is as follows:

	ENCLOSED					ARABLE OPEN FIELDS		
Copyholders	Arable	Meadow	Pasture	Unspec.	Total	East Field	West Field	Total
Wm. Hedges, m	2.75	1	4.75		8.5	14	14	28
Wm. Mercer, m	0.5	3	5.5	5.5	14.5	25	29	54
Alice Willis, m		3.25	5		8.25	16	16	32
John Dagger, m	2.25	1	2	4.5	9.75	6	6	12
Joane Browne, m	1	3	10	1	15	20	20	40
Laurence Smythe, m	0.5	4	10.5	9.75	24.75	3	6.5	9.5
Joan Awburd, m	0.125	1.5	7		8.625	14	16	30
Editha Reade, m								
1 yearde of land	3	3.5	7.75		14.25	16	20	36
Thos. Hudd, m								
1 yearde of land	7	3	12.25		22.25	9	20	29
Total (Acres)	17.125	23.25	64.75	20.75	125.875	123	147.5	270.5

This survey is of particular interest because it proves that the medieval 'open-field' system of agriculture was practised in the parish, and that it was a two-field arrangement (which was general in East Somerset), rather than a three-field arrangement (which was more widespread). The origins of this form of farming remain a matter of scholarly debate; it may have existed in pre-Conquest times but was certainly well established by the 12th century.

The extent of the West Field and East Field are not known. The former presumably embraced all the land south of the Wansdyke and west of South Stoke Lane; the latter, extending east of South Stoke Lane, probably excluded Horsecombe Vale. Field names seem to suggest that both fields extended down the slopes into the valley.

The Tithe Map of 1840 shows four long thin fields in what is now Plough Field. This points to the practice of strip farming at an earlier date. Over 100 years earlier, a minute of 1707 in the churchwardens'

accounts seems to confirm that at least the West Field was still being farmed as an open field; there had evidently been a problem with overgrazing. It reads as follows:

In the count of Sumerset in the Parish of Sothstoke March the 3 in 1707 The old cosstom Renewed by the Consent of the Neighbors to put three Sheep to an Acre and put no More upon the penalty of half a Crown to the overseer of the poor and a groat a Sheep to the Haward from the owner of the Sheep.

Mr John Gay in the West feld 35 acres
Mr Crowch in the West feld four acres and
* three yeards*
Jeames Chambury [sic] in the West feld 22 acres
* and 3 yeards*
Jeames Charmbury for his own in the West feld 13
* acres and half*
Edward Harris in the West feld 20 acres

William Willshear in the West feld 3 acres
William Clement in the West feld 7 acres and half
John Clement in the West feld 7 acres
Widdo Smith in the West feld 3 acres
Widdo Kelson in the West feld 15 acres
John Webb in the West feld 31 acres and half
William Meser in the West feld 2 acres
William Ward in the West feld 5 acres
William Robbines in the West feld half an acre.

(Notes: John Gay held the manor at the end of the 17th century; he died on 12 October 1706. Robert Crowch was the vicar from 1691 to 1739. Meser may be a misspelling of Mercer, a family name in the parish for a century or more. James Charmbury evidently ('for his own') owned 13½ enclosed acres, as well as being a tenant in the open field like the others, of presumably the Manor. A groat was a silver coin worth 4d. (10p) in circulation from 1351 to 1662: it is interesting to see it still quoted half a century later.)

The great wave of Parliamentary Enclosure Acts that peaked between 1750 and 1830 virtually ended the common field system; but for centuries before this, enclosure by local agreement had been taking place and enclosure in Somerset had been almost completed by the 16th century. It is therefore noteworthy that open fields endured in South Stoke into the 17th and 18th centuries: their final enclosure was effected by private agreement, so there was no enclosure in the parish by Act of Parliament. Thomas Thorpe's 1742 map of 'Five Miles Round Bath' (see page 24), which shows a surprising amount of detail, seems to indicate that enclosure was complete by that time.

The survey carried out in the late 1830s for apportioning tithe rent charges records in detail the area, owner, occupier and use of every plot of land in the parish, and the resulting map dated 1840 (see pp 38 & 39) is the first large-scale map of the parish. The preamble to the Tithe Award document includes a summary:

The said parish contains by estimation eight hundred acres or thereabouts, which are cultivated as follows (that is to say)
Arable about four hundred and twenty nine acres
Meadow or pasture about two hundred and ninety six acres
Garden and orchard about thirty two acres
Woodland about twenty two acres
There are also Twenty two acres of land the Estate of the Somersetshire Coal Canal Company...

It is noteworthy that over 90 per cent of the total acreage was farmed and that of this farmed acreage some 60 per cent was arable. Somerset was a predominantly pastoral county and it is surprising that this arable percentage is more than double the county average. Wheat and barley were the main arable crops.

The decades following 1840 were the time of high farming to be followed by increasing agricultural

depression in the last quarter of the century and beyond.

Gerald Hignett (1908–79)
(Courtesy Charles Hignett)

In the 20th century, the Manor Farm was again the largest in the parish. It was acquired by Gerald Hignett in 1936/7 and took in lands which his father, Geoffrey of Hodshill House, had acquired earlier in the century. These included the woodland south of Hodshill which he planted and Rowley Farm in the adjoining parish of Combe Hay (which was tenanted to the Moody family until the 1960s).

From 1937 to 1948, Manor Farm was in the hands of E.C. Masters as tenant and would no doubt have been subject to wartime regulations. Robert Masters, his son, says it was a mixed farm of milking cows, sheep and corn. Gerald Hignett took back the farm in 1948. An Ayrshire dairy herd was built up and the milking parlour moved to new buildings on the hilltop. There were four full-time employees. The herd was gradually expanded, changing breed to Pedigree Friesian during the 1960s, and with new milking facilities again in about 1970. Following Gerald's death in 1979, the farm was taken on by a partnership of his widow, Betty, and his two sons, Jeremy and Charles. Broadfield Farm at Hinton Charterhouse was incorporated to improve the economic viability of the unit and the dairy herd was again expanded with the concomitant building works. When Betty Hignett died in 1984, the farm remained in hand but the farmhouse was tenanted until 1991, when Charles and his family moved into it. At the same time, the dairy operation, which had been uneconomic for a number of years, was abandoned and the farm converted to suckler beef production and arable cropping.

With the agricultural depression striking from the mid 1990s, the decision was taken in 1998/99 to dispose of all 200 head of livestock and to contract out the farming to a neighbouring farmer. The one remaining full-time employee, Peter Marsh, went to work for the contractor, whilst continuing to live in the village of South Stoke.

At the turn of the millennium, there are still a few smaller agricultural units in the parish, but two of the long-established farms, Parsonage Farm and Pack Horse Farm, had closed by the 1980s. Grassland now predominates, arable accounting for perhaps only about one fifth of its area at the time of the tithe survey. The majority of the land in the parish may still be farmed as for centuries past, but under very different conditions and it now provides employment for very few.

GORDON TUCKER DESCRIBES ASPECTS OF FARMING IN MIDFORD:

The railway demolished Bridge Farm where Dick Hamlen used to milk. All that is left is a henge where I watched Dick. That henge is now converted into a house.

Before the First World War the Tuckers... made money... they developed dog biscuits. They also supplied hay, straw and forage for horses in the City, and poultry. During the First World War all the horses went to the Front. Only doctors and farmers were allowed to keep horses. So 99 per cent of the Tuckers' business went. After the war the internal combustion engine gradually took over and horses never really came back... as a means of transport.

During the Second World War the Tuckers did a bit better because everyone kept chickens. We collected swill from Bath three times a week and occasionally found things in that swill. For example, we found false teeth and advertised but no one responded.

Farming has changed a lot. Nowadays we all have wellingtons – so we never get wet feet. When I was a boy, farmers wore boots and breeches or leggings.

Even if the boots were waterproof the water got through the laces and holes. It was physically hard work. The sheer weight of sacks they carried was extraordinary. They built hay ricks and bound them by hand. They used to thatch the ricks, then they put bails into the rick and thatched them across. Farming was very labour intensive. There were vast numbers of people on the farms 'til the Second World War.

My father was very progressive with poultry in the '40s. We kept 800 chickens here. Every afternoon my mother, when she was pregnant with me, had to sit outside there and watch out for the fox. A pair of yokes were made for me when I was 10 or 11 to help Dad carry around water and swill.

We have 180 acres and have beef now – 34 cattle, a suckler herd. Now I'm selling pigs for less than I pay for their food. In the past farming promoted local employment, people stayed in the country; people went to the pub in the evening. That has gone... people expect cheap meat.

You have to do something with land otherwise it is quickly overgrown by docks and nettles and brambles. This process is speeded up by people grazing horses. Wars changed the fate of farming; farming is in depression now.

❖ Brewing in South Stoke ❖

Roman pottery dating from the 1st century found in the parish suggests that the land was settled and farmed quite early in the occupation. It is likely that, as was the case elsewhere around Bath, grapes were grown on southern slopes and fermented to make wine for local consumption. Cider making also has a long history in Somerset. This is illustrated by Richard Pole of South Stoke who, in 1794, offered 'ten hogsheads' (about 540 gallons) 'of last year's cider for sale at £2 per hogshead'.

Before the coming of the Industrial Revolution in the 18th century the brewing of ale in Britain was mainly a cottage industry. The process of brewing and that of malting barley were not necessarily done together. The malting process involved steeping of the barley in tanks with frequent changes of water. The wet grains were then spread on the malting floor to germinate or 'grow'. During this time the maltster kept a watchful eye on

An advertisement for Southstoke Brewery, c.1850.

the process and turned or 'raked' the barley grains to ensure even germination. At the appropriate time, a key decision for the maltster, the barley was transferred to a kiln where, with further turning, the grain was dried. The part-time maltster would sell on his product to a small-scale brew house that was often adjacent to the 'alehouse'.

The earliest reference we have to brewing in South Stoke is in a house sale advertisement in a *Bath Journal* of 1762 where Joseph Burden offered a 'house for sale with brewhouse'. A 1793 report of a tragic accident suggests that brewing in the parish was a regular activity: 'The two year old son of Cox [possibly John Cox] a farmer of Southstoke fell into a cooler of boiling wort [unfermented beer] and scalded to death'. And according to the *Parish Survey* of 1803 two South Stoke maltsters chose 'not to attend the Parish Meeting to fix upon a situation to defend the country nor would they give in any account of their stock.'

Thus small-scale ale production was normal practice in the area before the building of Southstoke Brewery in the 1830s by a certain Thomas Hunt (known as Thomas Hunt the younger).

The Hunts were an enterprising family living in Bathwick on the east side of Bath. Thomas Hunt the elder's business is described as that of a carver and gilder and according to *Keene's Directory* he was also a looking-glass manufacturer. In addition he was involved in property development and renting, as well as brewing and alehouses. The family may well have owned land in South Stoke before 1822. Certainly by 1840, the Tithe Apportionment shows a considerable swathe of land owned or occupied by the Hunts, including Pack Horse Farm and Hodshill Farm, and at this date Thomas Hunt the younger is described as 'farmer'.

Thomas Hunt the elder had two sons, Charles, who was a printer in the Market Place at Bath, and Thomas, who to start with followed his father's profession of carver and gilder. They owned and developed property in Bath including 19 St James Parade, later developed as an alehouse, and also The Gloucester Inn in Walcot, where a trade card shows T. Hunt as 'purveyor by appointment of beer and porter to his majesty'. We also learn that the beds at this establishment were well aired and the stabling good.

On 19 August 1822 Thomas Hunt the younger was married in St Mary's Church at Bathwick to a newly widowed lady called Ann Love. The marriage certificate refers to 'Ann Love of South Stoke, widow'. Her former husband Richard Love had been a parish officer in South Stoke responsible for the collection of land tax. He lived in the parish and, when he died on 30 October 1820, he was buried in South Stoke churchyard. We know that Thomas Hunt was 22 years old when he married, whereas his wife was nearly 40. Her baptism was registered at Wellow on 2 November 1783 where her parents, James and Ann Oxenham, were farmers. She must have been embarrassed by this age difference of 17 years as the census of 1841 shows her no less than a decade older and the census of 1851 six years older!

In January 1823 the bride and groom had acquired the lease of a smart and recently built house at No. l Argyle Buildings (now the Bath Rugby Club shop at the end of Pulteney Bridge). The Bath rate books show T. Hunt as ratepayer there until January 1838. During that time their only child Thomas Henry Hunt was born; he was christened at Saint Mary's Church, Bathwick, on 16 October 1824. The occupation of the father is recorded as 'carver and gilder'. So we see Thomas Hunt in the early years of his marriage, employed in his father's business. This was soon to change, however, when he saw the possibility of new enterprises in South Stoke. The land on which the brewery was to be built belonged to Ann Hunt, in that she had a life interest under the will of her first husband Richard Love. Both she and

Thomas Hunt must have been only too well aware that after her death it would revert to the trustees of Richard Love's estate. A legal agreement in the 1830s released the land to Thomas Hunt under certain conditions.

The precise date for the building of the brewery is not known. A later document states that by 1838 'he had already erected a dwelling house and buildings as well as a brewery and malthouse' in South Stoke. Thus we may infer that the new brewery was up and running by around 1835. This was a major building project, when the two earlier cottages on the site were converted and enlarged to make what is now Brewery House and in those days was known as Belle View Cottage. The three-storey brewery factory and the substantial malting house in what is now the top garden were completed, as was the vat and other equipment in today's Brewery Cottage. The previously sloping front gardens of the old cottages were reformed to make four huge storage tunnels going right back to the house. Water from a spring to the east of Belle View Cottage was channelled into a large stone-lined tank under the floor of the brewery. The tank remains to this day.

In 1839 Thomas Hunt raised a mortgage of £1000 from his brother Charles Hunt. There are three more agreements to borrow money dated between 1843 and 1850 and further sums of £1600 and £2400 were raised. This money was probably used by the Hunts for improvements to the brewery including, perhaps, the installation of the steam engine and possibly building The Priory. The Tithe Apportionment of 1842 shows Thomas Hunt owning Hodshill Farm and renting Pack Horse Farm Inn. He farmed a sizeable area of land in the parish, but it is unclear whether this was the father or the son.

It was Pack Horse Farm on Old Midford Road that had been the beer house for the village up to the 1840s and it might well be that Thomas Hunt was the man responsible for the move of the business to the present Packhorse.

All this enterprise came to an end when, on 19 August 1853, Thomas Hunt died of liver disease (probably sclerosis). Two days later, Ann Hunt, by this time aged 70, died of heart failure. In their obituaries both are reported as residents of Belle View Cottage. They were buried in South Stoke churchyard. Thomas Hunt had not made a will and, with so many parties having claims on his estate, it was only after a reference to the High Court of Chancery and a 14-page legal settlement, that matters were resolved. The brewery was sold at auction on 15 November 1853, as were The Priory, Snowdrop Cottage, the four Rose Cottages and five properties in Bath. The bill of sale for the brewery, of the same date, reads:

Lot 9. The Freehold BREWERY and MALT-HOUSE
In the occupation of Mr Thomas Henry Hunt, with
steam engine and fixed plant, the whole of which is

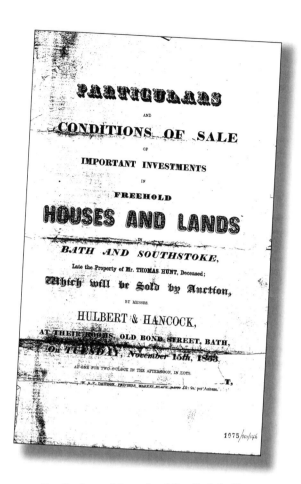

Particulars of the sale of Southstoke Brewery, November 1853.

new, and of the most modern and approved construction. The capacity of the Copper is Ten Barrels; the Malthouse cistern is capable of wetting Seven Quarters; and the cellar stores equal to 500 Barrels and upwards. These premises have been lately fitted up at a very large expence [sic] and from their compactness are considered a Model Brewery. To a Gentleman possessing energy, skill and a moderate capital, their possession would be the certain road to a fortune.

The brewery and goodwill were sold to Frederick Wainwright who ran the business until his death, aged 49, on 5 February 1876; his funeral service was conducted in Bath Abbey by the Vicar of South Stoke, the Revd W. Acworth. By 1856 Wainwright had advanced his status to 'Gent'. Judging from a series of advertisements published between 1864 and 1872 he appears to have been extending his clientele into the houses of Bath. One such read:

SOUTHSTOKE BREWERY, NEAR BATH
To Private Families and the Public Generally, F. Wainwright having found the BITTER and DINNER ALE brewed expressly for their use to have given such General satisfaction for several years, owing principally to the purity of the Beautiful spring of water with which the Brewery is supplied,

begs to inform them he has considerably enlarged his premises, whereby he is enabled to command a much larger supply of all kinds of Beer and Ale than before, and respectfully invites a trial from those who have not yet favoured him.

A local anecdote of about this time relates that a barrel was often left outside the brewery for people to sample on their way to work. The brewery continued in the Wainwright family with Frederick's widow Eliza taking the helm. The once thriving business was now in competition with the new and much larger facility of the Bath Brewery Company in the city. On 7 November 1898, Eliza's son Alexander Wainwright died in South Stoke, aged 48, and his coffin was carried to his grave in the churchyard by brewery employees. Eliza gave up the brewery in 1899 when she was in her sixties, just after the death of her son. The 1899 deed of sale mentions a steam engine, fixed plant, vats and machinery as well as the goodwill of the business under the names of Southstoke Brewery or Wainwright. All books associated with the brewery were passed to the purchaser Mr H.W. Treacher. If the books have survived they will be able to reveal a wealth of valuable information about the brewery's operations, including the number of staff employed and perhaps recipes for what was reputed to be a good drop. Following the sale Eliza went with her daughters to live at Pembroke Villa, Bathwick Hill. She died aged 90 in December 1916 and was buried at South Stoke.

Just two years after he had purchased the brewery, Harry Treacher was declared bankrupt, having insufficient working capital to run the business, and the brewery was sold once more.

Finally, under the ownership of the Lemon family, the business continued in decline and the buildings became dilapidated, until the brewery was closed in about 1909 and the works demolished in 1921.

Colin Wilcox with his baker's cart in front of the brewery's storage cellars in the 1940s.
(Roger Clifford Collection)

135

❖ *Fuller's Earth Mining* ❖

Wool manufacture is one of Britain's oldest industries and until the middle of the 19th century the West Country was a major centre of production. To remove fat and for general cleansing of the wool or cloth the material was 'fulled', that is, beaten, washed and treated with the highly adsorbent clay, fuller's earth, which is predominantly calcium montmorillonite. The fuller's earth beds around Bath were deposited in the Jurassic period and the clay is used, not only for fulling, but also for decolourising oils and as a pharmaceutical excipient. There are at least three suggestions for the derivation of the term 'fuller'. The Roman term for bath-man or laundry-man is 'fullo' and the Romans called the clay 'creta fullonica', or 'terra fullonia'. Robertson, on the other hand, makes claims for the Anglo-Saxon origin 'fullian', meaning literally to baptise – i.e. purify. It was certainly an important resource from early times. Dr Samuel Johnson in his *Dictionary* of 1785 wrote:

> *The Fuller's Earth of England very much exceeds any discovered abroad in goodness, which is one great reason why the English surpass other nations in woolen [sic] manufacture.*

He quotes Piers Plowman who in 1377 wrote:

> *Before newly woven cloth is fit to wear it has to be cleaned in fulling mills, trodden, combed with teasels and stretched. So also a new-born child, until it is christened in the name of Christ is still a heathen.*

Fuller's earth mining had been going on in and around South Stoke for centuries; in fact it is likely that in Roman times Ostorius Scapula (in AD47) from his encampment on a hill between Wellow and Dunkerton, had encountered the lightly covered clay at Wellow and in the fossae cuttings of the Fosse Way. It is possible that, even earlier, local fuller's earth had been used at the hot springs in Bath for washing.

During the years 1880–90, a flourishing market had developed for good quality blue earth in the USA, where it was employed to purify all manner of oils. Technology was changing and, to engage more effectively in this lucrative export industry, businesses in Britain started to amalgamate. In 1890, 11 small companies from Surrey and Bath joined to form a cartel called The Fuller's Earth Union (FEU) (which was later bought by Laporte Industries). The only local company not to join at that time was The Midford Fuller's Earth Co. which operated in Horsecombe Vale and at Tucking Mill. The company finally joined the cartel in 1914.

In June 1890, with the advent of the FEU, it was decided to construct a new processing plant, just

'Yorkshire' steam wagon belonging to the Fuller's Earth Union collecting pit props possibly at Bath railway sidings. On the left is James Staddon and in the middle to the right is 'Smacker' Gerrish (a well-known amateur boxer). (Broome Collection)

The fuller's earth factory windmill at Odd Down, c.1890. (Roger Clifford Collection)

outside the parish, near the extensive underground workings close to the Fosse Way at Odd Down. The Odd Down Works were equipped with two crushers, one louvred dryer, two grinding roller mills, two air separators and two fine-mesh dressing machines. Outside were the settling tanks and storage areas. The associated steam engine and drying ovens were coal fired. In the late 1880s a windmill 60 feet in diameter, a Halliday Engine made by the US Wind Engine & Pumping Co. of Batavia, Illinois, was erected. It was the largest windmill in the country at the time and the steam engine and windmill were connected to a drive shaft running the length of the factory. Both the tower and sails of the windmill were constructed of wood and this contributed in no small way to its destruction by fire in 1904. Fortunately, just before the fire, a larger steam engine, built by Fuller & Son of Leeds, had been installed and this was capable of supplying the full power demand even when the wind failed.

The Odd Down Works were fed from two main sets of mines known as the Upper and Lower Mines. From the Lower Mines, which were being worked before the advent of the factory, a pattern of parallel tunnels spread northwards towards Combe Hay Lane and across into the 'Park and Ride'. No permission was given to cross the boundary into the parish of South Stoke and extend the workings further east. Mining in this area re-started in 1968, the railway from the works was extended and a new adit (an inclined or horizontal shaft into a mine) to the east of earlier ones was opened. It was here that Roman artefacts were found (including two coffins) and Bronze-Age discoveries were made (see chapter 2).

On flatter land at the top of Dunkerton Hill in the field known as The Firs, where extensive mining had occurred over a long period, the Upper Mines started in the late 1880s just before the formation of the FEU. Both the Upper Mines and Lower Mines were owned by two brothers called Butler, one of whom lived at Caisson House, Combe Hay. The extent of the Upper Mines can be gauged by the fact that there were ten airshafts feeding the tunnel lattice. It was not until the 1930s that permission was given to dig under Duchy of Cornwall land to the west of the Fosse Way. A new tunnel lattice was then extended as far as Vernham Wood, some three quarters of a mile on, to join with old small mines. Initially the crude earth was moved through the tunnels by trucks or tubs, pulled along iron tracks by ponies to the main entrance from whence they were raised to the surface by winch.

The demand for fuller's earth increased after the Second World War and by 1978 output at Odd Down was 25 000 tons. In addition to the opening of the new adit, various technical improvements were made. Electric battery-driven locomotives replaced the ponies and mains power now fed the battery chargers as well as the fans and lighting in the tunnels. Digging was increasingly done with powered knives rather than hand tools. In the Lower Mines huge moveable hydraulic jacks were used to support the roof for a short time as the working face retreated, allowing the overlying roof to subside.

Unfortunately the new-found prosperity was not to last. Cheaper supplies from open-cast mines in Surrey and from overseas meant that Odd Down was no longer competitive and in 1980 the Fuller's Earth Union closed down.

Immediately on the south side of the Wansdyke, a little to the east of the boundary of Sulis Meadows, was the Wansdyke Mine. This short-lived mine was working in 1886 but does not appear on the OS map of 1904. As there was no easy ground-level access, a 25ft vertical shaft was dropped below the oolitic limestone and underground passages were dug to follow the clay seam to the west and south west.

Crude earth was pulled to the surface by winch and transported to Odd Down for processing. All mining operations are dangerous and in 1902 John Lamborn lost an arm after being caught in the winch chain.

The South Stoke Mine, immediately to the south of Hodshill, was an open-cast mine that started in about 1886 and ceased production in 1894. The mine, owned by W.H. Handley of Hodshill House, is believed to have been worked by Uriah Handley. The story goes that when the first load of earth was produced, Handley gave to each woman in the village enough cloth to make a dress. A gravity tramway from the mine led to settling and washing tanks that were fed by water through a pipe from a spring near the road just to the south of the house. In addition there may have been a coal-fired drying oven. Refined earth was bagged to be loaded onto barges on the canal. Anecdotal evidence suggests that there was an inclined road leading to a loading bay below Underhill Cottage; alternatively the earth may have been taken by cart to a loading place near the Bull's Nose. Even after work had ceased at Hodshill, W.H. Handley remained active in the fuller's earth business and his company, the Minerals & Mining Co., became a member of the FEU. Stone, in the form of good quality ashlar, was also mined at Hodshill from before 1904 and was used for the rebuilding of the house (1910–24) and the extensive stone work in the gardens laid out by the Hignett family. During the Second World War the disused stone quarry was used as a tip.

THE MIDFORD FULLER'S EARTH COMPANY

A patent was granted to Charles Dames in 1883 for improvements in the method and machinery for refining fuller's earth. This new process produced a better quality product than that of competitors and company invoices refer to it as 'washed and refined fuller's earth'. In the same year Dames established the Midford Fuller's Earth Co. with his brothers George and Henry (who lived at Farm Cottage, Wells Road) and Henry Newsome Garrett.

The annual output from the Midford business increased and by 1884 had reached 864 tons. However, in 1885 there was a setback when a large tank collapsed doing £500 worth of damage. Shortly after this Charles Dames sold up and Henry Newsome Garrett became sole owner. In addition to his partnership with Dames, Garrett had been running another, older fuller's earth business at Wellow. He soon decided to close the Wellow factory and concentrate his efforts at Tucking Mill. Equipment and staff were transferred and the Wellow foreman William Palmer took over the same job at the larger Tucking Mill works. The remains of the large kiln house at Wellow with its iron doors can be seen still below the Fox and Badger Inn.

Left: *Midford Fuller's Earth Company works at Tucking Mill, c.1905.* (Broome Collection)

Below: *At the entrance to a fuller's earth mine in Horsecombe Vale, c.1914. Back: ?, James Coleman; front: ?, ?, Ernest West, Jim Staddon. The word 'blunge' meaning rubbish stone is written on the side of the truck.*
(Broome Collection)

Right: *James Palmer in 1892, the foreman at the Midford Fuller's Earth Company.*
(Broome Collection)

Midford Fuller's Earth Company demolition of the chimney at Tucking Mill in 1968.
(Broome Collection)

Above: *The new boiler is unloaded (c.1914) for the engine house at Horsecombe Vale, top works. Left rear, James Palmer (foreman), right front (standing) James Staddon.*
(Broome Collection)

Henry Garrett was the son of one Richard Garrett of Leiston Engineering, a Suffolk firm, well known as makers of steam traction engines. Henry had all the ability to follow in his father's footsteps but, because of his womanising, he was kicked out of the family business and came to Somerset. He set his sights on producing fuller's earth of the highest quality. He had the very best raw material from his mines in Horsecombe Vale and, thanks to good management and a series of improvements to the process, he was successful. The Midford Fuller's Earth Works, as his business was called, produced a more refined product which fetched a higher price than that obtained by the FEU at Odd Down and was later to find a market in the USA for the food industry and oil refining.

The Midford Fuller's Earth Company mines were approached by a series of adits on the south side of Horsecombe Vale, just below and to the east of the junction of Old Midford Road and the B3110. The three most westerly were driven under Midford Road, the soffits being supported by stone arches that still exist. From there the mine tunnels spread under the field known as Combe Path Lawn and later under Packhorse Lane. Four more mine adits entered the same hillside further east and below the overlying oolitic limestone. From these a network of tunnels spreads out below the footpath, under Midford Road and then under the fields of Pack Horse Farm known as Long Breach, Milestone Ground and Little Breach, reaching as far as Old Midford Road. The total area mined from adits in Horsecombe Vale was between 15 and 20 acres. These are shown on the mine surveyor's map in the Bath Royal Literary and Scientific Institute.

After emerging from the mines, the skips full of newly dug earth converged at a point below the junction of Old Midford Road and the B3110. Here a large edge-runner mill was used to break up the earth; the cast-iron pan was some 7ft in diameter. The mill was driven by a steam engine which, after the First World War, was replaced by a hot-ball oil engine. Water was added to the earth and the thick slurry was lowered down a steep incline to a point just above the stream. The position of the engine house and the gravity tramway are clearly shown on the 1904 OS map.

The slurry was next transferred to storage or settling tanks and more water added until it was ready to be run down via a large earthenware pipe to the 'Maggie' at Tucking Mill. This was a very large tank fitted with a series of baffles so that, as slurry moved along, the larger impurities could be removed before entering one of several large settling tanks. Over three or four weeks the granules of fuller's earth slowly settled. There was a series of wooden plugs that could be removed successively as the water cleared, until only a thick layer of clay remained. This clay was then dug out by hand and spread on the perforated floor over the drying furnace and heated by hot air from a coal-fired boiler. Next the fuller's earth was loaded into a steam-driven grinder, then weighed and bagged up ready for despatch. In the early days before the closure of the canal in 1898 the 2cwt sacks of fuller's earth could be lowered straight onto a waiting barge, later going by road to Midford Goods Yard or directly into Bath.

Mining at Horsecombe Vale ceased in about 1920 but small amounts of fuller's earth from Odd Down were being carted to the Midford Works as late as 1945 for washing and refining. At a cost of £65 the chimney at Tucking Mill was dismantled in 1968.

❖ The Somersetshire Coal Canal ❖

Situated along the southern boundary of the parish the Somersetshire Coal Canal (SCC) is the most significant industrial feature in the vicinity of Midford and South Stoke. This huge engineering project started more than 200 years ago and, although it has now largely disappeared, some important vestiges remain. The canal was built to transport coal from the North Somerset coal fields to Bath and beyond. Its proximity to South Stoke and its passage through Midford were dictated by the topography of the hilly landscape and river valleys between coal mine locations and the most advantageous point for junction with the route proposed for the Kennet and Avon Canal near Limpley Stoke. Although there is now little to see along much of the route, abundant records and old photographs enable us to visualise a scene very different from the pastoral landscape familiar today. The story of the canal is of a fascinating struggle to surmount natural

obstacles with the limited engineering resources of the time, and to finance and manage a project on the success of which the survival of the Somerset coal industry depended.

The canal project was first discussed in 1792, at a time when canal mania was sweeping the country. News of the construction of a canal from Pontypool to Newport was seen by the Somerset mine owners as a threat that superior quality Welsh coal could be delivered to Bath by sea and river at prices which would undercut the Somerset product. Five sixths of the price of the latter was for carriage over unpaved roads that were often impassable in winter. Following meetings of colliery owners, a survey was made by John Rennie and a Bill to authorise the building of a canal, with two branches, was submitted to Parliament in 1794. It received Royal Assent on 17 April of that year authorising £120 000 maximum expenditure.

Construction of the canal began in 1795; however, geographical obstacles delayed the project and estimated costs were greatly exceeded. It was not until ten years later that the main route via Dunkerton was fully open for navigation as far as the Kennet and Avon Canal. The southern branch from Radstock was never completed as a waterway because it was clear that the costly and time-consuming engineering problems encountered at Combe Hay would have to be faced again at the steep gradient between Midford and Twinhoe. However, a tramway was constructed from Twinhoe to the valley bottom and thus Midford became an important junction and distribution point for coal both from the Radstock collieries and from those around Timsbury.

Between 1815 and 1840, the Canal Company became prosperous, carrying more than 100 000 tons of coal a year from 1820 onwards. The price of coal in Bath was very substantially reduced and the link with the Kennet and Avon Canal gave the collieries access to markets further east.

By the middle of the 19th century railway competition, particularly from the Radstock to Frome railway, began to affect profitability, which fell progressively between 1840 and 1870. This, and the projected construction of a railway from Evercreech to Bath following the line of the canal, precipitated the sale of the Radstock tramway to the Somerset and Dorset Railway in 1871. As profits dwindled further the Canal Company itself was offered for sale in 1894, but failed to attract a purchaser. Four years later the canal was finally closed and pumping ceased. By 1910 a railway had been laid from Camerton to Limpley Stoke by the GWR and this operated until 1951. The track followed the line of the canal in many places and consequently much of the canal bed and many of its features were destroyed. Obliteration of the canal continued through tipping, road building and farm developments during the ensuing years, with the result that little can be seen today. Fortunately, the increasing interest in industrial archaeology over recent years and a growing concern for the rural environment on the part of enlightened landowners has halted the progressive loss.

ROUTE OF THE CANAL

The junction of the Somersetshire Coal Canal with the Kennet and Avon Canal is close to the Dundas aqueduct, where there is a large basin. The line of the SCC here runs parallel to and below the A36 road from Bath to Warminster, near the bottom of Brassknocker Hill. From there the route was adjacent to the Midford Brook past Monkton Combe, Tucking Mill and to Midford, where the Radstock branch turned off to the south across an aqueduct, finally terminating in coal wharves and the tramway to Twinhoe. The Dunkerton arm followed the valley, past Hyver Kennels and on to Combe Hay beside the Cam Brook. Its eventual route climbed around the valley north of Bridge Farm, by an extensive series of locks making a hairpin curve known locally as the Bull's Nose. The canal passed through a tunnel to the north of Combe Hay village and on to Dunkerton, crossing the line of the present A367 road a little above the road bridge over the Cam Brook. It then passed to the north of Camerton to terminate at the Paulton basin between Paulton and High Littleton. A number of tramways from collieries brought coal for loading to canal boats here.

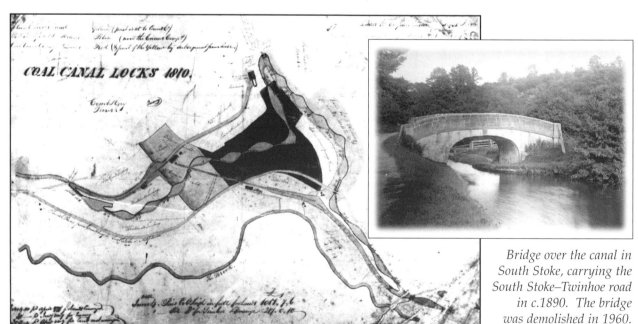

Map of the Somersetshire Coal Canal near Bridge Farm, 1810, showing the flight of locks round the Bull's Nose and the branch connecting to the inclined plane which terminated near Caisson House and carried traffic until the locks were completed.

Bridge over the canal in South Stoke, carrying the South Stoke–Twinhoe road in c.1890. The bridge was demolished in 1960.
(Courtesy Roger Halse)

The Radstock branch was never completed as a waterway due to the cost and problems encountered in the Combe Hay area on the Dunkerton branch. Insufficient funds remained to construct locks on the gradient from Midford to Twinhoe, so unloading to the tramway remained the means for transporting coal down to sidings and wharves at the Midford basin. The canal was completed from Radstock via Foxcote and Wellow to Twinhoe, where a basin existed, facilitating transhipment of coal to the tramway. Later, use of this canal section was abandoned and a tramway was installed along the towpath.

CONSTRUCTION

The SCC established a committee of management under the chairmanship of James Stephens of Camerton. William Smith, who was later to become famous as the pioneer of geology in England, was appointed its surveyor in 1795 and John Sutcliffe became Chief Engineer.

The first section of the SCC was opened for traffic on 1 October 1798 and five boats laden with coal sailed from Camerton to Dunkerton. The first two loads of coal were carried onward to Bath by road, using the same team of horses for both journeys. Within six months a wharf was in full operation at Dunkerton and it was found that a wagon could go twice from Bath to load there more easily than making a single journey to the coal works. Within a year the price of coal in Bath was reduced by this stage of the canal's completion from 14 or 15 pence per cwt to 9 or 10 pence.

The next canal section posed the problem of getting boats down and up the sharp gradient between Bridge Farm and the upper level of the Dunkerton to Combe Hay reach. The committee made the risky decision to experiment with an untried invention – the Weldon Patent Caisson Lock. Three would be needed to gain the required lift. It was hoped this would cost less than building a long staircase of conventional locks, but a catalogue of breakdowns during testing of the first installation proved intractable to remedy. Nonetheless, successful tests on a modified design were completed on 5 April 1799 and a further trial was arranged for 17 April. The Prince of Wales attended the trial and, in spite of continuous rain, His Royal Highness examined the device carefully and climbed to the upper level to see a boat, with three men, emerge from the cistern door. He 'condescended to converse very familiarly with Mr Weldon', the lock's inventor, to whom he gave a generous present for the men operating the lock. Further public trials took place on 27 April 1799 and over 60 people, including some ladies, made the ascent and descent in boats. Sadly for Weldon's brilliant invention, a month later, the walls of the cistern began to bulge, work on the Caisson Lock was suspended and an alternative

solution sought. Much time had been lost and heavy costs incurred, precipitating a financial crisis and for much of the year 1800 the SCC committee was assailed with competing and conflicting proposals for solving the Combe Hay impasse.

An inclined plane was hastily installed but double handling costs were such that it proved only an interim measure. Finally, a flight of conventional locks was the solution chosen and a Lock Fund was established under the third Somersetshire Coal Canal Act of 1802 to meet the extra cost. It soon became apparent that the cost of constructing the Combe Hay locks had been badly underestimated giving rise to serious cash flow problems. These and other delays are believed to have been responsible for a significant drift back to the overland transport of coal.

On 5 April 1805 the SCC were at last able to announce that water communication had now been achieved from the coalfields to the Kennet and Avon and the Wilts and Berks canals. Celebrations followed, and parties of ladies and gentlemen embarked at Timsbury Basin, with the Bath Forum Band, and proceeded through all the locks to Sydney Gardens in Bath where they dined and attended a ball. Welcome income by way of tonnage began to flow into the Lock Fund that, by then, had been seriously overspent.

THE CANAL IN COMMERCIAL OPERATION

The tonnage of coal handled on the canal increased from 66741 tons in 1813 to 138403 tons in 1838. These were prosperous years for the SCC and its shareholders but the railway age was beginning and would soon compete for the cargo.

A notable development at Midford was the installation of a weigh house, one of only four on British canals capable of weighing a loaded boat. The site of this remarkable device was below and behind the present Hope and Anchor Inn on the north side of the B3110. The machine was erected over a lock and had a roofed superstructure carried on six 8ft high Bath stone columns of classical appearance. A cradle was suspended from the superstructure by rods, in a submerged position, such that a loaded boat could be located over it. Water was let out until the boat rested on the cradle and was weighed by an elaborate arrangement of compound steelyards. Accurate weighing was important and the Weigh House clerk, who lived in an adjacent cottage, was a person of some responsibility. Records from other canals show that serious revenue losses occurred through fraudulent practices. The Midford Weigh House came into service in 1831 and was still in existence, albeit unused, within living memory.

Working on the canal was hard and could be hazardous. Extant accounts show significant expenditure on ice breaking during winter months.

Fatalities are on record at Combe Hay locks, where one woman lost two successive husbands, both of whom fell into the water and drowned. Deaths also occurred on the tramways and, where horse-drawn trains met away from passing loops, precedence of passage was sometimes decided by the drivers fighting it out. Balancing the hazards there were pleasure voyages, one of which is recorded by the Revd John Skinner, Rector of Camerton:

Before breakfast I sent my servant, Heal, to see whether the coal barge I had ordered to be prepared to convey the ladies to Combe Hay was ready. All being arranged according to my orders, the party arrived about ten o'clock and went almost immediately to the canal. To screen them from the sun there was an awning carried over the centre of the vessel and a table and chairs placed beneath. As all Mr Boodle's children and two nurses, with the man-servant, were of the party from Radstock we mustered fifteen on board. My horse, under the direction of a man from the coal works, towed us along. We first visited the head of the canal at Paulton basin, and then returned thence through Camerton and Dunkerton to Combe Hay. Having explored the beautiful grounds, etc., we partook of our cold collation under the shade of the elm trees near the cascade, and in the cool of the evening proceeded homewards. Passing the Swan at Dunkerton, the Camerton band came on board and played marches and Scotch airs the whole way home. The music and the dressed out coal barge attracted multitudes, who followed our course along the banks of the canal and lined the bridges under which we passed, which gave a novel appearance to the scenery and a pleasing termination to our rural fête.

Canal and Weigh House working in 1880. (Samler Collection)

THE COMING OF THE RAILWAYS

Once the Great Western Railway line between London and Bristol was opened on 30 June 1841, the Kennet and Avon Canal, whilst retaining local traffic, soon lost all its through traffic on that route. Because the Somerset collieries had no direct rail link, the Somersetshire Coal Canal was more fortunate and its coal trade was little affected. Tonnage carried on the SCC increased through the 1850s but the company was pressed to reduce tolls to help both the collieries and the Kennet and Avon. However, revenue and dividends fell and relationships with the collieries deteriorated because of the virtual monopoly of Somerset coal transport held by the canal. The SCC shareholders were receiving satisfactory dividends and became complacent, making no improvements to the canal nor to the service it offered. The result was that numerous railway schemes aimed at capturing the coal trade were canvassed and met with some support. A Bristol and North Somerset line was authorised in July 1863 between Bristol and Radstock and was opened to traffic in 1873.

The Midland Railway had reached Bath earlier in 1869 and, in 1870, the Somerset and Dorset Railway announced that it intended to extend a branch from Evercreech to connect with the Midland at Bath. It was to serve the parishes of Claverton, Limpley Stoke, Monkton Combe, South Stoke, Freshford, Combe Hay,

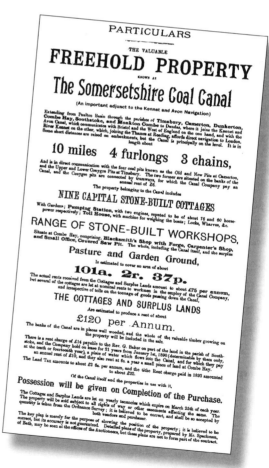

Notice of the sale of the Somersetshire Coal Canal in 1894.

Hinton Charterhouse, Wellow, Cameron, Writhlington and Radstock. This news came as a shock to the SCC and its proprietors decided they had no option but to sell their tramway to the Somerset and Dorset Railway. From about 1880 the SCC was unable to compete with the growing strength of the railways and traffic declined year by year until 1890, when the Company was trading at a loss and paid no dividend. In June 1893 the decision was made to present a petition to wind up the Canal Company on the grounds of 'Bad Trade'.

The last boat to carry a load of coal from Dunkerton to Midford was described by a passenger writing in August 1898. He recorded that there was at that time plenty of water in the lower reaches of the canal and that the Combe Hay locks seemed to be in quite good condition. The Weigh House at Midford was intact but could not have been in operation for some time as its lock was filled with reeds. He saw two pumping engines at Dunkerton because at some time the Combe Hay engine, installed in Engine Wood to make up water lost through the range of locks, had been transferred there and its engine house subsequently demolished. An order to cease pumping was finally given in November 1898 and the labour force was dismissed except for two men to look after the banks of the canal.

VESTIGES OF INDUSTRY IN SOUTH STOKE AND MIDFORD

At Dundas aqueduct near the bottom of Brassknocker Hill, the basin where the Somersetshire Coal Canal joined the Kennet and Avon may be visited. The first reach of the SCC has been excavated and enlarged to form a marina for canal craft. At Tucking Mill there is a plaque recording William Smith, who lived there when Surveyor and Assistant Engineer of the SCC. As previously mentioned, the plaque is on the wrong house; he lived at the larger house further along the lane towards Monkton Combe. The disabled fishermen's lake has obliterated the fuller's earth factory site with its settling ponds and nothing remains of the wharf where the earth was loaded onto canal boats.

Opposite the Hope and Anchor at Midford, the bed of the canal has been made into a garden. There is a gap in the wall leading to a public footpath. A short way along the road to Twinhoe the remains of the viaduct of the Camerton railway can be seen. The line went to Monkton Combe, passing underneath the much larger Somerset and Dorset viaduct, straddling the B3110, which carried the line by way of the Tucking Mill viaduct towards Combe Down tunnel. Walking westward from Midford on the footpath, the canal and towpath are well defined and one soon comes to the point where the Radstock arm branched south to cross over the Midford Brook. The aqueduct, now in ruins, is being restored. South of the brook is the area where the Radstock tramway terminated in multiple sidings from which coal was transferred to boats. A powder house has been restored but little else remains. North of the stream the public footpath follows the Dunkerton arm of the canal towards Hyver Kennels near which the remains of the elegant Accommodation Bridge are slowly deteriorating. Hyver, formerly The Boatman's Arms, was a thriving inn during the heyday of the canal.

The footpath passes under the line of the Camerton railway, where it crosses the brook over a fine bridge and then follows the canal towpath along the water meadows. The remains of one lock are visible before the path crosses the Twinhoe track and, just beyond the crossing, are the remains of a staithe (loading stage) thought to have been used for loading fuller's earth mined in the Hodshill area. The canal here was supported by a massive masonry retaining wall still partly visible and there are signs of a temporary branch that accessed the inclined plane before the locks were completed.

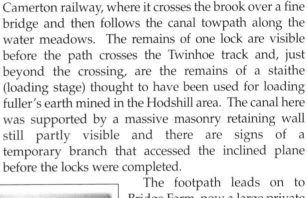

The footpath leads on to Bridge Farm, now a large private house, beside which it crosses the Midford to Combe Hay road. One path then proceeds under the railway bridge of the Camerton line and follows the canal beside the still impressive line of locks towards the Bull's Nose. A newer path follows the line of the railway, parallel to the Combe Hay road, on to which it emerges at Rowley Bottom. Following the path by the locks, some of which have been cleared of vegetation, a branching path to the left leads up into Engine Wood. Here little remains of the pumping engine site and the canal branch that fed it. The probable caisson lock site is in the private grounds of Caisson House, as is the site of the upper end of the inclined plane. However, recent investigations give rise to the alternative theory that the Caisson Lock location could have been under or near the engine house in Engine Wood.

From the top lock of the Combe Hay flight the canal ran westward by Rowley Farm, past the Wheatsheaf Inn and through the Combe Hay tunnel towards Dunkerton. There is little to see until it crosses the A367 and passes out of the immediate locality.

Inset: Road bridge at the bottom of the Combe Hay flight of locks. The cottage (known locally as the 'Blue House', now Bridge Farm), was the canal's toll house. Only the house remains to be seen today. (Edward Smith Collection)

❖ *The Railways at Midford* ❖

Early settlements in the area now known as the parish of South Stoke were essentially rural backwaters. For centuries two important roads, that from Bristol to Salisbury and the South Coast and the ecclesiastical route from Bath to Wells, crossed on the northern boundary of the parish, ensuring that the villages of Midford and South Stoke were not isolated. Midford, resting at the meeting of five parishes and two brooks, with a ford carrying the main road south, has always been an important junction. So it was to prove to be again with the advent of the canals and railways.

Industrial transport first came to the rural Midford Valley with the building of the Somersetshire Coal Canal between 1792 and 1805. The canal era was short-lived as by 1830–40 the railway age was beginning, with steam trains affording a more efficient way of transporting, not only coal, but other commodities and people around the country. The Somerset and Dorset Railway Company was authorised by Act of Parliament in 1871 to construct a new line from Evercreech to Bath, running through Radstock, Wellow and Midford. The track ran across the grain of the hilly country and required extensive heavy engineering works. To get from Twinhoe to Bath Junction (now the Green Park shopping area) two great viaducts were needed, at Midford and Tucking Mill, and three tunnels at Midford, Combe Down and under Devonshire Buildings (Bath). At a cost of over £400 000 and employing 3000 men, the construction was completed in two years. Stone excavated from the Combe Down tunnel was used to build the viaducts, with brick casings being added later. A shelf was hewn from the hillside behind the Hope and Anchor to accommodate Midford Station. The speed at which the work was executed led to faults discovered by the Board of Trade Inspector, but these were soon rectified and the first passenger train ran on Monday 20 July 1874. A goods yard on Tucking Mill Lane was completed in 1884 and was used by the Fuller's Earth Company and other local businesses.

Although Radstock coal could now be transported by rail and people of the parish were able to travel in comfort to Bath or Radstock, the high construction costs had left the Somerset and Dorset Railway Company close to insolvency. They were compelled to lease the new line jointly to the Midland Railway, which connected Radstock with Bath, and the London and South Western Railway which had connections at Wimborne and Templecombe.

The Company retained separate management until 1930, when it came under the direct control of the London, Midland and Scottish Railway (LMS). The line carried the prestigious 'Pines Express' from Bournemouth via Bath to Manchester and Liverpool; it was pulled by two engines because of the gradients to be climbed. After nationalisation of the railways in 1947 the line was first assigned to the Southern Region and later to the Western Region. By the early 1960s people were travelling less by rail and more by private car and bus, thus reducing the passenger traffic through Midford. In addition freight was going increasingly by road. The 1963 'Beeching Report' sounded the death-knell of branch lines throughout the country. Midford's goods yard ceased operations in 1963 and the station became an unstaffed halt in 1964. The line finally closed in 1966.

The impressive Midford viaduct is a constant reminder of the railway, but it is easy to overlook the second now-vanished railway in the parish. Following the closure of the canal in 1898, several schemes were proposed for a rail connection to transport coal eastwards from the Camerton area collieries. The Somerset and Dorset Railway was not interested, but the Great Western Railway Company purchased the canal in 1904 with the intention of connecting a new branch line from Camerton to Limpley Stoke following the line of the canal. Work on the line was completed in 1910. Camerton was already connected at Hallatrow to the Bristol–Frome line and the new single track passed through Dunkerton, Combe Hay, Midford and Monkton Combe to join the Bath to Trowbridge line near Limpley Stoke. The branch line operated until 1951 when the decline of coal traffic made it non-viable. At Combe Hay the line passed through the enlarged canal tunnel and fine railway bridges can still be seen at Bridge Farm and near Hyver Kennels. Remains of a viaduct are visible at Midford where the line ran through an arch of the Somerset and Dorset viaduct.

How ironic it is that, as we enter a new millennium, politicians are talking of creating railway branch lines and tramways of the kind destroyed following the Beeching Report, so that passenger and freight traffic can be diverted from overcrowded and polluting roads.

Inset: Percy Savage on duty in the Somerset and Dorset signal box at Midford.
(Copyright, Julian Peters, photograph, Ivo Peters)

Left: *A view looking north over the Midford viaduct on the Somerset and Dorset Railway, 1958. A tank engine is passing underneath on the GWR branch line.*
(Copyright, Julian Peters, photograph, Ivo Peters)

Right: *A freight train from Bath passes Midford Goods Siding before going under Tucking Mill Lane towards the station, 1955.* (Copyright, Julian Peters, photograph, Ivo Peters)

Right: *Somerset and Dorset railway viaduct at Midford, c.1905. Looking north along Twinhoe Lane before the building of the GWR branch line.* (Edward Smith Collection)

Right: *Midford Station looking south towards Midford viaduct and houses on Twinhoe Lane, 1959.* (Copyright, Julian Peters, photograph, Ivo Peters)

Runaway Train

At 10a.m. on 29 July 1936 a shunting engine was pulling empty coal trucks southward between Wellow and Radstock. Coming from the opposite direction, a northbound freight train over-ran signals and a head-on collision seemed likely. The driver of the shunter reversed his engine to reduce the impact and the crews of both engines took the expedient course of 'baling out'. As the freight train slowed, one of the drivers bravely scrambled on to the footplate of the engine, applied the brake and brought it to a halt. But the driverless shunting engine sped off in reverse through Wellow Station pushing its eight trucks ahead of it, and careering downhill and through Twinhoe at 50mph. The Wellow signalman contacted signalman Larcombe in the Midford signal box at the very moment the runaway came into his view. Larcombe just had time to shout a warning to stationmaster Tinney, who wisely dropped to his office floor.

The double track changes to a single line on the Midford viaduct and the points were set against the up line. This derailed the leading truck which then hit and smashed the signal box base. More trucks then collided with the end of the station platform and truck parts and debris flew everywhere, some crashing down the nearly vertical bank opposite the platform, through the trees and into gardens of houses below. The engine and one truck ploughed on, with the truck breaking up and leaving a pair of wheels under the long arch bridge where Tucking Mill Lane crosses the railway line. With two remaining truck wheels on the rails, the runaway steamed on through Combe Down tunnel and through the Devonshire tunnel. It finally came to rest under the Claude Avenue bridge, when part of the truck jammed the wheels of the engine. Miraculously nobody at Midford was injured; a dog and a parrot in Lynwood and a house below the station had narrow escapes. If the next passenger train from Bath had left Green Park Station, there could have been a catastrophe in one of the tunnels. Repair crews were very quickly on the scene and nine hours after the crash the line was operational.

❖ *Hamlen Hauliers of Midford* ❖

A familiar sight around the villages of Midford, South Stoke, the Twinhoes and Hinton Charterhouse in the early years of the 20th century was the postman, William Hamlen. Mainly on foot, but sometimes on bicycle, he humped his sack of mail around the parish and beyond. He did this until a fall made his job as a postman impossible. Clearly a man of initiative and in spite of his handicap, he saw an opportunity to take advantage of the busy wharf in his home village of Midford as a centre for a haulier's business.

Within a few years, with the help of a coal delivery contract from the Somerset County Council, he had three carts and a dozen horses and traded under the name W. Hamlen & Sons. As a child of five or six Ernest Hamlen recalls walking the gentle dray horses around the fields for his grandfather (William senr) and, in particular, the occasion when 'one took off and ended up in Freshford'. He also related how his father had a horse which 'won the Bath and West Show 1st prize at Frome.'

In addition to the coal contract Hamlen and his drivers, including Vic Southers of Tunley, delivered coal to households, wheat, milk and other farm produce to their markets, goods between farms and made ad hoc general deliveries. By 1930 Bill Hamlen had purchased his first Chevrolet lorry and soon had a small fleet of 'Chevs' and Bedford lorries and employed a staff of six. He had seven sons and of these Godfrey (Goffer), Bill and Walter were all involved in the business. Tom, who worked a pumping station at Tucking Mill, was known as 'Rattler' and is remembered as the 26-stone fairy in a carnival celebrating the building of the Royal United Hospital at Bath. Edward ran the Post Office in Midford for many years and Dick became a farmer near Southampton. After the death of William, the founder of the business, the brothers became joint proprietors. Ernie Hamlen recalls:

I was born in Combe Down but lived in Midford since I was six months old. In the '30s the Hamlens had an old farm there. When I was a kid we went out at 8.00a.m. and we wouldn't get back 'til 6.00p.m., when we were hungry. You could wander anywhere then – Twinhoe, Wellow. I'd go up to my Gran, she'd give me a big lump of tart then I had to take tea up to the hay makers in the fields. Then we went round the back and had a go at the booze – Ushers.

During the Second World War we used to sit in the bus shelter and watch them (the Germans) *giving Bristol a hiding. When Bath was blitzed we'd been dancing at the Avenue Hall (Combe Down). We ran round the corner just along the top and we heard the bomb that hit Prior Park. I dived on top of George Scott and Goffer dived on top of us and a window came out on the lot of us. Bombs hit the bank and half crowns were flying everywhere. Our mother could remember the Boer War – 'The Boers who got my Daddy', she sang. There were a few conchies about (conscientious objectors), they were on the farm. One blew his leg off on a tractor. If you were a conchie, local people made you feel bad. We had rations but we had plenty to eat round the farms and anything going on the black market… whisky, side of beef… go down to Andy's and get it.*

Hamlens had the barn that is now Monk's Barn and Friars Barn, now turned into houses.

My Gran came off of a farm. I never knew from where. She lay the stick into me when I was a boy. I had to carry the laundry basket 'cos she took in washing all over Combe Down.

Jim Summers in his memories as a boy in Midford recalls the Hamlen family:

The Hamlen family was a prominent family around Midford and South Stoke. I remember seven sons and a daughter. William [who was named after his father], Tom from Monkton Combe, Walter, who died about four years ago [making it 1996], Godfrey, Dick, Bob and Ted (who ran the Post Office at Hillside) until his call up [for the Second World War] when it was taken on by his wife and the only girl, Leila.

The boys ran the farm and haulage business in the early years using big horses for transport, but at the start of the war I remember an early Chevrolet lorry coming on the scene. Later Dick went to Kingsworthy near Winchester to start his own farm, calling it Southstoke Farm, and it is still called that today. Bob, Ernie's father, nicknamed Beano, died at a young age, and his widow married Len Cross who worked for the Hamlens after the war.

All the pit props for fuller's earth came into the rail sidings (at Midford) and of course were hauled by Hamlen's to the Odd Down works.

In the early '50s the Hamlens sold their haulage business to John Keeling who was the local agricultural contractor. Keeling lorries may still be seen today on local roads and motorways.

Epilogue: The Parish in AD2000

On the eve of the New Year 2000, there was no formal community festivity in the parish, but through the so-called 'millennium year' people collaborated to celebrate this milestone of history in a number of ways.

An ambitious project was initiated to present the local history of the parish up to the year 2000. The results of extensive research were first presented in the South Stoke 2000 Exhibition and now in the principal objective the publication of this book. The book was, as intended, a project for the parish, by the parish, about the parish. A private preview of the exhibition was attended by Don Foster MP, local celebrities and people who had assisted with the research. South Stoke 2000 Exhibition was staged in the Village Hall on 25, 26 and 27 May 2000 attracting huge interest, and a total attendance of well over 1000 people from near and far.

The Millennium Viewpoint was the other major parish project. The site, a high south-facing vantage point enjoying a 180 degrees view over open countryside for some 15 miles to Salisbury Plain and the Mendip Hills, was licensed to the Parish Council for 999 years by the landowners, the Hignett brothers, for use as a public open space. An appeal for funds was issued to the parish in April 1999 that raised nearly £4500, more than double the target. This included £750 from a very popular and enjoyable summer barbecue staged by Robert Hellard and his team in the grounds of Southstoke Hall by invitation of Trevor and Jenny John. The Parish Council met the balance of the direct cost which totalled about £7000. On the site a crescent-shaped stone seat with a backing wall was constructed, together with a toposcope indicating a selection of visible landmarks. The latter is mounted on a massive old stone pillar, originally in the yard of Manor Farm, donated by Charles Hignett. A millennium time capsule, organised by James Aldridge, is buried on the site.

SOUTH STOKE 2000

AN EXHIBITION CELEBRATING 2000 YEARS OF PARISH HISTORY

SAT MAY 27, SUN MAY 28 AND MON MAY 29.
10am-5.30pm
IN SOUTH STOKE VILLAGE HALL

Photographs Maps Stories Research
Roman, Saxon, Norman
The Church & The Manor
Medieval & Middle Ages
Plague & Civil War
People, Houses, Schools
Life in the 18-20 Centuries
Agriculture & Industry

DONT MISS THIS UNIQUE MILLENNIUM EVENT

ENTRANCE FREE   REFRESHMENTS

On 19 August 2000 the Millennium Viewpoint was inaugurated with a reception on site for many of those who had made the project possible. A most enjoyable evening was crowned by a spectacular sunset. This ambitious project was implemented by an ad hoc Project Group consisting of James Aldridge, Kirsty Banwell, Robert Hellard, Charles Hignett, Sandy Neill and Derek Satow. It was brought to a successful conclusion not only by the generosity of contributors, but also by the many volunteers who did hard labour on the site, often in disagreeable weather, during the spring of 2000. The viewpoint is now in frequent daily use by visitors and parishioners alike, as an objective for gentle strolls from the centre of South Stoke village and as a vantage point from which to enjoy the unspoiled landscape, which is part of the designated Cotswold Area of Outstanding Natural Beauty.

A Millennium Party for the parish, with hog roast, barn dancing and fancy dress, was held in the Tithe Barn on 24 June by kind permission of Charles and Pauline Hignett, arranged by Martin Davis and his Village Hall Committee and helpers. Brilliantly decorated for the event, the Tithe Barn provided a memorable setting for this festive occasion that was a highlight of the year. Midford held its own party, preceded, a week earlier, by a children's party organised by Bob Honey. A large marquee was raised in the meadows and villagers enjoyed a hog roast, dancing to a London band, and tethered balloon rides.

A handsome and worthy addition to the Church of St James the Great is a sculpture of its patron saint, embodying his emblem, the scallop shell, commissioned from Derek Carr, a sculptor from nearby Timsbury. This fine piece of art and craftsmanship is mounted over the outer door, replacing a stone that appears to have been left blank when the porch was built in 1662. The bas-relief was dedicated by the Revd Frank Brand at the celebration of the patronal festival on 23 July 2000, and was paid for by members of the congregation.

The Millennium Wood was initiated by The Woodland Trust as part of its 'Woods on your Doorstep' scheme – a millennium project to plant 200 new woodlands throughout the country, supported by lottery funds from the Millennium Commission and also by the Sainsbury Family Charitable Trust and the Forestry Commission. The Trust approached the Parish Council in February 1999, and the project was endorsed at a public meeting in April. An appeal launched in the autumn raised some £2000, following which the Trust completed purchase of the 2.2 acre site on the south side of the Midford to Combe Hay Lane, a little to the west of Upper Midford. In December, meetings were held on site and in the Village Hall to discuss the design of the wood. The culmination of this project was on the afternoon of Sunday 19 November 2000 when over 80 people turned up and planted some 400 mixed native trees. The remaining 500 or 600 trees were planted by the Trust.

Restoration of the canal aqueduct at Midford was also started in 2000. Since the canal fell into disuse some 100 years ago, neglect and the forces of nature had brought it to a state of near ruin. In the 1990s, the Midford Environmental Group under its Chairman, Peter Oliver, organised an immense amount of work to clear trees and ivy from the structure, and to retrieve stone that had fallen into the brook. They also secured, in partnership with the Somersetshire Coal Canal Society, the interest of the local authorities and the Avon Industrial Buildings Trust. In December 1996, in response to a bid submitted by the AIBT, the Heritage Lottery Fund awarded a grant of £750 000 for a full restoration of the aqueduct. This was double the amount requested, as English Heritage advised that the submitted proposal, which was limited only to stabilising and conserving the status quo, would be uneconomic. The work should have been carried out in 1997, but was delayed by legal and administrative problems. It was eventually started in August 2000 but was severely hampered by flooding and high river levels throughout the autumn. The award also included funds for a comprehensive survey of the remaining structures of the canal to assess the feasibility of their conservation.

These millennium projects were additional to the regular events in the parish calendar. The biennial Church Fête, run by Robert Hellard and held at Brantwood by kind permission of Diana Goodman on the perfect summer afternoon of 22 July, was attended by some 700 people and raised just under £5000 towards the cost of re-roofing the church nave, which was done in May. The annual South Stoke Show was held in the Village Hall on 9 September, and the Harvest Supper was enjoyed on 30 September.

The Church of St James the Great has been the centre of religious and secular life throughout the centuries, and continues to be so. It is therefore fitting that the last celebration during the second millennium of the Christian era was held on its very last day, Sunday 31 December 2000, when a special Millennium Service was conducted by the Revd Frank Brand.

Thus the year 2000 was an eventful one and many members of the community were involved in these projects and activities. It was a year that will be remembered also for its abnormally wet autumn, with the highest rainfall since records began 244 years ago.

There was serious flooding in many parts of the country that even this largely upland parish did not escape. For a brief period the valley of the Cam and Midford brooks from Bisham's Bridge to Tucking Mill was a continuous lake, but fortunately no houses were affected.

Changes over the centuries have been profound, albeit mainly gradual, but their impact has been greater during the last half of the 20th century, which has seen some encroachment and major and serious challenges to the integrity of the parish. The most obvious danger is that the parish may be overwhelmed by development and its rural nature changed out of all recognition to a characterless suburb. Less obvious but equally real is the indirect, insidious impact of the ever increasing number of motor vehicles, and the consequential demands for traffic management measures.

As the third millennium dawns, however, the Parish of South Stoke retains its distinctive character and the village remains, as Pevsner saw it in 1958, "still entirely 'unsuburbanised'". Away from the busy B3110, the hamlet of Midford is similarly quiet and unspoiled and both remain, within their ancient parish boundary, well-defined and active communities, although inevitably less self-contained than in times past. The people of the parish, and many others, walk the same lanes and paths trodden by their predecessors for centuries, and are privileged to enjoy the sights and sounds and beauty of this delightful patch of England. We can only pray that our successors will be similarly blessed.

Inset: *Millennium sculpture above St James' porch by Derek Carr.* (Photograph, Derek Satow)

Left: *South Stoke 2000 Exhibition preview, 24 May 2000. Derek Satow, Gill Carter, Bob Parfitt, John Brooke.* (Photograph, Judy Parfitt)

Left: *The Millennium Viewpoint plaque.*

Above: *South Stoke 2000 Exhibition preview, 24 May 2000. Don Foster MP and Anne Samler.*
(Photograph, Judy Parfitt)

Above: *South Stoke 2000 Exhibition, 25 May 2000. Roger Clifford, pictured here, was the first to sign the visitors' book.*
(Photograph, Judy Parfitt)

Above: *The Millennium Viewpoint seat and members of the Project Group.* Left to right: *Charles Hignett, Sandy Neill, Derek Satow, Kirsty Banwell, James Aldridge, Robert Hellard (with Bronte).*
(Photograph, Rollo Torrance)

Right: *Tree planting in the Millennium Wood, 19 November 2000.* From the left: *Sylvia Williams, Valerie Summers, Muriel Moon, Jim Summers, Ann Willson, Sheila Neill, Alastair Gourley, Betty Cavanagh.*
(Photograph, Derek Satow)

Bibliography

Addison, P., *Around Combe Down*, Millstream Books, 1998

Allsop, A., *The Somersetshire Coal Canal Rediscovered*, Millstream Books, 1993

Arlett, M., *Somerset & Dorset at Midford*, Millstream Books, 1986

Aston and Iles (eds), *The Archaeology of Avon*, Avon County Council, 1986

Bassett, S. (ed), *The Origins of Anglo Saxon Kingdoms*, Leicester, 1989

Branigan, Keith, *Roman Britain*, Reader's Digest, 1980

Branigan, K. and Fowler, P.J., *The Roman West Country*, David & Charles, 1976

Clew, K.R., *The Somersetshire Coal Canal and Railways*, David & Charles, 1970

Collinson, J., *The History and Antiquities of the County of Somerset*, 3 Vols, Bath, 1791, reprinted 1983

Commemorative Folder of a small exhibition to mark the Centenary of Parish Councils, '100 Years in South Stoke', 3 September 1994.

Costen, M., in *Aspects of the Medieval Landscape of Somerset*, Somerset County Council, 1988

Costen, M., *The Origins of Somerset*, Manchester University Press, 1992

Cunliffe, Barry, *Roman Bath*, Batsford/English Heritage, 1995

Gray, H.L., *English Field Systems*, Merlin Press, 1969

Grundy, G.B., *The Saxon Charters and Field Names of Somerset*, Taunton, 1935

Little, Brian, *Portrait of Somerset*, Robert Hale 1969

Major, R.A. and Burrow, E.J., *The Mystery of the Wansdyke*, Cheltenham, 1926

Pevsner, N., *North Somerset & Bristol*, Penguin, 1958

Robertson, R.H.S., *Fuller's Earth: A History of Calcium Montmorillonite*, Volurna Press, 1986

Stringer, A.H. (ed), *South Stoke History: The work of John Canvin*, 1988

Taylor, C.C., *Village and Farmstead: A History of Rural Settlement in England*, 1983

Thorn, F.R., 'The Hundreds of Somerset', in Williams, A. and Erskine, R.W.H. (eds), *The Somerset Domesday*, London 1989.

Thorn, F.R., *A Brief Early History of South Stoke*, Somerset, 2000

Toulson, Shirley, *Somerset with Bath and Bristol*, Pimlico County History Guides, 1995

Tunstall, J., *Rambles About Bath*, 1847

Watson, W.G.W., *Chronological History of Somerset*

Weigh House, The Newsletters of the Somersetshire Coal Canal Society 1995–97

Wilson, Roger, *A Guide to Roman Remains in Britain*, Constable, 1988

Ziegler, P., *The Black Death*, Folio Society, London, 1997

The SCC Weigh House, c.1880.
(E. Smith Collection)

Appendices

❖ *South Stoke or Southstoke: Two Words or One?* ❖

It may seem surprising that there is no consensus on the answer to this question. This note seeks to explain why the Parish Council uses the two-word spelling, South Stoke.

MEDIEVAL DOCUMENTS The Saxon charter of AD961, which is in Latin, is the earliest documentary record of the name: the heading refers to Sudstoca. There are no fewer than 14 other spellings in medieval documents: Southstoca, Sudstoc, Sustoc, Suthstoc, Suthstoca, Siccstoca, Suthstokeham, Southstok, Sustoke, Suthstoke, Sowthestoke, Southstoke, South Stoake, South Stoke – the latter appearing as early as 1286. (There are about as many spellings even of the name of Bath.)

MAPS The historic county maps of Saxton (1545) and Speed (1610), and virtually all subsequent maps use the two words, likewise Thorpe's 'Five Miles Round Bath' map (1742 and later editions); also the first larger scale (1 inch to 1 mile) maps of the county by Day and Masters (1782) and Greenwood (1822) both show two words. Two words were standard on Ordnance Survey (OS) maps from the '1 inch' 1st edition (1809), and the first '25 inch' and '6 inch' maps (1880s), and all later editions until about 1960 when a change to one word was introduced for reasons that are explained later. In 1902 the then Parish Council Clerk confirmed to the OS that South Stoke as two words was correct.

BOOKS In relevant books during the last 200 years the two-word spelling is almost universal. For example, Collinson, *The History and Antiquities of Somerset* (1791); *Kelly's* (and other) *Directories* (19th century); *Somersetshire Parishes* (1905); *The Victoria County History of Somerset* (1911); The Somerset County Council *Inventory of Parochial Records* (1938); Pevsner, *The Buildings of England: North Somerset* (1958); Young's *Guide to the Local Administrative Units of England* (1979); Avon County Council, *The Archaeology of Avon* (1986); and the county volume of such popular classics as The Little Guides series (1905), the Highways and Byways series (1912), and The King's England series by Arthur Mee (1940).

The entry in the authoritative *Concise Oxford Dictionary of English Place Names* – the 'Bible' of English place names – gives the two-word spelling, South Stoke.

OTHER DOCUMENTS The earliest extant written records are the churchwardens' accounts from 1662 onwards, in which both spellings are found. In manuscript deeds, etc., from the last two or three centuries it is usual to find the single-word spelling. The title page of the first Parish Council minute book has South Stoke, but both spellings are used in minutes, even by the same hand.

THE NAME OF THE PARISH In 1956, the then Ministry of Housing and Local Government (MHLG) noticed a discrepancy between the spellings of a number of names in their list of local government areas and the Ordnance Survey names, and wrote to Somerset County Council for clarification. The latter replied that Southstoke as one word was the correct spelling, and was 'used by the Rural District and Parish Councils as well as the County Council'. This information came to light only recently (1999), and raises several pertinent questions.

First, how did the MHLG come to have the one-word spelling and why did neither the MHLG or the County Council abide by the long established Ordnance Survey practice? Secondly, what was the basis of the County Council's statement that the single-word spelling was used by the Parish Council? (The statement that the County Council used the one-word form is open to question: indeed there is evidence to the contrary, including the 'Inventory' referred to above.) Thirdly, and importantly, why did the County Council not consult the Parish Council? Section 147 of the Local Government Act, 1933 (which was in force at the time) stated:

> *(4) In the case of a rural parish, the county council may, at the request of the parish council or of the parish meeting of the parish, change the name of that parish.*

Clearly the Parish Council had a statutory right to be consulted if there was any doubt about the spelling of the name, but neither the County Council nor the Parish Council has been able to produce any evidence of consultation. If there was no consultation, the County Council acted unlawfully.

The name of the village was changed to one word in 1968 by the senior rating assistant to Bathavon Rural District Council in the course of a map revision, and again apparently without the knowledge of the Parish Council. This only came to light in the OS reply to a letter from the late Miss Ena Clifford, a life-long and very knowledgeable local resident, who wrote to the *Bath Chronicle* in 1984 deploring their spelling of the name as one word.

As a consequence of these two decisions, OS maps have progressively changed to the single-word spelling; and, understandably, everyday use of 'Southstoke' has tended to become increasingly common and to be regarded as the norm.

LOCAL OPINION   These facts were set out at the South Stoke 2000 exhibition and local residents had the opportunity to express their view in an unofficial ballot. This resulted in 22 in favour of two words and 20 in favour of one word. Thus local opinion seems fairly evenly divided. The rather smaller than expected response perhaps suggests some indifference; but the sample, at 10 per cent of the total population, is statistically significant.

THE VIEW OF THE PARISH COUNCIL   The council attaches little weight to the phonetic and capricious spellings of the medieval scribes;

recognises that both spellings have long been in common everyday usage, but suspects the contraction to one word may sometimes be unwitting or casual;

considers that the two-word spelling had become the generally established public form of the name for some 400 years, thereby acquiring historical authenticity, and sees no good reason why it should be displaced by the one-word form;

considers that the County Council's ruling in favour of one word was, beyond reasonable doubt, unlawful due to lack of consultation, and the subsequent decision by the senior rating assistant was also improper;

considers that the two-word spelling better reveals the identity and meaning of the adjective and noun comprising the name, and notes that nearby North Stoke (which has a similar one-word Saxon charter origin) and the North Stoke and South Stoke pairs in both Oxfordshire and Sussex remain uncontracted;

notes the indication of local opinion from the exhibition ballot, marginally in favour of two words, perhaps with many in a 'don't know/don't mind' category;

and for these reasons, the Parish Council favours and uses South Stoke as two words.

South Stoke. (Drawing by Julia Ponsonby)

Field Names in the Parish

The names of fields may date from quite recent times or have much older origins; for example, Plough Field is a 19th- or 20th-century name, whereas Horsecombe is recorded over 1000 years ago. Their meaning may be obvious or obscure – what, for example, is the explanation of Nibble? Old names may have been corrupted through the written or spoken word over the centuries. Some field names consist of a single word, but most comprise a 'generic' word preceded by a 'specific' (or 'qualifying') word rather like a surname and a first name. Generic words include, for example, Acres, Batch, Close, Ground, Mead, Tyning, etc. Specific words include a wide range of descriptive adjectives, many of which are self-evident, or they may be personal names.

The Tithe Apportionment is the only complete documentary source of field names in the parish, recording as it does all of the names obtained by the surveyors in 1840. There are unfortunately no earlier estate or enclosure maps for the parish. Field name evidence from medieval documents is scanty, but there are a few records, although some of these include names that are not related to Tithe Map names. For example, a charter of 1305 refers to 'one acre at Clerereswelle', and there is a similar reference in 1342, but the name is spelt Celerereswell.

The following list includes all the names in the Tithe Apportionment, grouped mainly under generic words (in capitals). Identification numbers used on the Tithe Map are given in brackets. A meaning of the name is given or suggested wherever possible; where none is given, it is either self evident, or none can be suggested. Many derive from Old English (OE), or Middle English (ME). Probable personal names are marked * and some of these can be identified with local families mentioned in documents. The meanings in this list are not to be taken as definitive in all respects. Some are not in doubt, while others are more tentative or speculative and open to debate and further research.

In the 160 years since 1840, some field boundaries have disappeared; but apart from land used for housing and other development, the general pattern of the landscape has changed little and most of the fields and boundaries shown on the Tithe Map are still readily identifiable. Principal sources for this section include: J. Field's *English Field Names: A Dictionary* (1972) and *A History of English Field Names* (1993), and M. Gelling's *Place Names in the Landscape* (1984).

NAME	INSTANCE/S	NOTES
ACRES	The Four - (158, 235); The Five - (15, 157); Six - (100, 152); The Six - (78); The Eight - (2); Nine - (93); Ten - (25); The Eleven - (16); Thirty - (24)	The OE word aecer meant a plot of cleared or arable land, then as much land as a yoke of oxen could plough in a day. This was first defined by an Act of Edward I as 40 poles long by 4 poles broad (= 4840 square yards). Medieval names may reflect the old meaning and not a standard acre (see for example Wateleyesacre under LEAZE).
Barlands	(167, 168, 170, 171); - Wood (169)	Possibly ploughed land on which barley was grown – see LAND(S).
BARROW	Little - (175); - Hedge (124)	OE beorg meaning a small hill or hillock, hence also an ancient burial mound or tumulus. In this case the former is probable, as there is no evidence of any tumulus. **Hedge:** more usually and correctly Edge, from OE ecg meaning an escarpment.
BATCH	(110); Bumpers - (86); East Mead - (233); Long - (196); Orchard - (137); Pews* - (196); Squirrels - (184); Thistlands - (164); West Mead - (145, 149)	Modern spelling of bache, OE baece or bece meaning a brook or stream; hence a stream valley, land beside a stream. **Bumpers:** possibly a personal name, or possibly indicating land that yielded a prolific crop. Batch in this instance is strange; the Tithe Apportionment has 'Bumpers Path or Batch' and the latter could be a corruption of the former, or it could derive from 'Patch', applied occasionally to small fields. **Squirrels:** may refer to the animals or to a personal name. **Thistlands:** a meadow in which thistles abounded.
Bisham	- Bridge (147, 160); - Mead (162)	Probably a corruption of 'Bishop's Bridge' found on Thorpe's 1742 map.

NAME	INSTANCE/S	NOTES
Bislade, Binlade, Bickslade	- (38) Brake in - (34)	The various forms of the first element are obscure; with SLADE (q.v.)
BOTTOM	Rowley - (10); Wethercombe - (118)	OE botm meaning land in a valley, or at the foot of a hill. **Rowley:** (q.v.). **Wethercombe:** a wether is a castrated ram, but it might be a corruption of withycombe, a narrow valley where willows grow.
BRAKE	- & Bank (233); - in Bislade (34); - in Great Mumbridge (32)	OE braece meaning rough waste land covered with brushwood etc., a thicket.
BREACH	Great - (103); Little - (105); Long - (101)	ME breche meaning land (newly) broken up from grass by ploughing.
CLOSE	(84, 90); Ear - (173); Great Broad - (23); Little Broad - (25); Hill - (181)	ME clos meaning an enclosure, fenced or hedged piece of land.
DOWN	Harris - (14); West - (14, 17, 28)	OE dun, a hill, an expanse of open upland. **Harris:** a minute of 1707 in the churchwardens' accounts records that Edward Harris held 20 acres in the common West Field. He died in 1744 and has a chest tomb in the churchyard.
ENNOCKS	Lower - (165); Upper - (166)	ME inhoke meaning land temporarily enclosed for cultivation (during the fallow period of a common field).
FIELD	Home - (231); In Midford - (180); Further/Nearer Midford - (202/203); The Nut - (257)	Originally 'cleared land', a common field under the open-field system; one of the furlongs composing an open field; and later, an enclosed piece of land (c.f. close). **Midford:** often (and strictly more correctly) Mitford until quite recently. OE gemythe is a river junction, with ford, a river crossing.
Foxmoor	(7, 8, 11, 13)	Tract of open (waste) land frequented by foxes.
FURLONG	Hare - (156). See also under WADBROOK.	OE furlang, a main division of an open field in which the furrows lay in the same direction. **Hare:** may be a personal name; or refer to the animals, although they feature rather rarely in field names.
GARSTON	Cow - (27)	OE gaers-tun, an enclosed yard near a village used for rearing cattle.
GROUND	Crab Tree - (174); The French - (258), Long - (178); Milestone - (95, 104); Packhorse - (106); Rough - (12); The Well - (22, 79)	OE grund, usually a large pasture field formed by enclosures, but acquired more general meaning like close and field. **French:** possibly a personal name, or where a crop of reputedly French origin was grown, or even commemorating the Napoleonic Wars. (The same name occurs in Wellow.) **Milestone:** refers to the old milestone on the south side of the turnpike road adjacent to field 95. **Well:** OE wella, the original meaning being a spring (rather than the usual modern meaning of a shaft sunk in the ground).
GROVE	The - (20, 21, 29); Miles* - (176, 177)	OE graf, a small wood or group of trees.
HAM	- Mead (161); Mill - (214)	OE hamm, a (riverside) meadow, especially in a river bend.
Henleys	(88)	Possibly Hen Leys (OE aege, untilled land); a chicken run?
Hodshill	Great - (129, 130, 140); Little - (128, 142)	

NAME	INSTANCE/S	NOTES
HOME	- Field (231); - Piece (40); The - Piece (236); Below - Piece (250)	Land near a farm or settlement.
Horsecombe	(92, 94, 96); Little - (99); Lower - (246); Middle - (93); Upper - (102)	The earliest name in the parish supported by documentary evidence; the definition of the boundaries appended to the charter of 961 includes a reference to Horscum; OE hors and cum, a valley in which horses were pastured.
LAND(S)	The - (82, 83, 85); Combe - (87); Broad - (211)	OE land meaning a 'selion', i.e. the basic unit of ploughing in an open field; hence also ploughed land, which may explain the modern name Plough Field for 81, 82, 83.
LEAZE	Wall - (123)	OE laes, pasture, meadow land. **Wall:** A charter of 1296 refers to a 'croft called Curtmede, and one acre called Wateleyesacre' (also Wateleyes in a similar charter of 1342). Courtmede on the Tithe Map adjoins Wall Leaze, of which it is now the eastern part. Wall Leaze may well therefore be a corruption of Wateleyes, which could be a personal name, or a corruption of Water-leys. Wateleyesaker probably reflects a pre-standardisation use of acre (q.v.).
Longthorne	Further - (109); Home and Middle - (117)	Land of greater length than fields nearby containing or hedged by hawthorn bushes.
MEAD	Court - (122); East - (254); Ham - (161); Long - (234); Pews* - (192); Sheppards - Orchard (112); Shepperds - (121); Thistlands - (163); West - (111); Meadow (162)	OE mead, meadwe, grassland kept for mowing. **Court:** with or near a cottage or cottages: 'a croft called Curtmede' (1296); 'one croft called Courtmede' (1342). [Croft: an enclosed piece of land by a dwelling.] **East:** 'a certain piece of meadow in Estmede (1296)'. **Ham:** q.v. **Sheppards:** a personal name. (A Thomas Sheppard, who died in 1840, aged 75, is buried in the churchyard.) **Shepperds:** there could be a connection between this personal name and the reference in a charter of 1341 to 'William, son of John le Schepurde, of Southstok'. **Thistlands:** see BATCH. **West:** 'certain pieces of meadow called Lakes and Overes de Westmede (1296); an identical reference in 1342 has Labes instead of Lakes; 'all the arable land at Westmede' (1305). The meaning of 'Lakes (or Labes) and Overes' is unclear. Whether this Westmede is the same as the rather small West Mead (now in the grounds of Southstoke House) on the Tithe Map is unclear: the latter could have referred to a much larger area before enclosure.
Mumbridge	Great - (31); Rushy - (193); Sidelands - (18); - Wood (20, 21, 29); Brake in Great - (32)	Possibly a personal name. **Rushy:** land, probably badly drained, abounding in rushes. **Sidelands:** land alongside, or at the side of (Mumbridge). (Also occurs in Wellow.)
Nibble	(229)	
ORCHARD	- (114, 119); Batch - (137); Old - (39); Sheppards Mead - (112); Young - (41, 113)	OE ort-gaerd meaning a fruit garden. **Sheppards:** see MEAD.
Paddock	(111)	A common name for a small grazing enclosure.
PASTURE	Cow - (244)	ME pasture, grassland reserved for grazing (as opposed to meadow).
PIECE	Cross Post - (210); Home - (40); The Home - (236); Below Home - (250); Waste - (207)	OE pece, allotment or portion of land, often small.

NAME	INSTANCE/S	NOTES
PLANTATION	- (89, 116); Rowley - (19, 33)	Of trees planted, as opposed to natural woodland.
Rowley	- (35, 134); - Bottom (10); - Plantations (19, 33); Little - (132)	OE ruh, rough, and leah a wood, woodland clearing; thus more generally, grassland. Note that Rough Ground (12) adjoins (10).
Slades	(202)	OE slaed, a shallow valley; a piece of greensward in a long depression in a field, too marshy to cultivate.
Souls	- (3, 4); Lower - (6)	Possibly OE sol, muddy place, wallowing place for animals. This may seem unlikely from the present condition of these fields, but a little to the east were the springs in The Well Ground, and this area may once have been wet and marshy. The name occurs in Kent and infrequently elsewhere.
Twinhoe	- way (151, 153)	'Between the (Cam and Wellow) rivers', from 'Tween-yeo', the latter from OE ea, the standard word for a river.
TYNING	Clay Pit - (143); Lower/ Upper Clements - (198/200); Cross Keys - (80, 81); Culverhouse - (1); Doctors - (206); Gays* - (238); The Great - (159); Greenaway - (154); Little - (210); Lower - (143); Mercers* - (201); Saunders* - (209); The - (159)	OE tyning, (fenced) enclosure. Common in the parish, the term is generally confined to some western and West Midland counties. **Clements:** William and John Clement are both recorded as holding land 'in the West Field' in a minute of 1707 in the Churchwardens' Account Book, which they both signed together with Richard Clement. There is a Clement chest tomb in the churchyard and the earliest legible inscription is to James, who died in 1828 aged 19. There is also a tombstone in the south aisle to John Clements (who died in 1824 aged 54), his wife and four children. **Culverhouse:** enclosure containing a dovehouse, OE culver being a dialect name for a pigeon or dove. **Gays:** John Gay held the manor at the end of the 17th century. **Greenaway:** a notably green piece of land, probably marshy. **Mercers:** William Mercer is recorded in an early Jacobean survey (1610) as being the largest of 11 copyholders in the parish.
Wadbrook	Little - (229, 237)	A charter of 1333 refers to 'two acres of arable land in Bataylle Forlong, by Wodbrok'. The small brook (OE broc): originating in a spring at the north end of the fields may explain the second element. OE wad often refers to woad, widely cultivated in medieval and later times for the famous blue dye. Bataylle Forlong has vanished as a name. Bataylle was the name of a family (and perhaps there is a connection with 'Mr Battell's', the name given to Combe Grove in Monkton Combe Parish on Thorpe's 1742 map). This quote continues with a reference to 'two acres of arable land in Harpforlong, on the east part of the said land'; this is also a lost name.
Warren	Rabbit - (26)	A warren is land used for the breeding and keeping of coneys, by which name the adult animals were known until the late Middle Ages, rabbit applying only to the young.
Winterly	- Wood (247)	Probably woodland used for winter pasture: the suffix -ly from OE leah, woodland clearing or meadow, or from OE laes, pasture or meadow land (now called Priory Wood).
Withy bed	(194)	OE withthe, stream or pool-side land where willows of various kinds were cultivated and pollarded to provide withes, if not for basketry, then for hurdles and other crafts.

Subscribers

James and Diana Aldridge, South Stoke
Heather Ash, Combe Down, Bath
Miss A. M. M. Atchley
Ian P. Atkins, Midford, Somerset
Brian and Margaret Auty, South Stoke
Betty J. Bailey (née Dobson), Bath
Ted Bamsey, Combe Down, Bath
Patricia and Mike Banks, South Stoke
Joy Edwina Banks, Bath. Daughter of
    Edwin Curtis and Rosie Ellen (née Hamlen)
Mr and Mrs S. G. Banwell, South Stoke
Amy Barkshire
Robert B. Barrett, Packhorse Farm, South Stoke
Bunty Bartlett
Mark and Martha Bashore, Morgan's Forge, Midford
Edward and Laura Bayntun-Coward,
    Midford House, Bath
Mr and Mrs L. G. Bell, South Stoke
Dr R. G. Bell, Hampton Hill, Middlesex
Dr M. G. Bell, Caversham
Dr Peter and Dr Jen Bennett
Mr P. R. Blake, Coleford, Somerset
Stephanie E. Bowyer, Langridge, Bath
John Brooke
Sheila M. Brown (née Holley),
    formerly of South Stoke
Stella H. Bunn, Grundisburgh, Suffolk
Joan Carey Jones, South Stoke, Somerset
George and Janet Carter, South Stoke, Somerset
Paul Carter, Wellow, Somerset
Cdr and Mrs E. J. Cavanagh, South Stoke
David M. Chancellor, Adelaide, South Australia
Mike Chapman, Twerton, Bath
Steve Chapple, Combe Down
M. Elizabeth A. Chorley, Combe Down, Bath
Mr Roy and Mrs Jeanne Clifford, South Stoke
Roger Clifford, Sunnyside, South Stoke
Gerald Clifford, grandson of
    Edward and Lydia Clifford
Commander Alan Cobb, South Stoke, Somerset
Mr Richard Cobb, Edgbaston, Birmingham
Trish Conklin and Sydney Monkman, USA
Diana Coombs, Bath
David Copeland, Midford Road, Bath
Jacquie and David Coulby, Orchard Barn,
    South Stoke
Jean A. Cowley, South Stoke, Somerset
Dr and Mrs Martin J. Cross, Cromhall, Glos.
John P. Cross, Combe Down, Bath, Somerset
Maureen Cross, Bear Flat, Bath
Tony Davies, Peasedown St John, Somerset
Martin and Juliet Davis, South Stoke
Michael and Anne Davis, Bath
The Dawson family, Midford
Paul De'Ath, Bath, Somerset

Neil and Christine Dent, Felton, N. Somerset
Peter Duppa-Miller, Combe Hay, Somerset
Gordon Dyer, South Stoke
Kathleen M. Dyer (née Heal), Lanivet, Cornwall
Chris, Jo and Olivia Eke, Hinton Charterhouse, Bath
Mr and Mrs N. G. Eldridge, Romain, Midford
Shirley Ellenberg, West St Paul, Minnesota, USA
Margaret Elphinstone, Glasgow, Scotland
Mr and Mrs W. J. A. Erickson, Combe Down,
    Bath, Somerset
Richard T. Esam, South Stoke, Somerset
Edgar and Eunice Evans, Odd Down, Bath
Ruth A. Haynes and Mike I. Evans, South Stoke, Bath
Garth and Nikki Evans, South Stoke
Jane Fee (née Williams), Bath
David and Carola Fielden, South Stoke
Tania Fielden and Harry Hitchens,
    South Stoke, Somerset
J. Fishlock, South Down, Bath
Mrs Lindsay Freeson, Putney, London
Mary Fry, Midford Road, South Stoke
Rosemary Fry (née Honey),
    Upper Midford Farm, Bath
Ann C. Gallop (née Robinson), South Stoke, Somerset
Keith E. and Sheila M. Gammon, Combe Down, Bath
Tom and Rosemary Geake, South Stoke, Bath
Elisabeth Geake, Henley-On-Thames
Mr and Mrs M. Germain, Southstoke Road, Bath
Ian A. Gerrish, Bradford-on-Avon
Sheila and Danny Gibbs, South Stoke, Bath
Michael and Beatrice Godwin, Malvern House, South Stoke
Diana Goodman, South Stoke, Bath
Kitty and Leon Goodrich
The Gourley family, Midford Road, Bath
R. and J. Gray, Midford
Patricia H. Griffin, Combe Down, Somerset
Mr E. A. Hall, Jersey, Channel Islands
Roger Halse, Chairman, Somersetshire
    Coal Canal Society
R. Hamlen, Bathampton, Bath
The Harben family, lived at Southstoke Hall
    from 1995 until 1976
Mr and Mrs M. J. Harris, Combe Hay, Bath
Ruby D. Harris, South Stoke
Dora Harrison (née Clifford),
Valerie Hayward (née Hawkins),
    formerly of South Stoke
Whiteley Helyar, Bath
Gordon G. Hembury, Middlesbrough, Cleveland
Hester and Michael Henebury, South Stoke
Roger Hext, Longthorne, South Stoke
Tony Higgins and family, South Stoke, Somerset
Lance, Madeleine and Nicci Holyoake, Midford
Mark, Kirsty and Sophie Honey,
    Tetbury, Gloucestershire

Mrs Ann Hopkins-Clarke, Bath
Natalie James (née Hawkins),
    formerly of South Stoke
D. F. Jefferies, Twerton, Bath
Mr and Mrs Trevor John, Southstoke Hall,
    South Stoke
Dorothy M. Johnson, Twerton, Somerset
Deborah Jones (née Price), Ely, Cambridgeshire
D. G. and L. M. Keepen, Combe Down, Bath
The Kernick family and Rushen family,
    lived at Southstoke Hall from 1995 until 1976
Diane and Graham King,
    Bradford-on-Avon, Wiltshire
Mr and Mrs Leslie D. King, Hansford Close, Bath
Fiona Kingdon (née Parfitt), Perth, Australia
Pat and Jack Kingston, Midford, Bath
Jenkyn M. B. S. Knill, South Stoke
Tim Laney and Pam Nix, South Stoke
The Revd Paul Langham, Vicar, South Stoke
Eleanor Letheren, Combe Down, Bath
Marek Lewcun, Saltford
Daniel Lloyd, Easton, Bristol
Dr and Mrs J. M. Lynam, South Stoke
Mrs S. E. Mansfield, Bath
Richard and Margaret Masling, Combe Down
Robert Masters, Westbury, Wilts.
Neil Mattingly, Freshford, Somerset
Mrs Frances McLeod, Midford, Somerset
Jane Measures, South Stoke
Jeremy Moon, grandson of Edwin Heal,
    Postmaster, South Stoke
Karl Moon, grandson of Edwin Heal,
    Postmaster, South Stoke
Muriel Moon, daughter of Edwin Heal,
    Postmaster, South Stoke
Joan Morris (née Gaylard), Bath.
    Attended South Stoke School.
Beryl Murray, South Stoke
Dr and Mrs A. E. Neill, South Stoke
John E. New, formerly Midford and Home Guard
Noel and Ruth Newman, South Stoke
Barbara Newman (née Marsh), Bristol
Bridget O'Neale, Australia
Carole Oakes, Snowdrop Cottage, South Stoke
Marion B. Palmer (née Furley), South Stoke
Mark Palmer FBII, The Cross Keys,
    Combe Down, South Stoke
Robert and Judith Parfitt, South Stoke
Shan and Ian Parfitt-Roche, Vienna, Austria
Christopher and Ann Parsons, South Stoke
Nicholas and Trisha Parsons, King's Somborne
David Parsons and Andre Chadwick, London
Daniel Pennock, South Stoke, Somerset
Brian G. Perkins, Bath
Mrs Joan Peters (née Moors),
    formerly of South Stoke, Somerset
Mrs Anna Philpott, South Stoke, N. E. Somerset
Mrs Simon Pitt
Lieut Cdr R. J. Pitt MBE, RN

Mr Noel Pizey, Horsecombe House, Combe Down
Susan Platten, Faulkland
Lois Price, Ely, Cambridgeshire
Myrtle Price (née Furley), Bath
The Revd Parish Priest, SS Peter and Paul
    Catholic Parish, Combe Down,
Dusty and Marcia Rhodes, USA
Mr P. G. Ricketts, Thetford, Norfolk
Mr J. C. Ricketts, Chester
A. L. and E. E. Ricketts, Bath
Alex Roberts, The Stables, Midford Castle
Nicholas Robinson, Midford, Somerset
Paul F. Roker, Bath, Somerset
Jack Rose, Southsea, Hants.
Julie Rosevear, Midford
Elizabeth Rottenbury (née Glanfield), Bath
Jocelyn F. Russell, Shepherds Mead, South Stoke
Bernard and Patricia Russell, Combe Down, Bath
Rufus F. Russell, Shepherds Mead, South Stoke
Philip and Rosie Russell, Shepherds Mead,
    South Stoke
Tim and Ann Samler, Midford
Pat and Derek Satow, The Priory, South Stoke
Michael Shearn and Freddie, Combe Down, Bath
Carmel Shepherd, South Stoke, Somerset
Felicity Shimmin (née Price), Godalming, Surrey
Jill Skedgell, Midford
Ruth Skinner, Combe Down, Bath
Doris Smith, Weston, Bath, Somerset
Karen Smith, Golden Co.
Sheila Smith, Langabeer, Devon
Mary and Gerald Smith, Denton TX
Katharine (née Samler) and Richard Smith
Anne E. Smith, Washington D.C.
Gerald Smith Jr, Lebanon N.J.
L. Edward Smiths family, Tadworth, Surrey
South Stoke Parish Council
Gordon Spencer, Goring by Sea, West Sussex
Mrs Gwendoline Stainer (née Marsh),
South Stoke, Somerset
Revd Matthew Street, Combe Down
D. Strickland, Beech Cottage, South Stoke, Somerset
Jim and Val Summers
Brenda E. Swatton, Bath
Harry and Marjorie Tanner, South Stoke
Joe Tanner, Tellisford
John Tanner, Gastard
Stuart Tanner, Tellisford
Steve Tanner, Wellow
Jean C. Taylor, Doncaster, S. Yorks
Rosemary Elizabeth Taylor, formerly of South Stoke
Susan M. Tewson, Cross Keys Cottage,
    Midford Road, Bath
Mr and Mrs A. Thomas, Gosford, NSW, Australia
The Thorburn family, Old Wall, South Stoke
Mr and Mrs R. Torrance, South Stoke
Mrs D. M. Tracey, Southstoke Road,
    Combe Down, Bath
The Tucker family, Cleeve Farm, Midford

Mrs B. Turk, Winsley, Wilts.

Yvonne I. Tyler, South Stoke, Somerset

Mr Nicholas Udal, ex-Midford

Mr Adrian Udal, ex-Midford

Helen Geake and Angus Wainwright,
   Bury St Edmunds, Suffolk

Mrs J. Waller (née Blake),
   Midsomer Norton, BANES/South Stoke

John F. W. Walling, Newton Abbot, Devon

Margaret Wallis, Camelford, Cornwall

Eva Wallis, Odd Down, Bath

Adrian Wallis, Pontrhydygroes, Ceridigion

Jean Ellen Watts, Trowbridge. Daughter to
   Edwin Curtis and Rosie Ellen

Heather Anne Watts, Bristol. Granddaughter
   of Edwin Curtis and Rosie Ellen

Peter Weaver, Midsomer Norton, Somerset

Barry Weaver, Bath, Somerset

Rita Mary Webb (née Furley), formerly of South Stoke

Eddy and Fay Weeks, Bathampton, Somerset

John R. Weeks, Uddingston, South Lanarkshire

Margaret and Charles Weston, Bradford on Avon

Richard and Carole Whale, South Stoke

J. H. and V. M. Wharton, Ditteridge, Wiltshire

Mr Michael Whatley, Southwick, Wiltshire

R. J. Whitaker MBE MA, Bath

Alison White, Midford, Somerset

Isobel G. Whyte, Combe Down, Bath, Somerset

Andrew Whyte, St Paul, Minnesota, USA

Robert C. Williams, South Stoke

Sylvia M. Williams (née Heal), South Stoke

The Williams family, Glen Cottage, South Stoke

Ann Willson, Hillside Cottage, South Stoke, Bath

Mrs Nicola M. Willus (née Blake),
   Coleford, Somerset/South Stoke

Sylvia Anne Wilson, Carmarthen

John Wilton, Mendip Gardens, Bath

Christopher and Anne Winpenny, South Stoke

David J. Woods, Bath

Mr and Mrs D. Wright, Marnhull, Dorset

ALSO AVAILABLE IN THE SERIES

SOME OF THE MANY FORTHCOMING TITLES

For details of any of the above titles or if you are interested in writing your own community history, please contact: Community Histories Editor, Halsgrove House, Lower Moor Way, Tiverton Business Park, Tiverton, Devon EX16 6SS, England, e-mail: sales@halsgrove.com If you are particularly interested in any of the images in this volume, it may be possible to supply a copy. Please telephone 01884 243242 for details.

In order to include as many historic photographs as possible in this volume, a printed index is not included. However, the Community Histories are currently being indexed by Genuki. For further information and indexes to volumes in the series, please visit:
http://www.cs.ncl.ac.uk/genuki/DEV/indexingproject.html